Online Learning

by Susan Manning, EdD, and Kevin E Johnson, MEd

FOREWORD BY Joan Vandervelde

School of Education

University of Wisconsin-Stout

for **dummies**®

A Wiley Brand

Online Learning For Dummies®

Published by: **John Wiley & Sons, Inc.,** 111 River Street, Hoboken, NJ 07030-5774, www.wiley.com

Copyright © 2021 by John Wiley & Sons, Inc., Hoboken, New Jersey

Published simultaneously in Canada

For general information on our other products and services, please contact our Customer Care Department within the U.S. at 877-762-2974, outside the U.S. at 317-572-3993, or fax 317-572-4002. For technical support, please visit https://hub.wiley.com/community/support/dummies.

Wiley publishes in a variety of print and electronic formats and by print-on-demand. Some material included with standard print versions of this book may not be included in e-books or in print-on-demand. If this book refers to media such as a CD or DVD that is not included in the version you purchased, you may download this material at http://booksupport.wiley.com. For more information about Wiley products, visit www.wiley.com.

Library of Congress Control Number: 2020946839

ISBN: 978-1-119-75686-6; 978-1-119-75687-3 (ebk); 978-1-119-75688-0 (ebk)

Manufactured in the United States of America

SKY10021681_101220

Contents at a Glance

Table of Contents

Foreword

When I think of the sixty online instructors that I have supervised since 1996, at the top of the list are Dr. Susan Manning and Kevin Bowersox-Johnson. Both are award-winning online instructors with over twenty years of experience designing and teaching online courses and certificates using a consistent application of proven best practices in online learning.

Above all, the authors understand how to coach and mentor newbie online students in becoming proficient online learners.

As a Coordinator of Online Professional Development, I have watched technology tools dramatically improve and advance. Yet I continue to hear instructors and trainers say the same thing today as in past years: Instructors wish remote learners understood the expectations of learning online and had a step-by-step success guide.

This book is a valuable compilation of lessons learned and provides a resource for new virtual learners to navigate the complexities of online learning. It answers questions about how to make the experience produce meaningful learning that sticks for life. Also, it includes how to locate legitimate online training and avoid scams.

Following the steps in this book will help result in the completion of an online micro-course, boot camp, certificate, virtual corporate sales training, or employee onboarding, as well as a full degree program.

Yes, you can Google and get the same stuff online, but this book provides specific strategies to leverage learning now and in the future as adults find themselves changing careers and retooling for the future.

Online Learning For Dummies is a book that will guide and motivate you to continue learning conveniently from your tablet or laptop or even your smartphone!

Joan Vandervelde
Online Professional Development Coordinator, University of Wisconsin–Stout

Owner, InstructOnline.com LLC

Introduction

According to the Babson Survey Research Group, online enrollments had grown for 14 years consecutively. Nearly every college student accesses course documents and resources via online portals. One in three learners in higher education takes at least one fully online course. That's a lot of online learning! And, considering that college is no longer limited to advantaged 18- to 22-year-olds, that means a lot of those online learners may be older and less familiar with the tools that come with the territory. That's why we've written this book — for the many learners who find themselves in school, online, and confused.

And then there's the COVID-19 pandemic of 2020. Overnight, brick-and-mortar schools had to shift to online options. College students were told to finish the term online. Though this kind of emergency instruction was not ideal for faculty or students, it brought about a sensitivity to how different online learning is from face-to-face models.

Furthermore, the ups and downs of the global economy have sent more learners back to school to retool or add credentials to their résumé. However, balancing work, family, and civic commitments with school is an arduous task at best. Online options allow learners to address their professional development needs at a time, and in a manner, that may be more flexible with their lifestyles. This may be part of the reason that online enrollments have mushroomed over the past few years.

Fifteen years ago when we tried to explain to people that we teach college courses online, we were met with, "How does that work?" Today, we hear stories of family members or colleagues taking courses online, but many questions still remain. There's a bit of controversy, too, in that students may not have a choice but to take a course online, and too often they're left to flounder, with inadequate guidance from advisors and faculty.

Regardless of age or experience, learners who know what they want and are willing to work hard are the ultimate winners in the world of education. *Online Learning For Dummies* helps students become winners in the online classroom by explaining just how it works. We take you from the decision-making process of determining whether this venue is right for you to applying and enrolling and then to the skills you need to succeed.

About This Book

Online Learning For Dummies is not a highly academic book written for scholars. It's a book for everyday people who find themselves faced with online possibilities. You can trust this book when you need to quickly understand something about online learning. Consider these examples:

>> **If you're a working professional who needs to earn an additional degree or certification for career advancement,** we can show you how to put together your application materials and get started in a program.

>> **If you want to go to school full-time but lack the funding,** we can tell you whom to talk to regarding financial aid.

>> **If you want to take online courses but are unfamiliar with the technology involved,** we can walk you through the kinds of tools you'll use to support classroom discussion and submit your assignments.

>> **If you're a high school student thinking about nontraditional schooling,** we can give you the information you need. We also cover students with disabilities.

Depending on who you are and what you need in terms of online learning, you can easily skip around this book to find exactly what you need. (Don't worry — we won't complain if you want to read it from cover to cover!)

Conventions Used in This Book

We use several standard conventions throughout this book:

>> New terms are *italicized*. We try to use as little jargon as possible, but because online education utilizes some slightly new vocabulary, some terms are unavoidable. Italicized words are followed by definitions in layman's terms. (We also italicize any words we want to emphasize.)

>> Key words in bulleted and numbered lists are **bold** so that you skim what's most important.

>> You'll see a lot of web addresses — how could you not, when we're talking about *online* learning? Also, notice we don't always give the entirety of the address, just the basic information you need to type into your browser bar. For example, if you type www.vimeo.com, you'll get to the page!

>> We've used gender-neutral language throughout the book. You'll notice "they" as the most common pronoun. That's because teachers and students come in both varieties!

What You're Not to Read

Of course, our egos hope that you read and digest every word. But the realists in us know that you're busy and might want to read only the essential material. So, if you need to skip a few things due to time constraints, here are a couple of suggestions:

>> **Sidebars (in shaded gray boxes) contain information that is interesting but not critical to understanding online education.** You can skip these boxes, especially if you understand the context of the surrounding material.

>> **We use the Technical Stuff icon for any topic that may require a little more explanation of what it is and how it works.** However, providing an understanding of technical details isn't the purpose of this book. Therefore, paragraphs marked with this icon can be skimmed quickly or skipped entirely, if you prefer.

Foolish Assumptions

As a way of helping us focus on what to write, we made several assumptions about you, dear reader, when writing this book:

>> **You know how to use a computer for the basics.** We hope this is true about you. If it isn't true, perhaps you can skim Chapter 3 and then decide whether online education is really for you.

>> **You're considering going back to school and you're leisurely looking at alternatives.** Maybe you're curious about how online learning works and want to get a sense before you select a school or program. In that case, you have plenty of time and may read the book from cover to cover.

>> **You know which subject you want to study.** We know that not everybody knows exactly what they want to study or what career they want to have upon graduation. We've done our best to speak to those who want to participate in

a full-fledged online program as well as those who want to explore options and possibly take only one or two classes total.

>> **You're faced with an online course, have no idea what you're in for, and need the information quickly!** This is where the majority of online students find themselves the first time. If you're already enrolled, you may want to jump to Part 3 and learn what you need to excel.

>> **You're an online instructor (or were recently forced to become one) and are curious about the various ways in which online courses are structured and how students and staff interact in cyberspace.** This book can help you see online learning from the student's perspective, and it may inspire you to try a new idea or two. Heck, it may even inspire you to consider taking an online course as a way to grow professionally.

>> **You're an online instructor and you need your students to be better prepared for taking online courses.** Perhaps your students are coming to your virtual classroom unprepared, with false expectations about online learning. In this case, consider recommending this book to your school bookstore to help your future students settle in to your online course quicker.

How This Book Is Organized

Online Learning For Dummies is organized in five parts. The parts are organized so that you can start by looking at the big picture of online learning and then walk through the decision-making and application processes, dive into courses and succeed, and, ultimately, move out of the educational realm to apply your new-found skills and knowledge.

Part 1: Introducing a Different Kind of Learning

In this part, we give you the basic landscape of online learning. In particular, we discuss what you may need to consider about online learning to see whether this is truly a fit for you. In addition, we give you an overview of the technological competencies you should have before taking an online course.

Part 2: Preparing to Be a Learner

If you haven't gone to school in the past ten years, you're in for a surprise! Almost everything is online, from course catalogs to applications to live advisors. This part walks you through the processes you need to follow to select an appropriate program or course, apply, register, and enroll. We also tell you about why you need to have the right attitude for learning online.

Part 3: The Virtual Classroom: Being an A+ Student

This part is where we talk about the specifics of how online learning works. Drawing from years of helping new learners become acclimated to online courses, we walk you through the common activities and processes you need to know as an online learner. This includes communication skills, identifying important documents and resources in a course, and understanding your role and tasks as a learner. Even if you've taken an online course previously, you may be surprised at the details we address.

Part 4: Special Considerations in Online Learning

One of the truisms about online education is that it offers more educational possibilities for persons who may not have access to a more traditional educational system. This includes younger students (those in kindergarten through high school) and students with disabilities. Online classrooms are diverse, and we address special needs in this part of the book.

Part 5: The Part of Tens

Every *For Dummies* book concludes with a short summary of key information and tips. In our Part of Tens, we have included ten myths about online education and ten best practices for self-care while being an online learner.

Icons Used in This Book

As is customary in any *For Dummies* book, we've used a few standard icons. Here's what the symbols mean and how you should interpret them:

TIP

We use this icon to mark strategies and techniques we've learned from being online students ourselves or from our former students.

REMEMBER

Any information marked with this icon is worth remembering and taking away from this book.

WARNING

This icon denotes things you should be cautious of. Taking note of this info can help you avoid unnecessary headaches.

TECHNICAL STUFF

We use this icon when we feel the need to provide more background information on a topic — material that's interesting, but not essential to your understanding the big picture.

Beyond the Book

In addition to the pages you're reading right now, this book comes with a free access-anywhere cheat sheet that offers a number of online-learning-related pearls of wisdom. To get this cheat sheet, visit www.dummies.com and type **online learning for dummies cheat sheet** in the search box.

Where to Go from Here

We understand that your situation is specific to you and that you may not necessarily need the same information as other readers. Feel free to look over the table of contents and decide which chapter might best meet your needs. Our recommendation is that if you're brand-new to the idea of online learning, flip to Chapter 1 for an introduction and move through the book sequentially. If you're already taking an online course, head to Part 3 for pointers on succeeding in your class.

We truly hope that not only is reading this book enjoyable to you but that it also helps you make some important decisions, provides you with the right questions to ask on your academic journey, and better prepares you for your online adventures.

We wish you luck in your online journey and prosperity in your future careers and academic adventures.

1

Introducing a Different Kind of Learning

Chapter **1**

Planning for Your Online Learning Journey

Hello, and welcome to the world of online learning. We are excited that you picked up this book to help you jump into online learning and what it takes to succeed in the online classroom. In this book, we explore the ins and outs of online learning. We share personal stories, from both instructor and student perspectives, as a way to help you understand what is expected of learners and overcome the sometimes false expectations of new online learners. We want to be clear that this relates to learning via a college course as well as learning via workplace training; in either scenario, the shift to learning online requires new skills.

You may have some specific questions about online learning, such as these examples:

» What is online learning, and how does it differ from the traditional face-to-face classroom?

» Which institutions offer online programs or courses, and how do I find them?

» What type of computer and technological skills do I need in order to be a successful online learner?

> » What kind of work will I be expected to do, how will I complete that work, and how will I be graded?

> » What resources are available if I need help?

Our hope is that we have created a resource that answers these questions and more in order to help you succeed as an online learner. In this chapter, you begin your journey into the virtual world of online learning.

Examining the Characteristics and Advantages of Online Education

In a nutshell, online learning is using the Internet to support learning. It is about connecting the learner to educational materials by way of the Internet. Online learning combines a student (you), a curriculum (determined by the school or instructor or trainer), and an Internet connection. In this section, we introduce a few traits and benefits of online learning; we cover both topics in more detail in Chapter 2.

The nature of online education

The content delivered as part of an online course and the way in which you prove that you're learning that content may vary widely. This list describes a few common formats:

> » **Read material, engage in online discussions with classmates, and then submit papers or projects at the end of the term.** This is probably the most common design. You complete the work when it's convenient for you but within the guidelines established by the instructor. For instance, if the instructor says that you need to post discussions by Monday at midnight, you can work through the weekend and get your ideas posted to the discussion board before you begin your workweek. These courses are often facilitated by an instructor (they're referred to as instructor-led) who not only shares their expertise in the field but also helps guide you through the entire online learning process.

> » **Read material and then take a test.** This is our least favorite method, and many students find it horribly dull. However, for some subjects, you can zip through the basic background information quickly and move on. You typically

have little interaction with your peers. As a matter of fact, in some self-paced courses, you have no interaction with peers and little interaction with the instructor.

>> **Read materials, log in to a real-time web conference, and then listen to the instructor or interact with peers.** You may take a test or submit papers later to demonstrate your understanding. This *synchronous* (real-time) method of online learning has become quite popular, especially for workplace training and professional development. However, it requires you to adjust your schedule to accommodate the class, just as you would a traditional class. These courses are also instructor-led and sometimes include peer presentations as well.

REMEMBER

In Chapter 2, we provide more examples of how the nature of online education is unique. However, we want to emphasize an attitudinal shift in online learning: The learner (you!) must assume responsibility for learning the material. There's no cyberprof in the room to nag you or tell you when it's time to log in. Of course, wonderfully encouraging and compassionate faculty want to see you succeed, and they communicate with you regularly to keep you engaged, but the nature of online learning requires the student to take charge and complete the work.

So, what kind of learner thrives in this kind of educational landscape?

>> **A person who needs flexibility in terms of when courses are offered:** If you have no free moments until 11 P.M. because of competing life demands but you really want to learn, an online course you can complete at 1 A.M. may work. (We hope you get to sleep in until later in the morning!)

>> **A person who comfortably sets their own agenda and manages their time well:** If you're good at crafting a plan and sticking to it, online learning may be for you. Though the instructor may provide a schedule and deadlines for assignments, you have to work them into your lifestyle.

>> **A person who has strong reading and writing skills:** Because much of what you need to know comes by way of textbooks or web pages, you need to be a decent reader before taking an online course. In addition, the way you show that you know the material requires writing summaries and short essays. Clear, concise written communication skills earn you an A.

>> **A person who's comfortable with technology:** Later in this chapter, we say more about this topic, but the bottom line is that an online course requires familiarity with your computer. This isn't the place to learn about the computer.

A few pros of online learning

Online courses and opportunities to learn have been steadily growing in popularity for the past decade. Here are just a few reasons online learning is popular:

>> **You can work around your schedule.** Who isn't triple-scheduled these days with demands of work, family, and community? Few of us have large blocks of time available for classes, but we may have an hour here or there. In an online course, you can log in and work whenever it fits into your schedule. You may find that studying for an hour first thing in the morning or over your lunch break is just what you need to get you back into the academic groove.

>> **You can save time and money by not having to commute to school.** Even if your local college is five miles from your home, the process of packing up your gear, getting to the school, finding parking, and walking to the classroom takes 30 minutes. Save the gas money and time, and study from home!

>> **In some cases, courses are accelerated and you complete the degree or program sooner.** A mixed blessing, many online programs have accelerated a traditional semester-long course into 8 weeks. Though you may take only one course at a time (or two, over the course of a 16-week semester), these courses move fast! The good news is that these kinds of programs typically run year-round and advance students through degrees and certificate programs faster than they would otherwise. (Flip to Chapter 4 for more information on accelerated classes.)

>> **Some of the pettiness and bias between students in traditional classes gets left behind in the online world.** No one knows whether you are shy, speak with a lisp, or sport multiple tattoos when you're an online student. What others care about are your ideas and how you communicate these ideas about the course material. Many students find this situation liberating.

Knowing the Technology and Computer Skills You Need to Succeed

TIP

Many nontraditional or adult students shy away from online education because they're afraid their computer skills aren't sufficient or they worry that they need a state-of-the-art computer. Don't let these thoughts scare you away from reaching your academic goals. Most institutions provide technological support and detailed lists of hardware, software, and competency requirements. Family, friends, and your local library also can serve as excellent backups when technology breaks or your Internet access is lost.

Don't get us wrong, though: A few minimum requirements must be met in order to adequately learn online. Chapter 3 describes the technology you need and all the skills necessary to be an online learner. In short, persons taking online courses should have access to the following basic hardware and software:

>> A computer with monitor, keyboard, and mouse (a laptop counts!)

>> Access to a reliable Internet connection

>> A web browser (for example, Chrome, Microsoft Edge, or Safari)

>> Speakers, microphone, or headset with microphone (optional, but may be required by some programs)

>> Word processing software such as Word or Google Docs

>> Presentation software such as PowerPoint or Keynote

Additionally, you should be able to handle the following basic tasks before taking an online course:

>> Open your Internet browser and navigate to a given website address (or *URL*).

>> Send and receive emails with attachments.

>> Open a word processing application and format, save, and retrieve documents.

>> Read and scroll web pages efficiently.

>> Type quickly and accurately.

>> Organize folders on your computer's hard drive or an external flash drive.

>> Download and install software.

>> Run virus protection software.

Seeing How to Go About Becoming an Online Learner

After you have an idea of what may be involved in online education and a good grasp of the technological competencies you may need, you can turn your attention to finding the right program and school and grabbing your seat in the class. You also need to know the process for applying to a school and getting ready for class. We introduce the basics in this section.

Finding available courses

We assume you know what you want to study — for instance, you know whether it's art history or business administration. That said, do you want to take a course or two, or do you need a degree or certificate? We ask this question because it influences how you go about finding an online course. Setting your sights on a degree means investing more time and money in the learning process. If you're like most people, the stakes seem a little higher when money is mentioned, and you want to make the best decision.

TIP

Here are a few possibilities, and you may want to explore all four:

>> **If all you need is a course or two in one area:** Check with your local 2-year school. Many 2-year colleges offer online courses at a fraction of the cost of traditional 4-year institutions.

>> **If you're looking for a graduate level course in your professional area:** Go back to wherever you earned your undergraduate degree and see whether that institution offers online courses. You already have a relationship with those folks, and you may find that the application and admission processes are streamlined.

>> **If you need to brush up for a career boost:** Check with professional associations. More and more associations offer courses and certifications via online programs. Having an industry-recognized credential might be just what you need.

>> **If you have no idea where to start:** Use a standard search engine to explore the possibilities at major online institutions. We deliberately avoid listing popular schools, because the landscape changes quickly! Plus, every learner needs to do their homework in terms of researching reputable, accredited programs. That said, if you find an interesting prospect, be prepared to receive solicitations the minute you submit a web based form asking for more information.

WARNING

If you do a Google search, the schools listed at the top are most often for-profit schools. Be careful when it comes to for-profit schools! Many are far more interested in taking your money than in offering you a good education. Later we talk about how to look at accreditation. Top of the list may not equate to top in quality!

Jump to Chapter 4 for a more detailed explanation of the process of finding the courses and programs available online.

Evaluating programs

REMEMBER

Regardless of whether you want to enroll in a single course or a degree program, you must select a school that is respected and accredited. Don't sink your money into a diploma mill that teaches nothing and wastes your time. In Chapter 5 we detail how to determine a school's accreditation, but we can tell you up front that it should be obvious. When you visit the school's website or review its printed material, you should see accreditation credentials listed.

After verifying accreditation, you may want to consider other factors when you evaluate online programs (see Chapter 5 for more details and lists of questions to ask academic advisors, instructors, and other students):

>> **General course style:** Are these self-paced courses where you read and take tests, or do they engage the learner in discussion and active participation? You need to find a course that meets your expectations of what learning should be ideally. Also, consider whether you will work on your own schedule or schedule your courses with real-time meetings conducted via web conferencing.

>> **Class size:** How many students does the program squeeze into the virtual classroom? If you're one of 20, that's an acceptable ratio. If you're one of 50, expect the instructor to be harried and the quality of your interaction to be markedly different.

>> **Completion and retention rates:** This is a telling statistic. How many students actually complete the courses or degrees? If only 20 percent of starters reach the finish line, the courses may be poorly designed, too difficult, too boring — you get the picture. This area is worth exploring with a counselor or an advisor.

>> **Faculty background and training:** Who teaches at this school? What kinds of credentials do the instructors possess, including technology training? Surprisingly, you don't need to consider whether the faculty are full-time or part-time, because many online faculty are actually *subject matter experts (SMEs),* who have impressive professional credentials in their disciplines. The most critical issue is whether these folks know what they're doing when teaching online.

>> **Student support services available:** Who will help you register, select the right courses in the right sequence, and figure out the technology, for example? What if you need accommodation for a disability? Quality schools and programs address these student services from the beginning; you know you have a whole team behind you.

Applying to a program and securing the money you need

If you're an adult learner, you may remember the lengthy college application process where you filled in forms, wrote an essay, took exams, and so on. Your high school guidance counselor probably walked you through the steps. Some of that process is the same online, just web based. Other processes are slightly different. For example, you may not need entrance exams, such as ACTs and SATs. Transcripts can be sent electronically.

Chapter 6 provides an overview of the whole process. It may surprise you that applying to an online program and then following through with registration still involves a guidance counselor of sorts. In the digital world, this usually involves continual communication with a representative from the school. For example, if you need to know more about a program, you may be asked to fill in a web based form. That form generates a phone call, and you quickly have a personal counselor or advisor working with you.

REMEMBER

Not only do you have to think about the application process, but you also have to consider the cost of classes. College isn't cheap if that's the direction you're headed. However, just as you may consider financial aid for traditional courses, you should explore this area for online programs (see Chapter 6). Your financial options may include

>> **Scholarships based on academics, demographics, or other criteria:** These do not have to be paid back.

>> **Grants awarded by the federal government based on financial need:** To qualify, you must first complete the same financial aid paperwork as all other students, available at https://studentaid.gov.

>> **Loans, via either the government or private lenders:** When you need to pay these back and at what interest rate depend on the lender.

REMEMBER

Are online courses less expensive than traditional on-ground courses? Yes, probably. Tuition may be the same, but you save money by not having to pay transportation costs. Other expenses, such as childcare, may or may not affect you. For example, one parent may be able to study while children nap or do their own homework; another may need childcare to keep a busy toddler occupied so that they can focus on schoolwork.

TIP

If you study more than part-time at a regionally accredited institution that receives federal financial aid, you may be eligible for assistance. You have to be part of a degree or certificate program, however. Check with the school for the details of what may be available, as well as its process. This is where selecting a school with a full suite of student services pays off, literally.

Getting accepted and preparing for class

After you've applied to an institution, your application and supplemental materials (transcripts, letters of reference, and personal statements) are reviewed by the institution. Of course, smarty that you are, you're accepted. You receive notice of your acceptance via email; however, some institutions follow up with a more formal acceptance letter via standard US mail. If for any reason you're not accepted, don't panic: Would-be students may not be accepted for any of several reasons, many of which are merely administrative. In Chapter 7 we discuss in more detail what to do after you've been accepted and describe strategies for moving forward if your application is rejected.

After you've been accepted, you must enroll in courses. This process is also completed using the web. Most institutions, even those teaching face-to-face, require students to log on to a website where they access the institution's course catalog and register for classes they want. These sites also provide you with a list of the required textbooks chosen for each class. If you don't know which class or classes you should take first or in what order you should take them, contact your academic advisor to work out these details.

Imagine that you're partway between registering and actually starting class. What's left to do? Get oriented! Any decent school provides you with an orientation experience. It may be a series of prerecorded tutorials to guide you through common technology processes or an invitation to attend a live webinar to see and experience the same. Orientation in its simplest form may consist of your receiving a document with printed procedures. See Chapter 7 for full details.

Attitude is everything

Think about the last time you had to do something you had never done. What helped you succeed? Your attitude was probably a huge part of the equation. Having a *growth mindset* means that you're willing to try new ways of learning, even if it means you might not immediately succeed. And if you do fail, a growth mindset turns that failure around into another attempt. Having a growth mindset is all about taking baby steps toward a goal.

With a growth mindset, you'll take in all kinds of new terms related to online learning. You'll experience the learning management system (LMS), and you will work in the cloud. These are exciting new ways to learn!

Most importantly, you have to see yourself as capable. We cover the right mindset in Chapter 8.

Becoming a Star Learner

After you register for classes, it's time to begin learning. This task can be a little nerve-wracking, especially if you haven't been in school for a while. However, like most things in life, a little preparation goes a long way. We help you with the basics in this section.

Making your way around your classroom

To truly succeed in online learning, it helps to be prepared and take the necessary time to become familiar with your classroom. In many cases, institutions will even open your virtual classroom one or two days before classes officially begin. Take advantage of this opportunity by logging in to your course and becoming familiar with the following aspects:

» General course structure

» Instructor announcements

» Instructor contact information

» Syllabus

» Calendar

» Course policies (including grading)

Flip to Chapter 9 for plenty of help with navigating your classroom.

Meeting the instructor, fellow students, and other important folks

You may think you're alone on your learning journey just because you're not physically in the same room or building as your instructor and classmates. Nothing could be further from the truth. As a matter of fact, some of our students have shared with us that they feel *more* connected to their online peers than they feel about the people they work with daily.

When taking online courses, you have a plethora of academic and technical support. Not only can you connect with your instructor and peers, but most institutions also connect you with academic advisors, technical support staff, guest speakers, and more. Check out Chapter 10 for more information on meeting all the people in and around your classroom.

TIP

If you ever do feel alone, don't hesitate to reach out. One way to stay connected to peers is to form a virtual study group that meets in real time (synchronously) each week to discuss course content and upcoming assignments. You can do this by way of several free online tools, such as Google Meet or Zoom.

Communicating with clarity

Though you may have opportunities to communicate with your instructors and peers via voice and/or video, most communication occurs in text. Therefore, communicating clearly, concisely, and respectfully in writing is important.

REMEMBER

Online courses employ two standards of writing: formal and casual. Being able to follow the instructor's cue and write according to the standard of each particular course is important. For the most part, though, initial discussion posts and assignments use formal writing skills, whereas responses to peers and questions are much more conversational.

Chapter 11 has full details on how to communicate clearly online.

Strengthening your study habits

With freedom comes responsibility. This statement couldn't be more true when it comes to developing good online study habits. As an online learner, you have more freedom to choose the days and times that you study and complete assignments. This may sound appealing until family and friends want to go see the latest action film or your child begs you to read their favorite book for the 400th time. Developing a strict schedule for studying is important in order to keep up with readings and assignments.

Not only is it helpful to have a set schedule for studying, but you also need to establish efficient and effective study skills to maximize productivity. Looking for patterns within your course schedule, bookmarking important sites such as the library, and writing initial posts offline are all things you can do to use your time more efficiently. Flip to Chapter 12 for information on developing good study habits for online classes.

Working well in a group

Yep, you read that heading correctly: group work. The fact that your instructor and peers aren't in your geographical location doesn't get you out of completing group assignments. Research shows that working in groups is tremendously beneficial, and being able to do it in an online setting takes skill, patience, and a lot of communication. To some of you, this won't come as a surprise, because more and more people work remotely. Your job is one giant group project!

As with any group-based task, you can do a few things to help make group work more efficient and effective (as you can find out in Chapter 13):

>> Communicate as soon as possible and as often as possible.

>> Summarize the project and break it into manageable tasks.

>> Delegate tasks to group members.

>> Establish roles.

>> Document progress.

REMEMBER

Most conflicts among group members are about one or more members of the group not doing their share. Documenting progress, or lack thereof, and keeping your instructor in the loop helps keep each member accountable and helps your instructor better facilitate conflict resolution when necessary.

Being part of a bigger world

One of the most exciting aspects of learning online is that you can meet others from around the world and learn from them. The Internet has opened possibilities your grandparents could not have imagined. It is not uncommon to have students from multiple continents in one course.

Being a *global learner* means having respect for cultural differences. It also requires that you coordinate across time zones and that you are helpful, not critical, when it comes to resolving problems that may arise from language differences.

In addition to describing what it's like to be in a global classroom, we address in Chapter 14 how to work and study from afar.

Minding your online manners and ethics

One problem with communicating mostly by text is that anyone can misinterpret what is written. Therefore, keep humor to a minimum and avoid posting questionable content. You also need to recognize when and where to address individuals when problems arise. If you are having a problem with a peer, politely and privately communicate directly with that person. You will want to include your instructor, who can facilitate resolution if necessary.

If your issue is with the instructor, you might take a different approach. For example, have you ever been in a face-to-face course when someone questioned an instructor rudely or otherwise inappropriately? In most cases, the instructor wins and the student ends up looking like a fool. The same is true in the online environment. If you need to question your instructor or another peer, post the question or concern privately and respectfully. In return, your instructor should also communicate concerns privately, along with other personal information, such as your grade and assignment comments.

Part of being respectful and honest is posting original content and giving credit where credit is due when posting someone else's work. You should cite sources in formal assignments and in everything you post, email, or present. If the idea isn't yours, cite it! If you have a question about whether to cite something, or if you're unfamiliar with the proper way to cite sources, ask your instructor or a librarian. We discuss this topic and others related to ethical behavior in Chapter 15.

WARNING

Institutions often provide instructors with tools to check assignments for originality. These tools include comparing your assignments to a database of other assignments, web content, and dissertations. Know your institution's guidelines for quoting/citing sources and developing original work. Some schools consider it plagiarism to repurpose an assignment from one class for another. The penalties for plagiarism can be quite severe, including removal from a program. Again, if you have a question about whether you can do something, ask. Don't assume.

Completing and turning in assignments

Some people believe that when you take an online class, you simply read an assignment and then take a test. This is partially true, but not as prevalent as you may think. Online instructors use a variety of assessment techniques to determine your level of understanding. As an online student, you may be asked to answer questions about the readings, write an essay that analyzes and evaluates research, give an oral presentation, or create a project to share with the class. All these formal assessment techniques require you to create something in a scholarly manner with proper citation and style formatting, depending on your instructor's directions.

How you submit each type of assignment can also differ. You may be asked to post your assignment in a public discussion forum for others to read and respond to. Alternatively, you may be asked to submit your work via a private, virtual drop box that only the instructor has access to. Other types of submission methods exist as well. The method for submission depends on the assignment, the purpose of the assignment, and your instructor's preference. Most online classes use a variety of submission methods.

We discuss how to finish and submit different types of assignments in detail in Chapter 16.

Transitioning after you're done with school

Many online learners go to school to either start a new career or earn a promotion at their current job after graduating. Reminding yourself why you're going to school and tracking your progress can help you stay on track and prepare for that transition. Some degree programs require students to develop and maintain an electronic portfolio, also known as an *ePortfolio* — think of it as an electronic résumé that allows invited visitors to see your academic/work history, sample assignments, and other pertinent information. Find out more about this topic and others related to transitioning in Chapter 17.

Looking at a Few Special Situations in Online Education

Online education opens access for learners who struggle in other contexts. In this section, we show how certain groups of students can be served via online learning. We begin with a discussion of where the youngest group — homeschooled and high school students — fit in, and then move to learners with disabilities.

Students in kindergarten through high school

Sometimes young learners want or need a different structure for learning than traditional schools offer. This includes kids who fall into these broad categories (among others):

>> **Child actors and athletes who need to travel:** Whereas these kids used to have private tutors, now they can stay on top of coursework by enrolling in online schools.

>> **Kids who live in areas where the schools can't offer advanced or specialized courses:** This describes a good number of rural communities. Online courses can fill in the gaps.

>> **Learners hoping to avoid some of the high school influences of drugs or gangs:** Online students can focus on the academics.

>> **Students who fail a class and jeopardize graduating on time:** The process of making up coursework used to mean summer school; now it includes online courses.

In many cases, states support online education for kids from kindergarten through high school via charter schools. Students within the state can take online courses to supplement or augment traditional curricula. Or, they may choose to forego traditional education altogether and take online courses exclusively. In Chapter 18, we discuss online education for kids of all ages, including how it differs from online education for adults, the variety of online schools available for kids, and the K–12 enrollment process.

Learners with disabilities

Online classes provide an exceptional alternative educational opportunity for persons with disabilities. Learners with physical disabilities can avoid the hassle of traveling to campus and navigating the physical classroom. For those with learning disabilities, technology can assist in activities such as prolonging test times and spell-checking documents. However, depending on a person's specific impairment and the institution's knowledge regarding the creation of accessible content, online learning may still present difficulties.

State and federal laws continue to be created that require public institutions to develop all materials in an accessible manner. However, not all those responsible for creating online courses are aware of these regulations or are trained on how to implement the guidelines. Therefore, websites, LMSs, and course content can sometimes lack design structures that meet accessibility standards. In Chapter 19, we provide a list of questions you can ask to help determine whether an institution is prepared to accommodate your learning needs.

The law provides learners who have disabilities the right to equal access to information in a comparable format to their peers who are without disabilities. However, with this right comes responsibility. To receive appropriate and reasonable accommodations, persons must voluntarily disclose and document their impairment before accommodations will be made. Accommodations, which are based on each individual's needs, are usually determined with the help of the institutions' disability services department staff. Find out more about this process in Chapter 19.

Chapter **2**

The Traits and Benefits of Online Learning

Ask almost anyone in the civilized world to describe school and they will probably tell you about a physical place — a shelter with a roof, desks, and chairs — along with people who assume specific roles, like teacher or student. The teacher decides what is to be taught, passes on the information to students, and awards scores to indicate their progress. The students sit attentively, do the work prescribed by the teacher, and perform tasks or take tests that measure how much they've achieved. That's the old-fashioned model of a school, one that is familiar to most people. Even a one-room Amish schoolhouse fits that description.

Yet ask someone about online learning and you'll likely get a different perspective. Almost everyone learns online! Whether you log in to your company's compliance training, view a free course about personal finances, or watch a YouTube video on how to change a fuse in your car — you are learning online. With the arrival of the Internet, the world has increasingly shifted from classroom-based instruction to learning online.

In this chapter, we sort through the factors that make the online experience different from traditional education. By taking a look at who is learning online and what they're gaining from the experience, along with doing some honest self-assessment on your own, you'll be able to determine whether this type of learning is right for you.

What Makes Online Learning Different from Traditional Education?

You may not remember life without the Internet, but it hasn't been that long since the only choices for learning were attending a traditional school or taking correspondence classes by mail. In response to an increasing demand for alternatives, some colleges began offering classes in the evenings or on weekends to accommodate working adults. That changed when the Internet became available to everyone. Eventually, online courses came into vogue as a way to learn "anywhere and at any time." Still, their format remained similar to the one people had known for a century; the teacher directed the learning. Today, people know so much more about how to learn, especially online. In this section, we compare the traditional model of learning to the world of online learning.

Connecting to learning and people via the Internet

Online learning is using the Internet to learn. It is about connecting the learner to educational materials by way of the Internet. As we show you throughout this book, online learning can happen in a variety of forms and fashions, but the underlying use of the Internet and its technologies are fundamental. Lessons, communication, and assessment (grading) all happen by way of the Internet. In the following sections, we describe the two major models for this communication and assessment: instructor-led and self-paced.

You're not alone: Instructor-led and -facilitated courses

The most common model of online learning in formal educational programs is instructor-led or instructor-facilitated. That means an instructor determines the content and pace of the instruction. In a sense, this is really no different from a traditional classroom experience. In a quality online course, you interact frequently with that instructor, either privately via email or publicly in discussion areas, just as you would have open discussions in a traditional classroom or private conversations on the side. We talk more specifically in Chapter 10 about how online discussion works.

Sometimes online teachers are known as facilitators. In contrast to what you may think of as traditional education, with a professor lecturing and learners soaking up the information, a *facilitator* provides resources for learners to consider and then facilitates their understanding through a series of discussions or activities.

Although facilitation happens in traditional classrooms through face-to-face discussions, it takes on a special significance in online education. Typically, instructor-led courses require learners to interact with one another and everyone follows the same schedule, so they're always aware that others are taking the course with them. We explain more about whom you're likely to find in your online classroom in Chapter 9.

REMEMBER

Not every opportunity to learn is tied to a formal program. If you're taking a course by way of your local 2-year college, we count that as formal. If you sign up for a 4-week course by way of Udemy (an online self-paced education portal), that's informal. Nevertheless, in both cases, you're learning online.

REMEMBER

In most cases, instructors are present in the online environment just as they are in a traditional one. However, what they do with their time in the environment might be a little different from what you would expect an instructor to do in a traditional classroom. Instead of lecturing, the instructor might post a series of narrated slides they created. Or, they might draw out additional responses in discussion rather than tell the class the answers.

Okay, sometimes you're alone: Self-paced courses

Another prevalent model of online learning is *self-paced:* That means computer-based instruction is delivered to you without an instructor attached. You access the lessons, follow the instructions, and return the required products — a completed test on the material demonstrating your understanding, for example. A computer scores the test. You work through the lessons at your own pace with no intervention or guidance from a teacher, and you have no way of knowing whether other students are even in the class with you. You might be the only student or one of a thousand.

In the business world, self-paced learning is the most common form of online education. A lot of corporate training is delivered by way of web-based programs that look similar to PowerPoint slides, sometimes with audio or video attached. At the end of the presentation, you typically find a self-test worked into the program. As the learner, you make the decisions and control the pace of the instruction with a simple click of the mouse.

Here's an example: At one time, state employees were required to complete ethics training that was delivered online. Some employees completed the training in 20 minutes, whereas others needed two hours, depending on how fast they read and how comfortable they were with technology. The program summarized basic information about state laws regarding campaigning, accepting gifts, and so on. Then the employees were instructed to consider different scenarios and select the most ethical responses. The results were scored, and each employee received a compliance certificate.

Can you imagine the cost of calling together all employees to complete the same training in classrooms? Not only would time be lost on the job, but facilities would also need to be considered, and travel time could possibly be involved. The self-paced model was much less costly.

REMEMBER

In a self-paced course, you work at your own pace with little or no instructor input. In an instructor-led course, you follow an established schedule and interact with the other students and the instructor.

Working when it's convenient

In our opinion, one of the best features of online education is its convenience: You get to work when it works for you. Say you're a supervisor assigned to the third shift and you work from 11 P.M. to 7 A.M. You may be able to squeeze in a morning class, but chances are, your biorhythms put you in a groggy state after work. You could sleep a little and then wake up and take a night class before your shift, but then when will you do your homework? And, what about tomorrow night when your son has a Little League game? Wouldn't it be great to work your course around your schedule? In many cases, online learning can accommodate your personal schedule. In the following sections, we define two types of timing for online courses: asynchronous learning and real-time (synchronous) learning.

Asynchronous learning

One of the most common questions related to online learning is "When do classes meet?" To answer that question, you have to understand the meaning of *asynchronous*. When a class is asynchronous, it does not meet at an appointed time. There is no synchronization of schedules. You don't have to be at class at any given time, such as 9 A.M. or 6:30 P.M.

THE ROOTS OF DISTANCE EDUCATION

You may be curious about the origins of distance education. Online education is just an extension of what began in 1728 when Caleb Phillips started selling shorthand lessons in the *Boston Gazette*. In the United States, as soon as the postal service was up and running, schools such as Chautauqua College of Liberal Arts of New York and the International Correspondence School proffered correspondence lessons, the old-fashioned version of self-paced learning. Meanwhile in Europe, the University of London was the first to offer distance learning degrees, in 1858. Learning anytime and anyplace is not new!

REMEMBER

That's not to say that there's no schedule. Your asynchronous class may have a definite schedule of when assignments and activities are due. For instance, every week an assignment may be due on Monday at midnight. When you work on that assignment, however, is entirely up to you. If working at 5 A.M. when the baby wakes for a feeding is good for you, then that's when you go to class! On the other hand, if you prefer to study after the 11 P.M. news, you can go to class then. By not having synchronized schedules, students can attend to coursework when it's convenient.

You can see that asynchronous learning represents a big difference between online and traditional education. Though you may complete coursework on your own schedule, few traditional schools allow you to show up when it's convenient. On the other hand, most online programs assume that you will work when it's convenient, while submitting assignments according to the prescribed schedule.

Synchronous (real-time) learning

The other option in online learning, which has grown by leaps and bounds recently, is synchronous learning. Think about the explosion of online meetings, online webinars, and opportunities to look at other people while not being in the same physical space. In this situation, you're provided a schedule of times to be available and explicit instructions concerning the software you need to connect with others.

Real-time synchronous learning most closely approximates traditional education; the meeting time is specific. Courses and companies use synchronous time in a few different ways:

» **Some instructors require classes to meet so that they can lecture in real time.** This also allows them to interact with students and determine whether students are following along in class.

» **Many companies have moved training online as synchronous learning.** What may have been a face-to-face meeting is now a web conference.

» **Some instructors host online office hours or informal times when they're available to answer student questions.** These instructors may not have a specific agenda for that time, but are open to whatever the student needs.

» **As we discuss in Chapter 13, you may be involved in a group project.** A synchronous meeting is an excellent method to get a lot of work done in short order.

Keep in mind that these synchronous or scheduled meetings don't require you to be in the same physical place. Though you may have to get online at a certain time, you can do so from the comfort of your home, office, or hotel room. And, you can wear your pajamas if you want to, and no one will be the wiser (unless you stand up and walk away from the screen while your webcam is on)!

The business world loves synchronous meetings. Companies have been saving time and money by offering part of their employee training via synchronous webinars and online conference meetings for years now. Although staff may be in different cities, everyone shows up at the same time online. Here's a list of some common web conferencing software:

>> **Zoom:** https://zoom.us

>> **Microsoft Teams:** Available as part of Microsoft Office 365

>> **Google Meet:** https://meet.google.com/

>> **GoToMeeting:** www.gotomeeting.com

>> **WebEx:** www.webex.com

No loafing!

One surprise that online learners report has to do with not being able to loaf or fade into the background in an online course. Face it: In a traditional course, you could go to class, sit in the back of the room, and never utter a word. The teacher may or may not know you're present. In an online course, that's not likely. Chances are good that an instructor is tracking your logins and the quality and quantity of your discussion postings. If you don't log in for a time, many instructors will come looking for you. You'll receive an email or possibly a phone call asking about your inactivity.

Establish a regular schedule for logging in and working on the course. We recommend three to four times a week. That way, your instructor won't have to look for you.

Who Benefits from Online Learning?

Ask a few of the 6.3 million students who took online classes at a college or university in 2016, and they will tell you about the substantial benefits of online learning. Yes, you read that number correctly! In fact, the Babson Survey Research Group, along with their partners the Sloan Consortium, Pearson and Tyton, also states that more than two-thirds of all institutions offer some type of online course. Business is booming, but who is enrolling? This section explains what kinds of learners find online classes advantageous.

Adults beyond traditional college age

If you're working, raising a family, or trying to manage many different roles, chances are that you feel a little stretched when it comes to time. Busy adults, such as the ones in the following sections, flock to online courses because they can determine when and where to study.

Professionals enhancing their careers

Want to move ahead in your career? Earning an advanced degree or picking up courses that directly relate to your job can help you do so. Not only do you acquire the knowledge and skills you need, but employers will also label you as being much more motivated than the average worker. Consider these examples:

>> Sandra's boss wanted to move company sales online, but no one in the office understood how to manage web pages and the Internet. Sandra enrolled in a series of online courses at the local community college and became a valued asset in her office.

>> Karl worked as an engineer for a freight train line. His job took him all over the continent and made it difficult to enroll in a traditional class. Because he wanted to move into a managerial role, online classes fit his lifestyle perfectly. He was able to complete a degree and stay on track!

>> Caryn earned a masters in nursing online while working as a surgical nurse at a local hospital. Her additional degree made it possible for her to teach nursing courses and supervise others. That meant more money!

>> Michael was a successful mortgage seller but wanted to branch into human resources. Although he had taken college courses, he hadn't yet earned his bachelor's degree. Finishing his degree online allowed him to look for work in his field of interest as competitively as any other graduate.

TIP

If you're looking for career advancement and think that taking an online course might benefit you from a time management perspective, look for a program that caters to working adults. Take advantage of the opportunity to talk to a live representative either via the phone or online chat and ask how many students complete the course. That will give you a good idea of how many students are satisfied as well as how attentive the school and faculty are to making sure their offerings work for students. See Chapter 5 for more information on researching different schools.

THE GROWTH OF ALTERNATIVE CREDENTIALS

With the awareness of student loan debt and the financial crises of recent years, more adults recognize the value of alternative credentials. An alternative credential can be a certificate in graphic design or a short skills-based course in artificial intelligence from IBM. Completing the course may (or may not) mean earning credit hours. What is most important about an alternative credential is that it typically aligns with real skills and competencies sought by employers. It's a career enhancement that doesn't require a full degree.

Degrees can be wonderful; the authors have several! However, if you can earn an industry-recognized certification in less than a year and walk into a sustainable job at the end, why not?

In a study by the University Professional and Continuing Education Association (UPCEA) and Pearson, an industry leader in offering educational services, 73% of higher education institutions indicate that they're aware of and planning for alternative credentials. This will bring even more online opportunities to learners.

Where a degree may be represented by a transcript listing courses, many alternative credentials are represented as digital credentials or badges. These digital forms display specific information about the skills and competencies acquired and what the learner is capable of doing as a result. They are not self-reported by the learner, but are verified by the institution.

Busy parents

Raising a family isn't easy. Your children need and deserve your time and attention. They also need to be fed and bathed, have their homework checked, be driven to tennis class, and more! But what if you're a parent and want (or need) to return to school? What are the benefits of online education over traditional schooling for you?

>> **Childcare savings are possible.** On the one hand, we don't recommend trying to be a serious student with small children running around; you can't concentrate adequately when your attention is divided between keeping your child safe, loved, and engaged versus completing a discussion question. However, it's reasonable to think that there will be quiet times when you can concentrate on your schoolwork and not have to pay for a babysitter. Save the babysitting money for those times when you have to take an online test and absolutely cannot be distracted.

>> **You don't have to spend time commuting.** You can study from home or from your workplace (with permission, of course), but you don't need to add travel time to school. That means more time for the family, ultimately. Many parents study at the dining room table while school-age children work on their own homework. "School" starts right after the dinner plates are cleared.

>> **Speaking of school-age children, studying in their presence sends a powerful message about lifelong education, your values, and the need to balance work, family, and school.** Yes, maybe they can see that if you go to night class twice a week. However, we think it's qualitatively different when your children witness you logging in daily and truly keeping abreast of what's happening in class.

So, as a busy parent, when are you supposed to fit in your schoolwork? For parents of very young children, naptime means class time. Many parents who take online classes dedicate those quiet moments to getting on the computer and completing class assignments.

TIP

What if you're not available to your child during the day, but work from 9-to-5? You have a few options:

>> Get up earlier and work for an hour each morning before you wake up the kids.

>> If you're working outside the home, make arrangements with your boss to work online at your desk during your lunch break.

>> If you're a commuter (and not driving!), consider what coursework you can do during that time. Your "green" friends might not appreciate your printing off the whole course to read on the train, but what about your textbook? How about working through a discussion question the old-fashioned paper-and-pencil way and then posting it online later? Or, what about catching up on reading with the help of a tablet?

>> Pull out the laptop when your children do their homework. You will not only stay current in class but also model excellent study skills for your kids!

>> Stay up an hour past your children's bedtime to catch up on your class.

REMEMBER

Only by setting a schedule can you manage work, family, and school. That's true for traditional learning, too — to survive, you must establish a regular schedule for study and stick to it. (True story: Your humble coauthors went back to school online because we were working parents and it was the only way we could manage.)

People with transportation issues

No travel is involved with online education, so students with transportation concerns can take classes easily. For example:

>> If you live in a rural area and have to drive in wintry weather, commuting even 20 minutes to the local community college can become a dangerous ordeal in February. Contrast that to staying warm and toasty at home while you complete coursework. And you pay less in fuel, parking, and maintenance on a vehicle to boot.

>> What if you have a medical condition that makes driving impossible and you're reliant on others for transportation? Again, if you study online, you're completely independent and not in need of travel assistance.

>> Not everyone lives where buses and trains can easily transport them to the local college. Online education cancels the need to find and fund private transportation or to hitch a ride with strangers.

>> If you carry this a little further, you can see that online education opens the possibility to take classes from anywhere in the world. This may seem kind of silly to consider, but you can live in Iowa and take a class from a university in California with no travel costs incurred. In one university class coauthor Susan taught, she had learners log in from Great Britain, Korea, and Dubai as well as North America.

People with disabilities

Typically, disabilities come in two major fashions: physical challenges and difficulties processing information (learning disabilities).

If you're physically challenged, whether by mobility concerns, deafness, or blindness, you may find the online environment to be more conducive to studying. Here are a few highlights:

>> **Mobility:** Persons who use wheelchairs or other assistive devices, such as crutches, canes, or walkers, can stay at home and study. No need to worry about whether sidewalks and building entrances are accessible.

>> **Blindness:** If you're a person who is blind and you use a screen reader such as JAWS to complete your coursework online, you may have to ask for assistance with some areas of your coursework, but your campus should have staff who can help you work around any difficulties.

>> **Deafness:** Unless audio is a major portion of the course, such as in a language listening course, persons who are deaf can typically read their way through a class. When audio or video is part of the content for a course, alternative text versions are typically available.

Learners who have documented learning disabilities can also succeed in the online environment. Most institutions have a department that learners with accommodation needs can turn to. This department not only supports learners but also trains faculty and staff on how to make the necessary accommodations for all students to be successful in the online environment.

REMEMBER

Disabilities are not limited to what others can see. Learners with anxiety disorders, for example, may need additional time for testing. That can be easily addressed online as long as you follow the same processes for requesting the accommodation.

Flip to Chapter 19 for more details on how people with physical and learning disabilities can handle online courses.

Traditional college students

According to a report from 2018 entitled "Grade Increase: Tracking Distance Education in the United States," the Babson Survey Research Group — along with their partners the Sloan Consortium, Pearson, and Tyton — determined that more than 80 percent of the people enrolled in online courses in 2017 were undergraduate students. You can probably figure that means a sizable number are in the traditional 18-to-24-year-old age group. There are some real advantages to studying online for students of this age.

Supplementing coursework

A slight variation in online learning is called *blended, hybrid,* or *web-enhanced coursework.* That means some of your resources and activities are shifted from the traditional classroom to the online environment. For example:

>> You might be expected to review a presentation online before coming to the traditional class.

>> You might take all your quizzes online rather than in the classroom.

>> You might be asked to participate in an online discussion between class meetings.

In some cases, faculty who teach blended courses eliminate one of the class meeting times. For example, if your class meets on Mondays, Wednesdays, and Fridays, your instructor may have you meet only on Mondays and Wednesdays in the face-to-face environment and transfer the Friday materials online. For a traditional-age student, that means having a few additional hours available for other activities.

Taking extra credits

How would you like to finish school early and put that shiny, new degree to work sooner? If you have time in your schedule and can accommodate a credit overload, you may find that taking an extra online course can help you speed through your academic program. Or, you can use summertime to catch up online.

Consider the example of Allison. Each summer, she came home to her parents' house for the summer and worked as a lifeguard at a nearby camp. However, she also enrolled in six credit hours through her university. She was not a full-time student, but the extra work did require a little discipline. After three summers, she had shaved off nearly a complete year of college!

WARNING

Before you try taking summer courses from a different school, be sure to verify whether the credits transfer.

Sleeping in

If you're a classic college student (unmarried and without children), not all of your time is spent studying. You may have a job, or you may be involved in campus activities that take up a considerable amount of time. We don't address what you do with your social time, but it's a significant factor in the lives of most 18-to-24-year-olds.

Not many traditional-age college students like waking up for an 8 A.M. class. If you study online, you can establish a schedule that works best for you. That means you can sleep in if you need to. As long as you manage your time effectively, it's possible to be a student online and have a social life (and maybe a job!).

Seniors and retirees

Senior citizens and retirees enjoy active lifestyles these days. That includes using the Internet. Don't let granny fool you: As the Pew Research group reports, technology adoption among seniors has never been higher. Some seniors are taking online courses for personal enjoyment or to "retool" for careers after retirement.

Seniors benefit from online education for the same reasons everyone else does (see the previous sections for examples), but convenience and not having to deal with transportation issues rise to the top. In addition, seniors have an advantage over most others in that they seem to be better at managing their time.

For young retirees, online learning could provide an avenue to retrain for a new career. In particular, military personnel who find themselves looking for work in their 40s can begin to prepare for their future without having to leave base. For example, First Sergeant Earl earned a special endorsement for teaching while stationed in South Korea; the university was in the United States. After he was discharged and returned to the States, he had the credentials he needed for a successful job search.

Teachers, especially college faculty, like to retrofit themselves for teaching through retirement as well. By enrolling in online courses, retiring faculty can update skills and acquire new understandings of the teaching and learning processes so that they're more marketable as part-timers or adjuncts. A retiree can still travel and teach (with a stable Internet connection, of course).

High school and homeschooled students

Perhaps the hottest area of growth and development in online learning impacts high school and homeschooled students. We address this topic in Chapter 18, but we review the basics here, in particular, the benefits of online learning for kids.

Even before COVID-19 made its first appearance, school districts offered online options for their students. In 2017, nearly 60% of public schools offered at least one online course. (These numbers come from the National Center for Educational Statistics.) In today's digital age, learning online has these distinct benefits for young students:

>> **It advances kids' technology skills.** Consider that most white collar jobs now require technology skills. With the globalization of business and industry, collaborating with colleagues around the world is common for knowledge workers. Children who acquire computer-mediated communication skills already understand how to collaborate online. Online learning teaches 21st century skills.

>> **It helps homeschooling parents plan their curricula.** In North America, homeschooling is inconsistently regulated. Having a quality source for instruction allows parents to select and supervise the curricula. Though state-supported schools still meet state mandates, parents can determine the most appropriate courses for their children.

>> **It allows kids to work at their own pace.** Virtual schools for kindergarten through 12th grade are more likely to be self-paced with parental supervision. In other words, if your child is gifted and can finish algebra in eight weeks, they can move on to their next course without waiting. If your child needs more time, that can be accommodated as well.

>> **It facilitates the management of health issues.** For kids with medical needs or disabilities, online education allows the family to manage health concerns without disrupting learning. For example, a child with severe diabetes can monitor blood sugar levels by snacking while learning. In a traditional classroom, the child would probably have to go elsewhere to snack, resulting in lost instructional time.

>> **It offers greater scheduling flexibility.** Reducing the time children spend in school increases time for other activities. In some cases, teens work significant internships, acquiring additional skills that complement their online education. For kids who excel in the arts or athletics and need additional time for practice, online education fits their lifestyles. Not only can they schedule learning before and after workouts and rehearsals, but also schooling doesn't stop because of travel to performances and events.

>> **It fills specialized needs that traditional high schools can't.** One high school can offer only so many classes, particularly in rural areas. The availability and expertise of teachers and school district financial constraints sometimes determine what courses students take. For students looking for more variety, online education can serve it up. Students aren't limited to what's available at their own school, but can tap into a wide network of available courses. They may find many of these courses at a state-supported virtual school, which directly ties into graduation requirements because those courses and programs follow the same state mandates.

Advanced placement (AP) courses allow high school students to study more challenging subject matter at a higher level than traditional high school courses. Additionally, these courses often count for college credit. Virtual high schools put AP courses within reach of those whose schools don't offer them. Even students who don't study entirely online can have access to the kinds of classes they want and need through these online programs. Of course, buyer beware: Check with your local district to be sure they'll accept the online credits.

TIP

Want to look further at online education for K–12 students? Visit the Aurora Institute at `https://aurora-institute.org`.

Getting a Grip on Potential Pitfalls

Working online isn't without its pitfalls. One of those pitfalls, especially for kids attending online schools, is cyberbullying; we cover how to deal with this pitfall in Chapter 18. The following sections describe a couple more realities you should consider before enrolling in an online course.

Online learning isn't easier

Contrary to popular belief, online learning isn't easier than traditional education. As we explain earlier in this chapter, most online education is instructor-led and follows a specific schedule. Though you may have the opportunity to choose when and where you study, you don't get to choose the content. If you're taking an online history course, you're going to study the same material that you would if you sat in a traditional classroom. The subject matter isn't "watered down." However, there are significant differences in the way you get the information and what you do with it.

Because online learning requires students to take more responsibility for their own learning, it can be more challenging! You may have to work a little harder to understand the concepts, and chances are, you'll be asked to do more than read a chapter and take a test. You're required to use critical thinking, to share your ideas in writing (not just by talking), and to demonstrate that you understand the material in ways other than by taking tests. We talk more about this topic in Chapter 16, but you should be prepared to prove that you're learning!

Also, online learning is more challenging for those who struggle with time management and study skills. Some students find it easier to attend a face-to-face class because the teacher's physical presence motivates them to complete assignments. If that describes you, you may struggle with an online course. (We show you later in this chapter how to assess your own discipline and determine your chances of online success.)

WARNING

If you're considering enrolling in an online course because you think it will be an easy, independent study, think twice! Read the course materials carefully before enrolling. Chances are good that your course will require a substantial amount of dedicated time and that you will have to adhere to definite deadlines.

Spontaneous, face-to-face discussions are not the norm

Earlier in this chapter, we talk about asynchronous learning — accessing course materials and completing assignments on your own time. When this term is applied to discussions — a common feature of online courses — one learner may post a comment at 1 A.M. and another may not respond until 5 P.M. That means discussion takes longer and isn't spontaneous. As an online learner, you have to learn to be patient in these circumstances. (Later in this chapter, we discuss the importance of patience and tolerance for online success.)

Given the time delay, it can be more difficult to sustain a conversation in asynchronous settings. Absent body language and immediacy, misunderstandings can also take on a life of their own. If you read something John posts and don't understand what he means, you may inadvertently take the discussion off course at 1 A.M.! By the time someone notices and you all get on the same page, valuable time is lost. The focus may be lost as well.

Determining Whether You're Ready to Join the World of Online Learning

So, do you think you're a good candidate for online learning? In the following sections, we review some of the characteristics and qualities that will make you successful. See how you measure up!

Assessing your own discipline

REMEMBER

One of the first areas you need to assess is the quality of your self-discipline. Some of us have more discipline than others. Ask yourself the following questions to assess your level:

>> **Are you a self-starter?** When it comes to completing a task, whether or not you think you'll enjoy it, are you one who starts without a lot of prompting? If you are, you're more likely to succeed online. When you receive assignments from your instructor, you will have to establish a personal schedule for getting those assignments completed. The first step is starting! Procrastinators don't do well in online education.

>> **Are you persistent?** What if your computer crashes and you can't complete an assignment as instructed? What if it's supposed to be done on a word processor and you break four fingers? How likely are you to give up when tasks are challenging or things don't go as planned? There are times when technology fails, group members disappear, and documents get lost. Persistence and addressing problems creatively and expediently can carry an online student through these challenges. Just be sure to communicate with the instructor

early in the problem stage. Let them know what you're prepared to do to remedy your calamity. (By the way, in the case of broken fingers, ask whether you can record assignments in an audio file.)

>> **Do you manage your time well?** What tools and strategies do you use to manage your time? Do you utilize a personal calendar? Do you schedule times or routine activities? Managing your time online will make you a successful student. You will need to dedicate study time and follow through with regular logins. You may also be juggling work and family. Online education requires effective time management skills.

>> **Can you work alone?** Even though a lot of online work is done in groups or collaboratively with other students, the majority of your time online is independent. Can you follow through with tasks by yourself? Or do you need others to be present? To succeed in an online course, you need the ability to work alone and to think independently. For example: When a problem has you stumped, it's important to try to find answers independently before asking the instructor. It shows that you have an independent spirit that solves problems without whining — no one likes a whiner! It also shows a great deal of initiative — a quality that's always valued.

Knowing how you learn

Think back to how you learned in traditional school. Individuals access and process information in a variety of ways. In this section, we talk about how people learn. Knowing how you learn best can help you select the kinds of classes that best match your learning style — as well as help you target those study skills that are most effective for you.

Learning strategies can be described most simply by three preferences: visual, auditory, and tactile or kinesthetic. This means that you prefer to take in information using your eyes or ears or by physical movement. Your brain then helps you process information using your preference. That said, please be aware that not everyone agrees that learning styles make a significant difference in the quality of learning. It's more an indicator of your *preference*.

TIP

Here are a couple online learning style inventories you can take to help you determine how you best learn (you can find others in a traditional web search of learning style inventories):

>> **Education Planner:** See its inventory at www.educationplanner.org/students/self-assessments/learning-styles-quiz.shtml

>> **Vark:** It's at https://vark-learn.com/the-vark-questionnaire.

Visual learners

People who prefer to learn visually like to read and look at images. They like to work with words that are on a page. In the online environment, visual learners prefer to read content or articles, look at charts and images, and take in information through their eyes. The page may be either a real textbook or a computer screen. For the record, most people are visual learners.

TIP

If you like to access information visually, you will do well with reading requirements. If you don't find enough graphics or images to help you learn, ask your instructor whether they know of alternatives. Sometimes textbooks come with corresponding websites that offer PowerPoint presentations and other supporting materials.

Auditory learners

Auditory learners prefer to hear information, and their brains process the sounds. Have you ever met someone who listens attentively to you but never takes notes and still remembers what you have told them? Chances are, that person is an auditory learner. Their ears take in the information and the brain stores and processes it. Auditory learners love to hear stories, by the way. In an online course, auditory learners immediately gravitate toward programs with sound, such as slides with narration or videos.

Those who are auditory learners may struggle a little with the text-heavy nature of many courses. However, these days more faculty are including podcasts and audio files as well as video introductions as part of their courses. They also may narrate PowerPoint presentations to help auditory learners better understand the material.

TIP

Need a couple of strategies for working with an auditory preference? Read out loud to yourself. When you read your classmates' posts, give them each a separate "voice."

TIP

Don't be afraid to look for additional materials on your own. Can't quite understand Newton's third law? You'd be surprised what you can find on YouTube, such as materials that are prepared for middle school kids but still make sense and entertain at the same time.

Tactile or kinesthetic learners

Perhaps you're best described as someone who likes to take action before reading the instructions or listening to directions. If so, you may be a tactile or kinesthetic learner! People who are kinesthetic like to put their bodies into motion in order to learn. It's too simplistic to say that this means the individual has to move in order to take in or process information, but when opportunities allow that person to put new ideas into practice, learning becomes easier. Say you want to learn a concept related to chemistry. You may read about it or listen to a lecture, but once you begin to experiment, it makes more sense. It's the action of doing that helps embed that new information.

TIP

Clicking a computer mouse doesn't count as movement. However, regardless of when or where you're working, you can stand up and walk around, eat while you work, take frequent breaks, and otherwise keep your fidgeting and movement going while you work.

Being patient and tolerant

Seldom are we told that patience and tolerance are necessary qualities for academic survival. However, the classroom has gone global, and technology is now a factor. In the following sections, we describe the facets of online learning that require your patience and tolerance.

REMEMBER

Online learning differs from traditional schooling in many ways. It's the 21st century method of acquiring information, putting it into practice, and interacting with other learners. Having some doubts is natural, but only if you enter the virtual classroom with a sense of wonder and possibility will you truly learn.

Trying new learning methods and technologies

Online learning stretches most learners. Many of the procedures and processes feel awkward, and the instructor may throw in new technology tools. How well you adapt to these additional challenges can make a difference in your overall survival online. The following short list describes some of the tools or methods you may face online (see Chapter 3 for more details on technology and the technological skills you need):

>> **Group work:** Very common online. Instructors pair up students or assign them to small discussion groups to work out problems.

>> **Wiki:** A web page that different people can edit. It's a simple tool that is used in group work. If you can edit a Word document, you can handle a wiki.

>> **Blog:** A web page that you may use in two different ways. You may just be asked to go to a blog and read the entries. Or, you may be asked to keep a blog — kind of like a public journal — of what you experience in the class.

>> **Webinar:** A live session where you can hear a presenter and see images. Instructors who have live office hours often use similar software.

>> **Chat:** Instant communication when you need to ask a question or work out a group decision.

>> **Podcasts:** Audio files that you can download and play on your computer or on your portable MP3 device.

Recognizing different kinds of people in the classroom

Cast your mind back to your glory days in high school. Chances are good that someone in your classes was a know-it-all. There may have been a teacher's pet. And how about a class clown? Guess what? They've moved online.

If you were particularly annoyed with a certain personality type when in a traditional class, you should prepare to meet the same person online. This time, however, you'll recognize their characteristics via writing behaviors. The know-it-all will answer everyone else's posts with an American Psychological Association (APA)-formatted reference. The teacher's pet will suck up with glowing acknowledgments of the teacher's presence. The class clown will always have a pun.

REMEMBER

There are probably many more ways to describe people. Suffice it to say that this is where tolerance comes back into play. It's important to get along when online, refrain from engaging in hurtful communication, and focus on your own work — not everyone else's. Check out Chapters 9, 10, and 11 for plenty of pointers on working well with others online.

Counting to ten when you're upset

REMEMBER

When something doesn't go your way in the online classroom, count to ten before reacting. If you read a comment that seems unkind or downright mean, don't blast off a nasty response. We say much more about netiquette in Chapter 15, but the bottom line is that you need to write civilly in the online world. Emotions are often incorrectly "read" into written communication, and this causes definite problems.

This is where the asynchronous nature of online learning is a real advantage, too. If John writes something that is borderline offensive on Thursday evening, Kelly can wait until Friday to see whether others have noticed and diplomatically said something. If not, she can then respond with a cooler head.

Chapter **3**

The Equipment and Skills You Need to Succeed

When it comes to technology tools and taking online courses, two components are essential to being successful: equipment and technological competencies.

» Your *equipment* includes things like your actual computer and attached devices that help you interact online, such as your webcam, headset, and microphone. Equipment also includes the programs and applications that you use to surf the Internet, write documents, and perform other digital tasks.

» *Technological competencies* refers to the basic skills you need when learning online.

Don't let these words scare you. Knowing what is expected up front helps you be more successful later. We explain in this chapter what you need for online learning success.

Checking Your Technological Readiness

The first thing you need in order to take an online course is a reliable computer that meets the minimum standards of your course or program. Most new computers meet many institutions' minimum standards for hardware and software out of the box. For programs and courses that require you to meet in real time over the Internet, you may also be asked to have a speaker, a microphone, and, sometimes, a webcam. Few programs require a camera, but having one can contribute to feeling more connected to your instructor and peers when meeting in real time. Additionally, more technical courses, such as those focusing on video creation, may require you to purchase more specific hardware and software. And, of course, you need a dependable connection to the Internet.

In the following sections, we explain what you need to meet minimum hardware and software requirements for most online classes, and we describe the importance of a fast, reliable Internet connection. With the rise of mobile devices such as tablets and smartphones, we would be remiss not to also talk about the use, pros, and cons of these devices for learning online.

Meeting minimum hardware requirements

Each online course has minimum hardware requirements. These standards are determined by the technology used to deliver course content. Courses using a lot of audio and video materials require better hardware than those relying solely on text-based materials.

Most institutions have a web page where they display the minimum and recommended hardware requirements. If, after a few minutes of searching, you're unable to find the computer requirements page on an institution's or organization's website, don't hesitate to pick up the phone and call them to ask. A good program also provides a list of minimum requirements and a list of additional hardware and software you might encounter when learning from them. Otherwise, once you start a course, your instructor will provide you with a list of any additional requirements that go above and beyond the organization's advertised list.

Table 3-1 shows an example of what you might see on an institution's computer requirements page. The columns note different types of hardware and the requirements for both PCs and Macs. Most computers two years old or newer meet these requirements.

TABLE 3-1 **An Example of Hardware Requirements**

Hardware	PCs — Windows	Macs	Chromebook
Processor	2 or more GHz	Dual-core Intel i5 or better	Intel Core m3 processor or better
RAM (random access memory)	4–8GB	4–8GB	4–8GB
Hard drive	256GB	256GB	32GB minimum
Monitor resolution	1024 x 768	1024 x 768	1024 x 768
Speakers	Sound card with headphones or external speakers	Sound card with headphones or external speakers	Sound card with headphones or external speakers
Microphone	Required in order to attend instructors' virtual office hours; a headset with microphone is highly recommended.	Required in order to attend instructors' virtual office hours; a headset with microphone is highly recommended.	Required in order to attend instructors' virtual office hours; a headset with microphone is highly recommended.
Webcam (optional)	720p	720p	720p

As we introduce different hardware components in the following sections, keep in mind that this information is simply an overview. Each operating system uses its own navigation method to find information, so as we talk about whether your computer meets certain requirements, you may need to reference your computer's manual or an additional resource to help you determine how to locate needed information. We suggest looking into other For Dummies books specific to your computer — you can peruse available titles at www.dummies.com/store.html.

TIP

If you plan on purchasing a new computer in order to take an online class, check with the institution to see whether you can purchase the computer at a discounted price. Many institutions have deals with computer manufacturers to provide their students with discounted hardware and software. For example, several schools use Microsoft 365, which is an online version of Microsoft Office Suite. As a part of this arrangement, students can often download a free, desktop version of the software to their personal computer while they are enrolled. If the institution doesn't offer discounts, you should still find out its minimum requirements before making a purchase. It's a good idea to print out the minimum requirements and take the printout with you to the retail store of your choice. Doing so can help the salesperson guarantee that you purchase a computer to meet your educational needs. If you have a student ID, take it with you and ask whether the store offers a student discount as well.

Processor speed

The *processor speed* refers to how fast your computer is able to process information and provide you, the user, with the output result; it's measured in gigahertz (GHz). The more complicated the task, the longer it takes the computer to provide you with output. Online courses that use more complicated materials, such as audio and video files, require a faster processor speed — in other words, more gigahertz.

Computers purchased within the past two years should have no problem meeting the processor speed requirements. If your computer is an older model, you should double-check to be sure its processor is fast enough.

TIP

Most computers have a screen that summarizes its physical makeup:

>> **If you're using a computer with Windows 10:** You can type **system** on the search bar at the bottom of the Windows desktop. Then click the System Information app when it appears. If you have a File Explorer window open, you can also right-click directly on the This PC link in the navigation pane on the left (see the sidebar "A quickie on right-clicking," later in this chapter) and then choose Properties from the menu that appears. This takes you to a screen that summarizes the computer's operating system version, processor speed, and memory amount. (See Figure 3-1.) Note that other versions of the Windows operating system may require different steps to find the same information.

System Information			– □ ×
File Edit View Help			
System Summary	Item	Value	
⊞ Hardware Resources	OS Name	Microsoft Windows 10 Pro	
⊞ Components	Version	10.0.19041 Build 19041	
⊞ Software Environment	Other OS Description	Not Available	
	OS Manufacturer	Microsoft Corporation	
	System Name	DESKTOP-RU4HJNB	
	System Manufacturer	Microsoft Corporation	
	System Model	Surface Pro 3	
	System Type	x64-based PC	
	System SKU	Surface_Pro_3	
	Processor	Intel(R) Core(TM) i5-4300U CPU @ 1.90GHz, 2501 ...	
	BIOS Version/Date	American Megatrends Inc. 3.11.2650, 4/30/2019	
	SMBIOS Version	2.8	
	Embedded Controll...	32.00	
	BIOS Mode	UEFI	
	BaseBoard Manufact...	Microsoft Corporation	
	BaseBoard Product	Surface Pro 3	
	BaseBoard Version	1	
	Platform Role	Slate	
	Secure Boot State	On	
	PCR7 Configuration	Elevation Required to View	
	Windows Directory	C:\WINDOWS	
	System Directory	C:\WINDOWS\system32	
	Boot Device	\Device\HarddiskVolume1	
	Locale	United States	
Find what:			Find Close Find
☐ Search selected category only	☐ Search category names only		

FIGURE 3-1:
A summary of the physical makeup of a computer with Windows Vista.

>> **Mac users:** You can click on the apple (top left of the menu bar) and then choose the About This Mac option from the menu that appears, to see a similar summary. (See Figure 3-2.)

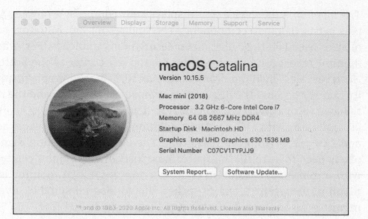

FIGURE 3-2:
A summary of the physical makeup of a computer with Mac OS X.

Memory

The role of computer memory is to assist the processor by temporarily storing instructions and other information for faster processing. Computer programs, also known as *applications* — Microsoft Word, for example — require computers to have a specific amount of memory available for their use. Memory is measured in gigabytes (GB).

Your computer's current memory capacity can be found on the same page as its processor speed. (See the preceding section and Figures 3-1 and 3-2.) Most newer computers come with plenty of memory, right off the shelf. However, if your computer is a few years older, it may not meet the minimum requirements for taking an online course. If this is the case, talk to either the institution's technical support team or a computer retailer about increasing your computer's memory. Depending on how old your computer is, increasing its memory may be all you need to do.

Hard drive

Your computer's hard drive is where all your files are stored. This includes the files required to run the computer's operating system and your installed applications. Think of the hard drive as a digital filing cabinet. How much information can be stored on your computer's hard drive depends on its size. Newer hard drives are measured in gigabytes or terabytes (TB). Older hard drives were measured using megabytes (MB).

Institutions may require that you have a hard drive with enough space to install additional programs and store your documents, such as homework assignments.

Monitor

The *monitor* is the device that displays your computer's output. A monitor's display is based on two components: size and resolution. Monitors come in a variety of sizes based on their diagonal measurements in inches. For example, a 20-inch monitor measures 20 inches from the top left corner to the bottom right corner. However, a 20-inch monitor has only an 18.8-inch viewable display. This disparity matters because the picture is developed using pixels, and the number of pixels that can fit in a given space is measured in terms of width by height. For example, on a monitor with a 640 x 480 resolution, there are 640 pixels across the screen and 480 pixels from top to bottom. The larger the monitor size, the bigger the pixels need to be to fill the space. Most institutions require you to have a monitor with a minimum resolution of 1024 x 768. A 17-inch monitor is best; however, monitors between 15 and 21 inches should also be suitable. Even the 13.3-inch monitors on our laptops display 1024 x 768 pixels just fine.

Speakers and microphone

Many online courses use audio and video files to support the curriculum. To hear the speech portion of each of these files, you need a good pair of speakers or a headset. Most computers come with speakers upon purchase. The speakers should work fine. However, your family and other housemates may prefer that you use a headset, to reduce distractions. Don't rush out and buy anything expensive. The headset you use to listen to your music player will work just fine. Your computer should have a built-in sound card and a round headphone jack for plugging in. The headphone jack may be located on the front or back of your computer. Or, if you use a laptop, the jack may be on one side. Most headphone jacks have a small Headset icon either above the jack or directly next to it.

Some instructors also may ask you to participate in a web-based conference using Internet applications. These applications allow instructors and students to communicate in a variety of ways, including via voice over the Internet. To do this, you need to have a microphone. Many computers, especially laptops, have built-in microphones. These can work, but we recommend that you purchase an inexpensive headset that incorporates a microphone. Look to spend about $50 for the basic set.

Webcam

Some programs or courses may require you to have a *webcam*, which is a camera for your computer. When you turn it on, the members of your audience see you sitting in front of the computer, as if they were looking through your screen. A webcam may be required for a couple of reasons:

First, you may be required to give synchronous presentations, and you may be asked to share an image of yourself during the presentation.

Second, an institution may require a webcam if a proctoring service is used for testing. Some proctoring services have you log in to a site and share your webcam so that they can confirm your identity and monitor your environment during a test. Most laptops and Chromebooks come with a webcam built in. If you have a desktop machine, you may need to purchase a separate camera.

Laptop and Chromebook

A *laptop* is a full computer system that is compact and easy to take on the go. You can buy laptops with either the Windows or Mac operating system on it that either meets or exceeds the minimum requirements we mention in the previous section. The *Chromebook* is a type of laptop that uses the Google Chrome operating system. It is specifically designed to run cloud-based applications, much like smartphones and tablets. Due to the limitation of relying solely on cloud-based applications, a Chromebook is often dramatically cheaper than a laptop. For the most part, you can accomplish much of your coursework on a Chromebook, though we recommend that you check the minimum requirements of your institution before making the investment. Many specialty programs cannot be installed on a Chromebook. Most Chromebooks and laptops come with a webcam built in.

Mobile device

Believe it or not, most mobile devices meet the minimum requirements needed to accomplish a lot of online learning tasks, including participating in synchronous sessions. For example, many institutions deliver their online courses using a specific learning management system application, where students log in to their virtual classroom and access course content. Most learning management systems — Canvas, for example — have a student mobile app that can be used on a smartphone or tablet to access the course. The same goes for synchronous communication tools such as Zoom. Students can use a mobile application to log in to a live session with their instructor and peers and participate in real time directly from their phone or tablet. This can be convenient for those on the move who want to watch a video on their bus commute to work or read a required article under a tree at lunch. Though these devices bring a lot of convenience and access to the learning experience, they aren't always the best tool for the job; therefore, we recommend that they not be used as the primary device for participating in your online course. For example, mobile devices often have problems when it comes to creating content such as essays, taking quizzes and exams, and participating in online discussions.

Some newer computers have webcams built directly into the monitor. If your computer doesn't have a built-in webcam, you can purchase one for $50; maybe less. When purchasing a webcam, the most important thing is to make sure it's compatible with your computer's operating system. Webcams that work with Mac computers don't necessarily work with Windows 10 machines. If a webcam is required by your institution and you're unsure which one to buy, contact the institution's technical support team. They can probably recommend one or two.

Meeting software requirements

After you have your hardware equipment, you need to install the right software (if you don't already have it on your computer). *Software applications* are the programs used to complete specific tasks. The two most important applications you need to have installed on your computer to take an online course are an Internet browser and a program like Microsoft Office or Google Suite (both of which are "productivity suites" that include components like word processing, email, and spreadsheets). Other applications may also be required by either the institution or an individual instructor, depending on the course content.

To check software requirements for a course, check the course description. Most institutions advertise software requirements there if they go beyond the standard requirements, to give you plenty of time to purchase the software before class begins. Don't forget to check the online bookstore for possible discounted purchasing.

Internet browser

The application that allows you to connect and interact via the Internet is called an *Internet browser.* Every computer purchased at a standard retail store these days comes with an Internet browser. Windows-based machines come with Microsoft Edge preinstalled. Macs come with Safari, and Chromebooks come with Google Chrome. These browsers, in most cases, work just fine, but we also encourage you to look at which browsers work best for your organization. (Later in this chapter, we explain how to obtain a reliable Internet connection.)

For example, some learning management systems, such as Canvas, work better with Google Chrome, and you may need to install it as another option. It's a good idea to have at least two browser options, just in case.

Unfortunately for Mac users, a few web-based tools — including those used in online courses — work only on Windows machines. This is becoming less and less of an issue and, hopefully, won't affect your ability to register for an online course. However, be sure to check the institution's software requirements before registering.

Email access

For academic programs, you communicate with registration and advising staff before you even start courses. After your application is accepted, some institutions provide you with an email account and instructions on how to access that account. These institutions often require that this account be used for all school business. On the other hand, allowing students to use an external email account of their choice is becoming increasingly popular. We recommend setting up a free account with Google (http://gmail.com) strictly for school communication. This helps separate your personal materials from your school communications.

TIP

Communication with academic institutions can become a part of your academic record. Therefore, if you are able to use a personal email address, choose one that's more professional in nature than certain personal addresses — for example, KevinJohnson@gmail.com rather than TheGoofster@gmail.com.

Word processing

The assignments that you don't complete directly online will most likely be completed using a word processing program such as Microsoft Word. For example, you may be asked to write an essay and turn it in directly to your instructor. To do this, you would use a word processing program to write your paper, save the file, and then upload it to your instructor.

TIP

If you don't have a word processing program installed on your machine and your institution doesn't require a specific program, you can choose from multiple online word processing applications nowadays. You may want to consider using an application such as Google Docs or Word (Microsoft 365). The biggest difference between these two web-based applications is that Google is free and Microsoft 365 requires a paid annual subscription. Both come with a suite of programs that include a word processor, spreadsheet, and presentation applications. They both also allow the sharing of files and collaboration in real time. This means that you and a peer can edit the same document at the same time from different computers in different locations.

Virus protection software

Whenever you're surfing the Internet, you should consider using virus protection software. Virus protection software, such as Bitdefender Antivirus (www.bitdefender.com) or Norton Antivirus (www.norton.com), protects your computer from malicious applications created to harm your computer hardware and files.

After being installed on your computer, antivirus software can monitor incoming communications and attachments from other computers. It can also check sites you're visiting to see whether they pose any danger. When viruses are found, the software alerts you to the danger.

TIP

Because computer viruses are always changing, you need to purchase an application that keeps up with those changes. Some programs have the option to update automatically, whereas others require you to update the software manually. We recommend that you update your antivirus software at least once a week.

REMEMBER

To reduce the risk of getting viruses, follow these guidelines when surfing the Internet:

>> Stay away from sites you don't know.

>> Don't open email attachments from people you don't know.

>> Don't open email attachments that seem suspicious, even if they're from people you know. For example, don't open an attachment that has no name in the subject line or that seems goofy or out of context.

>> Don't forget to turn off your computer (or at least its Internet connection) when you're not using it.

Additional programs

Depending on what class you're taking, your instructor may require you to acquire and install additional programs. For example, if you're taking a business class, you're likely to need a spreadsheet application, such as Microsoft Excel. Or, if you're a doctorate student, you may be required to install a statistics software package like SPSS for carrying out research. Many software companies have moved to a subscription-based purchasing structure. Gone are the days when you purchase a program, install it on your computer from a disc, and then use that version of the software as long as you want before updating to another version. Now, you purchase a monthly or annual subscription and are required to create a profile on the vendor's site upon purchasing their software. When running the software on your computer, you're required to log in, and the software checks to ensure that the software is up-to-date and paid for. Though you can no longer go on for years — skipping versions if you want to save money — you're at least guaranteed the latest version of the product at all times.

Establishing a reliable Internet connection

When taking an online course, the Internet is your lifeline to your instructor, peers, and course materials. Therefore, reliable Internet service is essential for your success. Not only do you need a fast, reliable Internet connection at home, but you should also have alternative options, just in case your connection fails.

Internet speed is measured in megabits per second (Mbps). This is also how most Internet service providers (ISPs) determine cost. The more Mbps you want, the faster your Internet goes — and the more it costs. Before signing a contract with an ISP, make sure the one you choose can deliver the speed and service availability needed to take an online course. Some institutions tell you the minimum upload and download speeds you need in order to connect to their system. Even if you don't know what these figures mean, you can still ask prospective service providers whether they're capable of meeting those requirements. Some general speed recommendations based on standard online learning activities include the ones described in this list:

>> **0–5 Mbps:** This speed is good for basic functions like surfing the web and checking email. This is roughly equivalent to 3G cellular service, if you're using your phone as a hotspot. This is not recommended for online courses that require synchronous communication in real time using video.

>> **5–50 Mbps:** Works pretty well for more complex functions (including video calls) if only one device at a time is accessing the Internet. This is roughly equivalent to 4G/LTE cellular service and can work with many online courses.

>> **50–100 Mbps:** Good for more complex tasks, including streaming video and making video calls while the Internet is being accessed by multiple devices. Though much faster speeds are available, this should be plenty for typical online learners.

WARNING

It has been our experience that connecting to the Internet using satellite equipment can be problematic. The delay between earth and satellite may cause the system to time out. Sadly, the result is that you can't log in.

If you live in an area that has limited options for connecting to the Internet and are concerned that the connection speed may not be adequate, you should

>> **Contact the institution and explain your situation.** See whether their technical support staff has any ideas.

>> **Arrange for a 30-day, money-back trial with any prospective Internet service providers.** Then you can test the system without having to a commit to a 1- or 2-year contract before knowing whether it will meet your needs.

REMEMBER

Trust us when we tell you that sometimes when an assignment is due, your Internet connection — even one that's typically reliable — will die. This can be frustrating and keep you from being able to turn in assignments and/or participate in synchronous meetings. Therefore, you must have a backup plan for accessing your course. Some ideas for backups include the use of your phone as a temporary hotspot, your public library, an office, or a nearby coffee shop.

Testing Your Technological Abilities

After you have the right hardware, the right software, and a reliable Internet connection, you need a few technological skills to match. Understanding your technological competencies up front can help you determine whether it would be a good idea for you to take an introductory computer course or read some computer books before enrolling in an online class. The following sections describe the skills you need.

Reading and scrolling efficiently

Much of the information you receive when taking an online class is provided to you directly on the screen. Although printing it is always an option, you're not always provided with reading assignments in the form of a word processing file that you can save and print easily. Therefore, you need to be able to read onscreen information quickly and know how to scroll when text goes off the screen. To scroll, simply find the scroll bars on the bottom and right side of the window. The bottom scroll bar allows you to scroll left and right, whereas the scroll bar on the right lets you scroll up and down. Some computer mice have buttons, scroll wheels, and touch capabilities that allow quick scrolling functionality.

Having the window maximized to fit the entire screen is also helpful because it reduces the need to scroll. If you're a Windows user, you can maximize the screen by clicking on the Maximize icon in the top right of the active window. Mac users can click on the green button in the top left of the active window. Both buttons are located in the active window's border.

TIP

Knowing how to zoom text within your web browser may be helpful as well. For most browsers, you can find Zoom In and Zoom Out options on the View menu. However, your Internet browser may work differently.

REMEMBER

Take frequent breaks. This helps reduce eyestrain, which can lead to higher levels of productivity in the long run. A simple 2-minute break to get a drink of water or use the restroom does wonders for your efficiency.

Typing quickly and accurately

Because most communication in online courses occurs via text, you need to be able to type quickly and accurately. Speed and accuracy are even more important during synchronous meetings, where you may be trying to answer questions in real time. (We explain synchronous learning in detail in Chapter 2.)

REMEMBER

Being able to type quickly reduces the time it takes to complete assignments and participate in online discussions. Though the spell checker is a wonderful tool, accurate typing skills are always more desirable. A spell checker with automatic correction often "corrects" misspellings erroneously, replacing the word you intended with a similarly spelled one that changes the meaning of the sentence. So, no matter how well you type or how much you use a spell checker, always proofread your work before submitting it.

Whether you have your fingers properly placed on the keyboard or use the 2-finger, hunt-and-peck method doesn't matter. No one will know how you type. However, if you need practice, you may want to consider a typing program that helps you learn how to type and provides timed tests that report your speed and accuracy. Examples are Typesy at `www.typesy.com` and TypingClub at `www.typingclub.com`.

Dictation is also an option for those who may experience painful carpal tunnel syndrome in their wrist or have arthritis. You used to have to purchase specialty software in order to take advantage of dictation features, but nowadays this capability is built into most operating systems — including mobile devices. (You may have used this feature for helping send text messages.) Dictation capabilities allow you to use a microphone to translate your speech to text. For example, all newer versions of Microsoft Word, including the online version, have a Dictate command that translates your speech to text, so you can do this on Windows, Macs, Chromebooks, and mobile devices. Some programs and devices come with accuracy training support to help learn your specific speech patterns.

Organizing folders

Have you ever gone looking for a file on your computer and been unable to find it? This tends to happen for two reasons:

>> Learners are unorganized and save their files in different places on their hard drives.

>> Learners save different files on several devices, forgetting which flash drive or folder the file was saved in.

We recommend that you have one place where you save all your course files, whether it's your computer's hard drive or a cloud drive (see the nearby sidebar for more about these devices), and perform backups frequently. We also recommend that you organize your digital files the same way you would organize physical files in a filing cabinet, using folders and subfolders.

Image a 3-drawer filing cabinet. In the top drawer, you want to store personal information. In the middle drawer, you want to store work files. And in the third drawer, you want to store school files. In the digital world, we think of these drawers as folders. Therefore, you might create three folders on your hard drive with the titles Home, Work, and School, respectively.

Now imagine opening the bottom drawer, where you want to store your school information. Inside the physical cabinet, you might create a hanging folder titled with the name of the institution. For example's sake, assume that you're attending Smarty Pants College. Then, inside that hanging folder, you might create a file folder for each of the courses you take at that institution. Your digital file structure should follow the same concept. Therefore, inside the `School` folder, you need to create a subfolder named `Smarty Pants College` and then a sub-subfolder inside for each of the courses you take — for example, `ENG101`.

By having a standard organizational structure on your hard drive, you can quickly and easily save and retrieve information when needed. Consistency is the key. Figure 3-3 is a screen shot of the drive structure where Kevin saves his school files. Notice for each term, he creates a folder for each course. Within each of those, he then creates four subfolders: `Admin` for administrative files such as the course syllabus, `Assignments` for course assignment files, `Discussions` for original discussion posts, and `Resources` for additional files provided by the instructor throughout the term of the course.

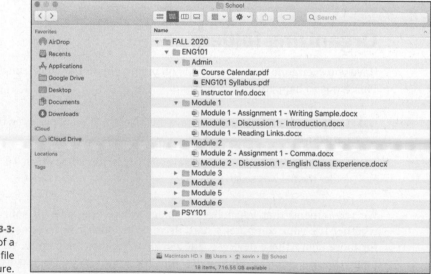

FIGURE 3-3:
An example of a computer's file structure.

SAVING YOUR FILES TO A CLOUD DRIVE

Cloud computing is a way of offering services related to data where the end user (you) can access files and programs as long as you are connected to the Internet. "The cloud" is the ethereal place where this data is stored. Services such as Google and Microsoft now offer hard drive space in the cloud. These storage spaces act just like the hard drive that's connected directly to your computer; they are simply located elsewhere and are accessible via the Internet. The advantage to using cloud storage is that you don't have to worry about accidentally leaving your files at home when you want to work on them during lunch or while traveling. These programs often have a bridge program that connects to your computer and makes them look and act just like any other drive on your machine. This allows you to create folders and work on files locally and then save them back to the cloud so that they stay up-to-date at all times.

Navigating the web

Being able to access and navigate the web is one of the most important skills you need when taking an online course. Specific navigation skills you should have include these:

>> **Opening your Internet browser:** Locate and click on your browser's application icon on the Start menu (Windows) or Dock (Mac).

>> **Navigating to a given URL:** Type the HTTP address in the address bar at the top of the browser's window — for example, `http://google.com`. In most cases, you can leave off the `http://` and simply type the address — for example, `google.com`. The browser automatically assumes that you mean an HTTP address.

>> **Navigating to the previous page:** Use the browser's Back button at the top of the screen, which has an arrow pointing to the left.

>> **Opening a hyperlink in a new tab or window:** Right-click on the link and select whether you want to open a new tab or a new window.

>> **Switching between open tabs or windows:** To open a new tab or window, click on the File menu and choose the New Window or New Tab option. To switch between tabs, either click on the desired tab with the mouse or hold down the Control (Ctrl) key and press the tab key on the keyboard. To switch between windows, click on the desired window on the taskbar.

>> **Refreshing the current screen:** Click the Refresh button in your browser or press the F5 key on the keyboard.

A QUICKIE ON RIGHT-CLICKING

Just in case you've never heard the term *right-click,* a PC mouse has two sides. Most of the clicking you do when surfing the web is left-clicking (and right-handed users do this with their index finger). But the other side works, too! You usually use the right side when you want to display a menu of options that can be executed depending on the location of the cursor. So, when we say "right-click," you should use your mouse or trackpad to highlight or select the words or icon and then click on the right half of the mouse. For the "lefties" out there, we recommend that you locate your computer's Control Panel (Windows) or System Preferences (Mac) and change the primary button to the right side, where your index finger is positioned. For you, when we say "right-click," we really mean "left-click." Confused yet?

Mac users, you can also use Control+click. Laptop and Chromebook users, you can place two fingers on the track pad while pressing down on the click bar.

>> **Resizing the browser window:** Click-and-drag the bottom right corner to resize the window to your liking, or use the Resize button in the top right (Windows) or left (Mac) of the browser window.

>> **Locating and opening downloaded files:** Navigate to the Downloads folder on your hard drive and double-click on the downloaded file.

>> **Conducting a web search using Google or another search engine:** Navigate to http://google.com and enter your search criteria in the search box. Then click on any of the links provided on the search results page.

TIP

If any of the preceding skills is unfamiliar to you, don't worry: None of them takes long to master — it's just important that you know how to do them. If you need help, you may want to check out the latest edition of The Internet For Dummies, by John R. Levine and Margaret Levine Young (Wiley).

Downloading and installing software

Earlier in this chapter, we discuss the possibility of having to purchase or download and install software. You have to know how to do this. Most commercial software programs can now be purchased online. Even if you buy them at a retail store, you receive only the instructions and an installation code to take home with you. Typically, you need to download and save the software to your hard drive, browse and locate your file, run the file by double-clicking on it, and follow the step-by-step instructions displayed on the screen. Chromebook users, you go to Google Play and purchase applications (apps), just like you do on mobile devices.

By finding out which software will be needed early in the process, you can better determine whether you can install it yourself or you need assistance. If you need assistance, you can try calling technical support at the institution, but depending on the program needing to be installed, they may not be able to help you. (Chapter 10 details which tasks technical support can help you with.) However, you can always find a local retailer that has technical staff on hand who can help you for a fee. That tech-savvy family member or friend can also come in handy.

REMEMBER

When purchasing and downloading software, know which operating system your computer uses, how much memory it has, and how much hard drive space is available. Refer to the "Meeting minimum hardware requirements" section, earlier in this chapter, to determine your computer's profile information.

Using email

One of the most common forms of communication occurs by using electronic mail, also known as email. Email is used to communicate with your peers and instructor. As we mention in the earlier section "Email access," some institutions provide you with a new email account for school use. Others may require you to provide them with a personal account. In this situation, we recommend opening a free email account with a service such as Google's Gmail (mail.google.com) for school use only.

Here is a list of common email-specific tasks that you should be able to complete:

>> **Open your email application:** Locate and click on your email client/application on either the Start menu (Windows) or Dock (Mac) — for example, Microsoft Outlook or Mail. If you're using a web-based email account, open your Internet browser, navigate to your email provider's website, and log in using your username and password.

>> **Check for new messages:** New messages are usually automatically downloaded and listed in bold print. To force your computer to check for new messages, click either the Send and Receive or Get Messages button.

>> **Check the Spam folder or Junk folder for misplaced messages:** Click on the Spam folder or Junk folder to open it and then check for any mislabeled messages. If a message has been mislabeled, click the Not Spam button or Send to Inbox button to reclassify the message. When you do this, your mail

program should start remembering which messages should not be sent to the Spam folder or Junk folder.

» **Compose new messages and address them to one or more recipients:** Click the Compose New Message button or New Message button. Type the recipients' email addresses in the To text box, separating each address with a space, comma, or semicolon, depending on your email application. Enter an email in the BCC (Blind Carbon Copy) text box if you want to send a message to multiple people but don't want the recipients to see to whom the message is being sent.

» **Attach a document to a message:** Click the Attach Document button, browse for the desired file, and click the option to attach the file to your document.

» **Open messages with attachments:** Click on the desired message in the inbox. Click on the attachment and download the file to your computer. Locate the Downloads folder and double-click on the file.

» **Edit a document and resend it as an attachment:** Edit the document, choose File ⇨ Save As, and save it to the desired location on your hard drive. Return to the email application and click either Compose New Message or Reply within an existing message. Follow the procedures for attaching a document to a message.

TIP

If you need help learning how to use email, there are a few resources you can explore. If the application is on your computer, you can use the application's built-in Help feature, found on the menu bar at the top of the screen. If you use a web-based mail system, you most likely have on the screen a Help link that transports you to a site with detailed descriptions, screen shots, and video tutorials on how to use the application. When all else fails, go to YouTube (www.youtube.com) and search for what you're looking for and add the word **tutorial** after it. For example, searching for **Google mail attachment tutorial** brings up several videos on how to attach files to a Gmail account.

Staying Safe Online

As you start using the Internet more, it becomes even more important to understand when and where to provide certain information in an online context. In the following sections, we explain how to make secure payments, remember and protect your passwords, and ensure your personal safety.

Making secure payments

REMEMBER

You need to be sure that you're truly protected when making online payments. This may be when registering for classes, purchasing books, or ordering study supplies online. Before entering your credit card or contact information into any web page, be sure that you trust the vendor and that you're entering your information on a secure site. There's a quick way to ensure that the site you're viewing is secure: Look at its website address. If the letter *s* appears after `http` in the address, you're visiting a secure site.

For example, if you visit Amazon.com to look at items to buy, you can see that the address, `http://www.amazon.com`, always starts with `http://`. This is because you're simply looking and you aren't being asked to share private information. However, when you're ready to check out and make a payment, you can see that `http://www.amazon.com` changes to `https://www.amazon.com`. This means that you're now connected securely and that any information you share is private between you and Amazon.com.

The following screen shots provide examples of unsecure and secure websites. Figure 3-4 shows an example of a site that's on an unsecure page. Notice how the site address, also known as the *URL*, begins with `http`. Figure 3-5 shows a secure page of the same site. Notice how its URL begins with `https`. The letter *s* means secure. Don't forget to check for it before sharing private information, especially financial information. As this example shows, websites don't need to secure every page, only those where private information is being entered or displayed.

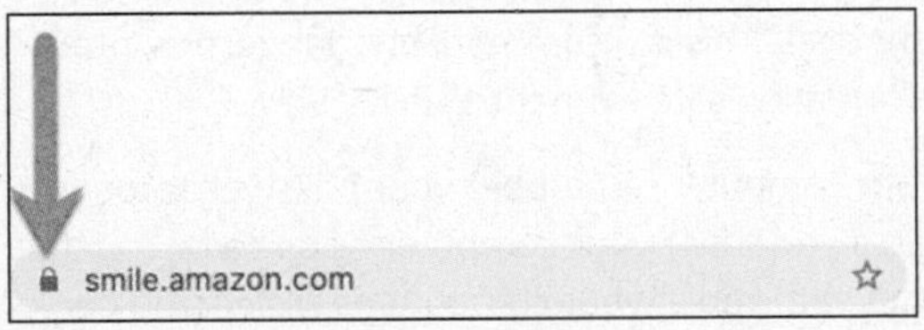

FIGURE 3-4:
A sample URL of
a secure site.

🔒 smile.amazon.com ☆

Remembering and protecting passwords

One thing that never fails when you become a part of the Internet community is the number of logins and passwords you need wherever you go. It's not uncommon for online students to have three or four different passwords just to access school information, depending on the technologies used.

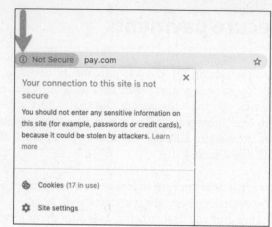

FIGURE 3-5:
A sample URL of
an unsecure site.

REMEMBER

Thinking of a password can be fun! Most institutions require 8 to 12 digits for a password, and many ask for a combination of letters, numbers, capitals, and, sometimes, symbols. For your own security, don't choose the obvious; instead, think of something unique to you, similar to a vanity license plate. You'll have a chuckle every time you log in. For example, a ghost hunter might select "ICg0sts2!" (I see ghosts, too!) The password "2kds1DG*" might be perfect for someone with two small children and one big dog.

REMEMBER

When it comes to passwords, here are a few dangerous practices to avoid:

>> Don't write your passwords on a sticky note that you attach to your monitor or on a piece of paper that's the first thing you see when you open the top drawer of your desk. This is a common, but dangerous, practice. Be sure to keep your information safe from the public's view.

>> Don't have your computer remember your passwords for you. This is especially true if you share your computer or use a laptop that you take different places with you. If your computer is stolen, the person who stole it now has access to your secure information.

>> Don't use the same password for all protected sites. Though it seems harmless and efficient, having the same password for everything makes you vulnerable if your information is ever compromised. Choose a different password for each site, and change your passwords frequently.

TIP

One way to remember all your passwords and keep them secure is to store them in an encrypted password manager program such as 1Password (https://1password. com. These programs also help generate random passwords to help make your password more secure. The advantage to such programs is that you have to remember only a single password — the one that's used to unlock the password manager program. Most password managers come with secure browser plugins that allow you to access passwords immediately upon visiting a site where a password is needed. After you enter your program password, it automatically fills in your login credentials and password for you. These programs can also be accessed online or via mobile devices so that they're with you at all times.

REMEMBER

Never give your password information to anyone, even technical support staff. They may have to reset your existing password in order to solve a particular problem, but they should have access to everything they need without asking you to share your password.

Ensuring personal security

REMEMBER

In the previous section, we discuss protecting your personal information and your passwords, and ensuring that you provide only certain information on secure websites. There's another type of security you should be aware of when participating in an online course: your personal security. We don't want to scare you; we simply want to remind you to stay safe when communicating online. Here are some important guidelines:

>> **Keep private information private.** Don't reveal too much about yourself. Almost every online course asks students to participate in an icebreaker activity. Many times, this includes revealing personal information about yourself, including your family, hobbies, and geographical location. Be sure to share this kind of information wisely. For example, feel free to say that you're married with two kids and live in Illinois. However, don't post your children's names or their elementary school photos. Disclosing medical conditions is also inappropriate. Your classmates really don't need to know you have irritable bowel syndrome.

>> **Guard your contact information:** You may need to provide contact information to your instructor or peers when working on a group project. Again, provide only the information that's necessary to complete the project. For example, you may want to give out your email address and possibly even a phone number, but not your street address. An instructor who needs to mail information to your home should have access to that information via the academic institution. If asked to provide that information, feel free to politely question why it is needed and who it will be shared with.

>> **Stay safe when meeting classmates in person:** Occasionally we find students who live in the same geographical location enrolled in our classes. In this situation, students often ask whether they can meet face-to-face to complete group projects. As instructors, we think this idea is fine; however, be safe when meeting classmates for the first time. We recommend always meeting in a public place, such as a restaurant or café, during common business hours. As a precaution, you may also want to notify your instructor that you're planning to meet, and provide the day and time. Afterward, you can provide your instructor with a summary of what you accomplished.

2

Preparing to Be a Learner

Figure out how to evaluate your institutional options

Learn the ins and outs of the application process

Control your educational costs with the help of financial aid

Register for courses and prepare for your first class

Chapter **4**

Discovering What's Available Online

After your appetite for learning online has been whetted, where should you go to find the right course offering? You may be surprised at the variety of institutions and organizations that offer online courses and how these courses have been packaged together for degrees. This chapter walks you through the many places you can find different kinds of online courses, and the various ways in which they are organized. Finally, we look at accelerated courses and how they work online.

Examining Different Types of Online Programs and Courses

Let's face it: Most adults avoid school because it means hard work. However, they have good reasons to continue learning, including job promotions, higher earning potential, elevated status, and personal enrichment. The surprising thing is that school and learning are becoming synonymous with online learning. That said, in this section we discuss aspects you should consider when looking at online programs and courses.

How important is it to you to earn college credit for your work? Do you have the time and resources to take enough courses to complete a degree? Or do you need only a few courses for professional development or skills enhancement? Would a specific certification be the professional seal of approval you need? Maybe you want to learn about a topic to help you in your personal life, like faux painting or dog training. How you answer these questions determines the kinds of online programs that are best for you.

Earning traditional credit

If you've decided to take an online course at a college or university, chances are good that you're looking to earn some sort of traditional credit for your work. As you should! This section describes the kinds of credit you can earn for your efforts — specifically, credits toward undergraduate or graduate degrees, credits toward academic certificate programs, and high school credits. You can earn traditional college credits at 2-year and 4-year higher education institutions (which we cover later in this chapter) if you have completed your high school education. If you're still working on high school, you can earn credits via accredited online programs that serve your unique needs.

Credits toward undergraduate and graduate degrees

Yes, you can earn an entire degree online! You can find programs that award associate's (2-year), bachelor's (4-year), master's, and even doctoral degrees online. You also can use online classes to supplement in-person coursework at a traditional institution. If you follow our suggestions for searching for a course at different institutions (they appear later in this chapter), you'll probably see this in the marketing information you find.

REMEMBER

Schools package courses together for an online degree just like they do for a degree you would earn in a traditional fashion. The degree consists of required courses you must take and a handful of elective courses. Only when you earn the necessary number of credit hours in the right mix of required and elective courses is the degree conferred. How many hours depends on the type of degree you're seeking, the state you're studying in, and the individual institution. However, in general, these are the expectations:

>> **Associate's degree:** Typically requires around 60 credit hours and may represent the first two years of a bachelor's degree

>> **Bachelor's degree:** Requires 124–128 credit hours

>> **Master's degree:** Requires 32–36 hours beyond a bachelor's degree. Some programs require as many as 44 credit hours

>> **Doctorate:** Requires around 60–75 credit hours beyond a bachelor's, plus successful completion of a comprehensive examination and a written dissertation of original research

When you enroll in a college course, the number of credit hours you'll receive upon completing it should be evident in the course schedule or the marketing information. Schools are typically transparent about stating how many credit hours they attach to a particular course, because this can make a difference in the total number of hours awarded that count toward a degree. A typical semester course awards three credit hours. By looking at the course number, you can tell whether those credits are undergraduate or graduate hours:

>> Any course with a number between 100 and 400 in its name (for example, PSY101) indicates undergraduate credit, which is what you need for an associate's or bachelor's degree.

>> Courses named with numbers 500 and higher grant graduate level credit, suitable for master's degrees and doctorates.

You may have seen or heard commercial ads claiming you can finish a degree in as little as 18 months. These programs target adults who have previously earned some undergraduate credit and are now ready to complete a bachelor's degree. This newer twist in online education is actually a continuation of a former adult education model. This model, which started a couple of decades ago, established a night-and-weekend schedule for working adults. Some programs "accelerated" their courses by compressing a 16-week course into 8 weeks, but not always. The point was that you could go to work during the day and catch up on coursework on the weekend. Today's model of online education offers even more convenience in that you don't have to push it all off to Saturday or Sunday. Because you work from the comfort of your home or office, you can engage in learning throughout the week.

TECHNICAL STUFF

One factor you may experience in online degree programs is the use of *cohort* groups. Simply put, this means when you begin a series of courses toward the completion of a degree, you progress with the same group, or cohort, of students through the entire degree. If John is in your first class, John should be in your last class — and every class in between! Many people believe that the bonds formed among a cohort group of online students are stronger than those in and face-to-face cohort and more likely to influence students to positively persist through programs. If John is your friend, he might talk you out of dropping out when times get tough. Plus, from an administrative perspective, cohorts are easier to track and often allow an institution to offer more start dates so that students don't have to wait several months to begin taking classes.

High school credits

High school credit functions a little like college credit in that you need to earn the right *number* of course credits and the right *types.* This requirement varies from state to state in the United States, however. For example, in one state you may need four years of English, whereas you may be able to squeak by with only three in another state. Depending on which state you live in and whether you're home-schooled or attending a traditional school, you might earn all or part of your high school credits by way of online schools.

REMEMBER

Make sure that any online high school courses you investigate will count toward graduation in your state. Start by checking your local school district's policies in accordance with the state requirements. A visit or phone call to the district office should scrounge up the information you need, but you can also search your state's department of education for policy statements concerning online education. Parents can also visit www.k12.com to see a list of tuition-free and tuition-based online programs for K–12 students based on state.

Obtaining certifications and other credentials

Maybe you're interested in a career change or you want to branch into a new direction within your current field. A certification, sometimes referred to as an endorsement, may be just what you need, and you can earn many of these online.

A *certificate* is sort of a miniature degree that signifies continuing education following a planned and purposeful curriculum. It offers only what you need for a specific professional field or task. For example, if you study for a certificate in web development, you don't have to take computer science courses in COBOL programming, but you do need graphics and multimedia instruction. If you're studying for a certificate as a dental assistant, you don't have to take an English composition course, but you need courses in radiology and diagnostics. Just the facts, ma'am.

Typically, a certificate is much shorter than a traditional degree. If you think of an associate's degree as a 2-year degree (60 hours) and a bachelor's degree as a 4-year degree (124–128 hours), the certification is a 1-year degree. For example, you can earn a certificate in medical transcription for an average of 44 credit hours. Interested in private security? A certificate is available for as few as 50 credit hours.

Another point to keep in mind is that some certificates can lead to other degrees. For example, if you earn a certificate in eLearning, some of those courses may count toward a master's degree at the same institution. Ask the school officials about this issue if you think the certificate may take you further.

More and more institutions offer certification online, including traditional 2- and 4-year institutions. Quality programs are truly beneficial in that they allow students to extend their professional development while continuing to work full-time. Every institution defines its own requirements for degrees and certificates based on standards set by the institution's accrediting agency. You need to compare carefully when looking at multiple programs. Drill down and see which courses are required and whether they hold your interest.

One of the best sources of information for a certification program is your professional association. Read professional newsletters and ask practitioners about the kinds of certificates and credentials valued in that field.

Staying current or retooling for work through MOOCs

We don't have to tell you how competitive the world of work has become. Most employers are looking for clear evidence of up-to-date skills, including technical and soft (interpersonal) skills. More employers are hiring based on skills (versus using a degree as the primary requirement). As a learner, you have many choices to learn by way of online vendors such as Coursera and Udemy. These companies sometimes offer free versions of their courses; or for a minimal payment, you can obtain a verified certificate of completion. Topics like big data analysis and artificial intelligence are definite career-boosters. If you don't need the academic credit but do need the background and some hands-on experience, these might be good options. Whenever you enhance your professional skills, you stand to profit via promotions and salary boosts. (In Chapter 17, we discuss how you can document your experience and work through an ePortfolio; this enriches the basic certificate.)

The majority of these courses are what we call *massive open online courses*, also known as *MOOCs*. You may be one of ten thousand learners. MOOCs do follow a schedule — don't be fooled. Sometimes you're asked to submit assignments and to peer-review other students' work. The principles of good online learning apply just as much to MOOCS as they would to any other online learning experience.

Continuing your education with a few classes for fun or profit

Online courses aren't limited to degree or certificate programs. You can actually have fun online! For example, you might take a course in *feng shui*, the ancient Chinese practice of orienting objects to achieve desirable outcomes.

Personal interest

Ever wonder about your genealogy but don't know how to start researching and documenting your heritage? There's an online course for that. How about picking up a second language? Digital photography? These examples show the diversity of online courses.

What kinds of institutions offer such courses? To be honest, you may find a course for free or very little money by starting up your favorite search engine (such as Google or Yahoo!) and typing **online course** + *<name of topic>*. Try it — you'll be surprised! These courses may not be supported by an institution, and you won't earn credit, but you will find the information you seek. For example, coauthor Kevin recently took an online photography course, where he learned the nuances of digital photography. He paid a fee to the photography school and completed the work online. If you are concerned about quality, you can conduct a Google search to see if there are any course or program reviews specific to the course you are interested in taking.

If you're looking for an institution to back you, you may find that your local college (2-year or 4-year) offers quite a few online courses geared toward personal interests. Topics may include the ones listed earlier in addition to art history, nutrition, parenting, and much more. These courses are usually part of the institutions' community development catalog or noncredit courses.

Professional development

In many fields, professionals are encouraged or required to complete professional development courses annually. For example, in the state of Illinois, per state funding guidelines for grant-funded adult education programs, faculty are required to complete six hours of professional development per fiscal year. So, if you want to keep your job, you have to complete those six hours of training somehow. If you're a practicing medical or dental professional and want to maintain your licensure, you have to earn a prescribed number of continuing education credits per year. These kinds of courses may be found at institutions that award degrees in those fields. For example, if you need credits for teaching, a college that awards degrees in education is a logical place to look.

In addition, more and more professional associations offer professional development online. They know that professionals appreciate the convenience of learning anytime, anywhere. You can find many opportunities by conducting a search for *<your field>* + **online courses**. For example, the Young Adult Library Services Association offers its members online courses related to their professional needs. You can find these opportunities by searching for *<your association>* + **online courses** in your preferred search engine.

Just make sure that any professional development course credits you earn will be accepted by the professional association that requires you to earn them. To find out, visit the association's site and search for statements concerning acceptance of online credit. For example, if you're a dentist and you visit the American Dental Association's continuing education page, you'll see a clear statement regarding states' limits on the number of hours that can be earned in self-paced online courses.

Compliance training

In business and industry, compliance training accounts for most course offerings. What kind of compliance? It might involve ethics training, safety and material data, or emergency preparedness. Other examples include processes and procedures for requisitioning funds, or must-know policies. All these are courses you may find online. The most common provider is your company's human resources department.

TIP

Compliance training works well as a self-paced course, so you shouldn't be surprised if you're in a course all by yourself. However, keep in mind that your participation, what pages or content you read, and how well you score in follow-up tests may be reported back to the company. We discuss self-paced courses in more detail later in this chapter, in the section "Instructor-led courses versus self-paced courses."

Finding Out Which Institutions Offer Online Programs and Courses

Whether you're interested in taking one or two online courses or completing an entire degree online, the process of searching for online education offerings isn't much different from researching traditional education options. First you need to determine what kind of institution best meets your needs. Are you seeking a bachelor's degree or higher? Then you need at least a 4-year school. In this section, we walk you through your choices according to the type of institution so that you know what to look for.

Four-year colleges

Many 4-year colleges and universities, both public and private, offer bachelor's degrees and graduate degrees online. They may also offer certificates and personal enrichment courses. Some are traditional schools with real brick-and-mortar campuses; others are completely virtual with no physical place to go. We discuss how to get course information from both of these types of schools in the following sections.

TIP

Hold on there! Before you go randomly searching, considering the following recommendations may save you time:

>> **If you're completing a degree that you previously started at a traditional school:** We recommend that you go back to the institution where you were a student and talk to someone about what courses may be available online. Jump ahead a little to the section "Brick-and-mortar schools."

>> **If you're starting an entire degree from scratch:** You have to decide which of the two types of institutions that we talk about in the following sections you want to earn it from: brick-and-mortar or wholly online. Read both of the following sections to find out how to find necessary information.

>> **If you simply need a course or two for personal interest or professional development:** We recommend that you look at your local state institutions. Not only do you keep your money in-state, but you're also closer if you need to drive to the campus for any reason. Also, don't forget online options like Coursera, Udemy, and EdX.

Brick-and-mortar schools

If you type *online courses* into a search engine (such as Google, Yahoo!, or MSN), only some of the schools in the resulting list are traditional institutions with physical campuses. For example, you might find Colorado Technical University or DeVry University. They offer their programs and classes both on traditional campuses and by way of online counterparts.

Traditional brick-and-mortar schools, such as your local state university, don't seem to pop to the top of the search results. They're competing against the online giants, and their marketing dollars aren't going as far. However, the brick-and-mortar model is still worthy of consideration — you just have to take a different route to gather the information you need:

>> Rather than suggest that you conduct an open search, we recommend that you go directly to the local school's website. Once there, look on the home page for links labeled Online Learning, Online Education, Online Courses, Distance Learning, or Distance Education. If finding information about online options isn't obvious, look for a link labeled Academics or Future Students and see whether online courses are mentioned there.

>> It helps to know the kind of degree you're looking for and the school, college, or academic department it typically falls under. For example, if you want to become a teacher, look in the College of Education or something similar. If you want a degree in business, look for the College of Business or a similar-sounding name.

>> After you find your way to the correct department, you can begin sorting through the course listings. Look for links to course schedules rather than the course catalog.

WARNING

A school's catalog tells you which courses you need to put together for an entire degree, but it may not tell you whether the entire degree is available online.

>> See whether the school gives you the opportunity to sort through the ways in which a given class is offered. This is usually described in the institution's course schedule. The best schools state clearly and unquestionably the modalities each class is offered in. For example, the course schedule will usually have a code that indicates whether the course is offered face-to-face, fully online, or in a blended format. (We talk about blended learning — a combination of online and traditional teaching methods — a little later in this chapter.)

>> After you have determined that the school in fact offers online courses or a degree in which you're interested, follow up. Send an email or make a telephone call to the department you're interested in. Ask for more information.

Wholly online schools

When you look up *online courses* at your favorite search engine, other names besides those of traditional institutions pop up. Private schools like Western Governors University (WGU), Phoenix, DeVry University, Southern New Hampshire University, and other wholly online 4-year schools have grown in popularity, and are now mainstream in the media and online search worlds. When looking at colleges and universities, be sure to do your research and ask the questions we discuss in more detail in Chapter 5. You don't want to end up spending money on a program that doesn't meet your needs or conduct courses in a manner that doesn't align with your learning preferences. For example, after researching a school, you might find out that the program operates in more of a self-paced manner where you receive little to no interaction with the instructor. If access and engagement with the instructor are important to you, you will want to shy away from self-paced programs.

Listings from the major players will come up in a general search for **online courses** plus the field you're interested in, as well as agencies that market online programs for a variety of schools. An example of an agency is onlinecolleges.com (www.onlinecolleges.com/). This particular site represents universities you may recognize as well as some that may be unfamiliar. They reach the top of the search engine results by way of strategic marketing and ads.

In most cases, you're asked to complete an online form with your name, email address, phone number, and other basic information such as the type of program you're considering. You will then likely receive a phone call — like, right away (these schools are frighteningly fast) — or receive more information by email.

Filling out online forms, emailing the institution directly, or calling in order to find out what's available are great ways to get information, but they have some drawbacks:

>> You're put on everyone's mailing list, and your email inbox grows exponentially.

>> You begin receiving phone calls during the dinner hour.

>> You may hear from institutions that are not accredited. (Chapter 5 explains the importance of accreditation.)

>> You may have so many choices that it becomes overwhelming.

You may also see a pop-up box with a seemingly friendly face asking whether you have questions. That's most likely a *bot*, which is an artificial intelligence tool at work to answer questions and help you find more information. We have nothing against bots; just be aware that you might not be speaking with a real person.

Two-year colleges

The search process for online courses at a 2-year college is similar to the one you would experience at a 4-year school, but you're more likely to be able to go directly to course listings that specify online delivery. In short, you might see a glowing icon that reads Online Courses Here! on the community college's home page. That means you won't have as much difficulty finding information about the online courses available.

If you don't see an obvious link to Online Learning, Online Education, Online Courses, Distance Education, or Distance Learning, follow the same steps that you would for a 4-year brick-and-mortar school. (We list these steps earlier in this chapter.)

REMEMBER

Two-year colleges are famous for tying their course offerings and programs to local industry needs. If you're looking for the latest-and-greatest courses that connect to local job opportunities, 2-year schools know how to deliver.

Competency-based education

Imagine that you don't have to take a specific course (or sequence of courses) to walk away with credit for basic business skills. Maybe some suggested learning activities are available online, but what really counts is your ability to prove what you know — or what you can do, by way of a body of work, or *ePortfolio.* (See Chapter 17 for more on that topic.) This is competency-based education at its best.

Competency-based education is available online. It allows students to select learning activities that support competencies. For example, perhaps you need to study three separate areas in supply chain management in order to pass the assessment in that area. Often, rather than take a traditional course with an instructor, the learner has a coach who guides the learner toward self-paced learning. When put together, the coaching, learning activities, and assessments result in credit. Western Governors University has been working in this area for decades. The concept isn't new, but it has gained favor because it is quite accommodating for working adults and often includes an assessment of prior learning (through life experiences) that can give the adult a boost.

Other institutions for certificates, professional development, and training

Finding an online certification program is similar to searching for online courses through 2-year or 4-year institutions. Again, you have to know what you're looking for, and you have to know what kind of institution will serve you best.

Say you want to earn a certificate in medical transcription. Using your standard search engine, you'll find that you can earn such a certificate through 2- and 4-year schools, some with brick-and-mortar operations, and others that are wholly online. (You'll even find programs that are sold by companies and don't offer traditional credit, but we don't recommend those.)

Here are a few questions to help you decide:

>> Is the area of study mostly introductory and associated with a 2-year degree, such as medical transcription or allied health? If so, look to a 2-year school.

>> Is the area of study more closely aligned with a field requiring a bachelor's degree? This includes fields like computer science and education, where certificates and endorsements often mean job promotions. In this case, be sure to ask questions about transfer of credits or look to a school that can offer graduate degrees to begin with.

>> Do you need to earn *continuing education credits* (CEUs) to maintain a license or for employment? Maybe a professional association in your field has recommended schools. It's just as likely that the association offers the training or certification. Start with the association's website.

>> Has your employer recommended specific skills training (for instance, database management)? Your human resources department may already have a subscription to a provider that delivers such training online. This is big business!

REMEMBER

When you search for any individual course, read the prerequisite information carefully so that you know whether that course is available to you independently or whether you can take it only if you're enrolled in a specific degree or certificate program.

Virtual schools for children and teens

A growing number of high school and homeschooled students are seeking online education, either to make up credits, work ahead, or study completely online as a homeschooled student. Where would you find a virtual K–12 school? Here's a list of suggestions:

>> If you're a traditional high school student and you need to retake a course you may have failed (called *credit recovery*), go to the school's office. Seriously, start with the local office and see whether anyone there knows of state programs that might meet your needs.

>> If you can't get the answer that way, we recommend that you search for <*your state*> + virtual school at any of the major search engines. For example, entering *Texas + virtual school* led us to the Texas Virtual School at www.txvsn.org and entering *Illinois + virtual school* led us to Illinois Virtual High School at www.ilvirtual.org. Both are state-supported virtual schools.

TECHNICAL STUFF

By the way, most state-supported virtual high schools require their faculty to have the same state credentials as any other public school teacher. Hiring state-certified instructors guarantees the hiring of faculty that are familiar with state standards and helps students better prepare for successfully completing standardized tests and graduating.

>> If you don't find a site that is directly state-supported, you may see a link to a private group. K12 at www.k12.com and Connections Academy at www.connectionsacademy.com are two examples. Believe it or not, a majority of K–12 online education has been outsourced to private agencies. School districts contract with these groups to provide online courses. For the money, they get trained faculty teaching well-developed, interactive courses.

WARNING

Make sure that whatever K–12 program you examine will count for credit — you don't want to waste your time on courses that won't count toward your high school diploma! A good school can tell you immediately what counts or doesn't count toward your state's requirements.

Imagine that you're looking for specific online courses through a virtual school. After you get to the school's website, you should be able to find a link to Courses or Curriculum. To be truthful, most K–12 sites are easier to navigate than those of colleges. You can read the course descriptions, application procedures, and more from these sites. As always, make sure you consider only accredited programs.

Flip to Chapter 18 for more about online education for children and teens.

Checking Out Different Structures of Online Courses

After you know that you can find a class you need at your institution of choice, your next consideration should be the structure of the class. By *structure,* we mean whether the course is completely online or a blend of online and face-to-face time, instructor-led or self-paced, and synchronous or asynchronous. If you have recently searched for a college course, you may already recognize that quite a variety of structures is available. This section helps you sort through some of the differences.

REMEMBER

Before we get to the different course structures, it's worthwhile to establish a baseline for classes in general. Every course typically has these two components:

>> **Content:** The guts of the course, or what you are to learn. The content of an accounting course is accounting. The content of a history course is the history of whatever era you're studying, and so on.

>> **Evaluation:** A nice word for figuring out which grade you earn. In many cases, testing determines your grade, but it may also be determined by a final paper or project.

Ideal courses also include a third component: Practice. In other words, somewhere between content and evaluation, the student gets to practice what is being learned, either by way of homework assignments, short papers, or other activities.

Just you and the monitor (fully online) versus blended courses (partly online)

One major consideration for courses should be whether they're completely online or a blend of online and traditional class time:

>> **Completely online:** A course that's completely online means just that — you complete all the work online. You might enroll in a course at a school that's physically located across the globe, because you wouldn't need to travel. (You can find other benefits of fully online classes in Chapter 2.) Because of the popularity of online courses, institutions readily identify which classes are online.

>> **Blended learning:** This different form of online learning is quite popular. Blended courses are a combination of online screen time and traditional seat time (the amount of time a student sits in a seat in a classroom). Faculty

appreciate blended formats because they can move portions of instruction online, thus freeing up class time for other activities. For example, the instructor may ask you to read articles, complete quizzes, or watch prerecorded lectures online. In the class time on campus, instructors may have groups work on projects, conduct labs, or host class discussions. (Blended learning is also known as *hybrid* learning.)

The major benefits of blended learning are human contact and accountability. Students aren't likely to slip through the cracks or procrastinate when a teacher has real face time with them every week. And yet, the student can work on other course materials in the asynchronous realm and may benefit from the independence and reflective thinking that often accompanies online courses.

WARNING

An obvious downside of the blended format is that you need to live close enough to drive to campus for the regularly scheduled meetings. If you enroll in a course at a college that's three hours from home, this might be a significant nuisance, not to mention an undue expense.

WARNING

Some colleges fail to advertise the blended requirements of traditional classes appropriately. For example, you could enroll in a business management course that meets Mondays and Wednesdays, only to learn during the first week that you're also required to log in twice a week and complete activities online. For this reason, we strongly advise you to ask about the structure of a course before enrolling and putting your money down. If the academic advisor or registrar can't answer your question, go directly to the instructor.

Instructor-led courses versus self-paced courses

In Chapter 2, we briefly outline the difference between instructor-led and self-paced courses, but we look a little deeper at the differences in the following sections.

Instructor-led courses

An *instructor-led* course is just what you think it is: An instructor determines what happens with the content, pace of instruction, and evaluation. Here are a few distinguishing traits of this type of course, which is the most common type out there:

>> In an instructor-led course, students follow a distinct schedule, and the whole class works through the content at the same time. While you're reading and completing activities for "module 2," so is the rest of the class. Typically, you find the schedule posted as a calendar or within the class syllabus. (See

Chapter 9 for more about these documents and how to locate them in your online classroom.) If you're a procrastinator, an instructor-led course can keep you on task.

>> Not only do you get to interact with your peers, but you also have regular communication with the instructor. The instructor is present and virtually "visible" by way of regular announcements and interaction in public discussions.

>> If you're enrolled in a synchronous course — real time, with a web conferencing component — it's instructor-led. The instructor is present and "visible" by way of web conferencing software. This is common in business settings.

TIP

Be sure to read the regular announcements posted by the instructor. Doing so not only keeps you on task and on time but also helps you avoid looking silly by asking a question they may have already addressed.

You also see the instructor via private communication. As you complete assignments and turn them in, the instructor communicates with you and provides feedback. This may come via private email or the electronic grade book. This communication reminds you that the virtual classroom has a live instructor and that you aren't alone. (We discuss all the different methods of online communication in Chapter 11.)

>> You don't see the whole course at one time. This fact may be one of the most distinctive features of an instructor-led course. Many instructors prefer to "time-release" the content according to when the students need it. In other words, if you're in the fourth week of an 8-week course, you may not be able to see the content for weeks 5 and beyond. You see only the week you're working on. This strategy keeps all students in the same place and prevents discussions from becoming disjointed and confusing.

TIP

If you find yourself in a course that uses the time-release method and you know in advance that you'll be traveling, let your instructor know the dates you'll be on the road. Ask whether it's possible for you to view some of the content in advance so that you won't fall behind if you experience technological difficulties getting connected to the Internet.

REMEMBER

Earlier in this chapter, we mention three basic components of an online course: content, evaluation, and practice. An instructor–led course is more likely than a self–paced course to have the practice component, because someone is available to check your homework and smaller assignments. Your learning can be evaluated by means other than traditional testing. If you think about it, it takes the capacity of a real human to read someone's essay and determine whether it makes sense. A computer can't possibly evaluate that kind of assignment as well as an instructor can. If practicing what you're learning is important to you, an instructor–led class is just for you.

Self-paced courses

In a self-paced course, you're on your own to determine your schedule, so if you're a self-starter, you may find this type of course to your liking. The content, or what you are to learn, is predetermined. When you access the course, you usually find that it has been divided into modules or units. You click on the first unit, read the content, and move through the course at your own pace. You can spend more time in the challenging areas and breeze through those that are easier for you.

In a business setting, self-paced courses are often prepackaged with simple software interfaces. The window loaded on your screen might look like the one in Figure 4-1.

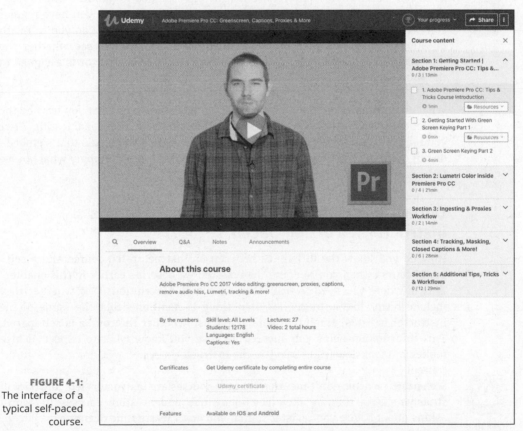

FIGURE 4-1:
The interface of a typical self-paced course.

Source: "Leadership: Effective Critical Skills," PD Online course, Alexandria, VA: ASCD. ©2009 ASCD. Reproduced with permission. Learn more about ASCD at www.ascd.org. ASCD® and PD Online™ are trademarks of ASCD.

These courses have navigational tools to help you move through the content. You'll probably see arrows at the bottom to help you advance and a menu on the left. You use these tools to help you move through the content at your own pace.

Just because a course is self-paced doesn't mean that an instructor isn't waiting in the wings to help you with questions or concerns. Consider the case of Alex. Wanting to learn better keyboarding skills, he enrolled in an online course via his local community college. The introductory information came from an instructor who guided Alex through the process of downloading and installing special software for working through the lessons. All the lessons were made available when the course started, and they could be completed at any time during the 8-week period. There were no scheduled meetings, and Alex could work at his leisure.

TIP

Even self-paced courses often have instructors assigned to monitor what's happening. What you want to know is what that person does. Will you have regular contact throughout the course or just at the beginning or end? Can you call with questions? When you identify a potential self-paced course, see whether the instructor has an email address available and ask. If no instructor is assigned to the course, be wary.

What about evaluation? How does the person in charge know that you learned the content? In the business world, most often this comes via traditional testing. After you read or listen to a portion of the content, you take a short quiz that's embedded in the program. These quizzes test your ability to recall or apply what you've just heard.

Determining whether the course you want is instructor-led or self-paced

How do you know the difference between an instructor-led course and a self-paced course when you're doing the research we describe earlier in this chapter? This is where you need to drill down to course descriptions. See whether they include terms like *instructor-led.* If nothing is mentioned but the name of the instructor is listed, email that person and ask whether the course is self-paced. This information helps you succeed because you know what to expect. It also makes you look downright savvy in the instructor's eyes.

WARNING

Sometimes schools don't mention that the courses are instructor-led, and a lot of students sign up thinking they'll be taking independent-study courses. It's worth asking about before you register so that you don't waste time or money.

Resources you're expected to access even for face-to-face courses

It bears mentioning that even face-to-face courses require some online learning savvy. You may be asked to access the syllabus in the school's learning management system (LMS). Additional learning resources, like slides and study guides, might be posted online. Or, you may be asked to submit assignments or take quizzes online. This isn't the same as taking an online course, but it requires the skills of being able to access the site, navigate efficiently, and communicate appropriately.

Asynchronous courses versus synchronous (real-time) courses

As we explain in detail in Chapter 2, most online courses are *asynchronous* in nature: You do the work when it's convenient for you. As long as you meet the deadlines for assignments, all is well. However, instructors may also have synchronous components to their courses, such as weekly meetings, and some instructors require attendance or participation. For example, when coauthor Kevin teaches, he hosts a weekly office hour during which he reviews assignments and introduces extra material. Though his students aren't required to attend, they like the personal contact. These sessions are recorded so that those who can't attend can watch a movie of the synchronous event.

REMEMBER

Specifics about the synchronous and/or asynchronous components of a course should be available in the course description that we explain how to find earlier in this chapter. However, be sure to ask an academic advisor about the possibility of a synchronous component if you don't see any reference to such sessions. Better safe than sorry.

Finishing Your Schooling Faster with Accelerated Programs and Courses

Teachers (your humble coauthors included) would love for you to believe that learning is fun, but the truth is that it can be a major headache and disruptive to real life. For that reason, you might truly appreciate the speed at which you can finish schooling online.

Now that colleges and universities have discovered a ready market of busy students who want to learn on their own time, they want to enroll and keep those customers. An effective way to achieve this is to make sure the courses hold the students' interest and move quickly. With this in mind, many institutions offer accelerated courses, which are traditional 16-week courses that have been condensed into half the time. In fact, 8 weeks is a common length for an online course.

In this section, we describe the pros and cons of accelerated online education and provide a few pointers for surviving such programs and courses.

TIP

Do course catalogs and descriptions specify which courses are accelerated? Nope, not necessarily. It's up to you, smart reader, to do the math. If you see a 3-credit-hour course with start/end dates indicating that it runs 8 weeks, it's accelerated. A traditional course would extend a semester, or 16 weeks.

Also, if you see marketing materials that recommend taking a single course at a time, it's probably because the courses are accelerated and *demanding*. After all, you're fitting 16 weeks' worth of content into less time.

The benefits and challenges of accelerated programs

The good news is that accelerated courses generally teach you information you can apply right away. Have you ever heard the phrase "Use it or lose it"? That's the mantra of instructional design for accelerated courses. Courses require students to apply the content right away via ongoing assignments. The more you use the information, the more likely you are to learn and retain it.

Obviously, if a course is accelerated, you learn more information in less time. In theory, you can complete a degree in half the time. However, the reality is that how much information you take in depends on your own capacity to absorb information. In other words, if your jug (brain) is full of holes (distracted or disorganized), it doesn't matter how much water (knowledge) you pour in. You'll never hold it all!

REMEMBER

So it is with accelerated courses. Yes, you receive more information in less time, but you have to be sure you have the time and the study strategies to process this information.

Tips for successfully completing accelerated classes

TIP

How do you succeed in an accelerated course? Here are a few handy guidelines:

>> **Enroll in only one course at a time until you know what you can handle.** You may even find degree programs that limit the number of courses you can take simultaneously at first, for this very reason.

>> **Establish a definite schedule for study.** Procrastination doesn't work well online, even for self-paced courses. We recommend daily logins. (We provide general guidelines for good study habits in Chapter 12.)

>> **Set reasonable goals for participation.** You don't have to answer every discussion post. Check your course requirements, and exceed them slightly, but not extremely.

>> **If you're crunched for time and have discussions to read, address the first posts from the original authors.** Unless your instructor says that "you must read every post," you can get by skipping a few responses here and there.

>> **Develop a method for saving links and resources you want to go back to later.** For some people, this means keeping a running document where they paste links and URLs. For others, it means opening an account on a social bookmarking tool, like historious (`https://historio.us/`). The point is that you don't have to read everything immediately.

>> **Save projects from one course to the next.** This isn't necessarily so that you can repurpose them, but rather so that you can draw on the resources and methods that you've previously employed.

>> **Align assignments to work projects.** When it is possible, complete school projects that also benefit your work. By doing this, you can potentially use work time to complete school work and school time to complete work.

>> **Work ahead, if you can.** Take advantage of a slow week to get a head start on the next one.

>> **Keep in mind that the intensity will last only eight weeks.** You can find great comfort in knowing that it won't go on forever, even if you love the class.

>> **If you're working on a degree that involves a thesis, try to connect all your assignments to your thesis.** Pick a topic early in your studies, and investigate different angles throughout the various courses.

>> **Set aside time at the beginning of the course for the basics.** Read the syllabus, become familiar with the course navigation, and begin reading the text.

>> **Take advantage of synchronous tools.** Using the phone, web conferencing tools, and other items is more productive than writing emails when you're conducting group work, especially during the organizing process.

Chapter 5

Doing Your Homework: Evaluating Schools

One of the hardest decisions you have to make when deciding to go back to school is which institution to attend, especially when considering online education. During the COVID-19 pandemic, institutions moved many of their programs and degrees to a fully online format. Though the change was intended to be temporary, these programs were restructured to work well online, and some of them stayed permanently online, with students never returning to the physical campus. Students therefore have more options for fully online certificates and degrees both domestically and internationally. This also means there's more competition for colleges. As a result, there's also more pressure to develop quality online courses that focus on learning and student satisfaction. More, more, more. It's supply and demand!

No matter which school you choose to attend, a few universal guidelines apply that can help you in the decision-making process. This chapter provides important information on what to look for and questions to ask as you evaluate various schools.

Focusing On What You Need in a School

When considering the financial investment of going to school, you should view yourself as a consumer. Approaching education in this manner helps you organize your thoughts and prioritize your wants and needs.

Consider the process of buying a car. When money is tight, what you really need is a reliable vehicle that will get you from point A to point B. Though you may want power doors and windows, keyless entry, heated seats, a navigation system, and a sunroof, you don't really need them. Therefore, you're forced to prioritize features according to ones you must have, ones you'd like to have, and ones you can do without. You also have to decide how much you can afford to spend. By making these decisions before heading to the dealership, you ensure a smoother interaction with the salesperson and protect yourself from being swindled into buying more than you really need or can afford. You also help the salesperson better match your needs with the right car.

Preparing to go to school, especially online, is much like purchasing a vehicle: You need to prioritize your needs and determine how much you're able to pay, whether it's now or by making loan payments later. For example, if you're a working parent with limited resources for childcare, fully online courses with no face-to-face obligations may be your top priority.

In the next section, we help you develop a checklist of elements to consider when looking to participate in online programs or courses. These considerations include evaluating the program/course offerings, types and sizes of classes, how much time they take, and whether your previously earned credits will transfer.

Considering the program you're interested in

The first thing you must decide is what you want out of your education. If you want to advance professionally, check with career professionals about the kind of degree you need. For example, if you're a registered nurse (RN) who wants to teach, you may be required by your state board of health to have a masters of nursing degree. You can't get one at a 2-year college. Similarly, if you want to be a paralegal, you don't need a law degree. Knowing specifically what you want can help you choose an institution with the right degree and concentration that meets your needs. (The *concentration* is the specific area within the field you want to focus on; for example, within education, concentrations include curriculum and instruction, organization and leadership, and instructional technology and distance education, to name a few.)

If you're unsure what you want to do professionally and you want to explore multiple options, consider an institution where you can gain diverse experience. One suggestion is to enroll in the general education courses that are required by almost every major and then take elective courses in a variety of fields that you may be interested in.

Secondly, decide whether you want to attend any of your courses on a traditional campus. If so, research the schools in your surrounding area to see whether they offer a program that meets your academic goals. You might need to do some digging to learn what percent of the courses within the program are offered online and how frequently. Otherwise, you need to look for programs that are offered fully online.

When researching a school (for pointers on this topic, see the later section "Talking to the Right People to Find the Answers You Need"), remember to find out whether the institution requires students to be on campus during any part of the program. Some institutions require a face-to-face orientation program at the student's expense. This can be quite a helpful experience for the student, but attendance incurs travel and other expenses.

Determining whether a program is affordable

Education isn't cheap. Therefore, cost may be a major determining factor as to whether you're able to attend a specific institution. Even though different institutions offer similar degrees and courses, they may vary in cost by a large margin, especially among community colleges, public universities, and private institutions. Not only is it important to know whether you can afford to pay for tuition, but you must also find out whether the program you want to enroll in has additional fees for supplies and services. If you choose to take advantage of financial aid (see Chapter 6), you need to know the estimated cost of your program and what the monthly payments will be upon graduation. We provide some questions specific to cost later in this chapter, and we detail financial aid options in Chapter 6.

Checking out class size (and the student-to-instructor ratio)

After you narrow your search to a few selective institutions that meet your academic needs, you can start focusing on other important details, including class size. You want to consider schools that offer classes that aren't too big or too small but are just right. In the online environment, class size matters. If the class is too big, the instructor may have a difficult time providing adequate amounts of feedback and managing course discussions, leaving you with little or no guidance. If the class is too small, you may struggle to keep the dialogue going and the course may seem dull and monotonous. From the instructor's perspective, we like class sizes between 18 and 25 students.

If you're looking for a more independent program with less interaction, a smaller class size may fit your learning style better. However, most research indicates that interaction, communication, and collaboration are all important pieces to successful online programs. Independent models, also known as self-paced instruction, tend to be more common in the corporate education setting, though some do exist in the academic setting. If a high level of independence is important to you, be sure to discuss this with your academic advisor up front.

TIP

Self-paced courses aren't eligible for financial aid reimbursement as determined by the federal Department of Education. This means you will be required to pay full tuition out-of-pocket for these courses.

When online education first hit the scene in the mid-1990s, many institutions saw it as an opportunity to make a lot of money by putting several hundred students in one class because they weren't restricted by physical space. This idea was disastrous. Instructors were so overwhelmed by the numbers that they were unable to provide any kind of personal attention or quality feedback in a timely manner. Courses became self-paced, and the instructor was simply used as a contact person for answering questions.

A lot has been learned since then, but some institutions still have unrealistic class sizes that prevent instructors from providing quality instruction. Therefore, find out how many students will be in your class before enrolling.

Where can you find this information? Ask to speak with a program representative or academic advisor. They'll know class limits and historic enrollments.

REMEMBER

In an academic setting, we recommend that classes have one instructor for every 18 to 25 students.

Knowing how much time you can commit and how it may be spent

One of the most underestimated aspects regarding online education is the amount of time needed to complete a course. The exact amount of time it takes to successfully participate in an online course is different for each person.

A common calculation for determining how much time you should expect to focus on coursework is to take the number of credits the course is worth and triple it. For example, a 3-credit course should require a minimum of 9 to 12 hours of your time per week. This calculation is made assuming that the course runs 16 weeks. Therefore, if you're considering an accelerated program (see Chapter 4 for more information), think about how much more time this adds and determine whether your schedule allows for that level of commitment.

Several factors can affect how much time you spend on your online education. We outline those aspects in the following sections.

The technology learning curve

Most institutions have some kind of formula for determining how much time students will need to spend on assignments in order to earn the respective number of credits for a course. However, they don't consider an individual's computer proficiencies, which can have a dramatic impact on the time it takes to complete assignments. Students who take longer to navigate the web or learn new technologies need more time to complete assignments.

TIP

When investigating programs and courses, ask about what technologies are used and how consistent those technologies are from week to week and class to class. This helps you understand what kind of learning curve you may need to account for when scheduling your time. You can also ask whether the institution offers a student orientation on how to use their technology tools. For example, many institutions offer online orientation programs teaching learners how to use their learning management system (LMS), the main source for delivering course content. Ask whether you can access the system before your courses begin and refer to it as often as needed. (We talk more about LMSs in Chapter 9.)

TIP

Ask whether courses are "opened" before the official day of class. Sometimes, this is an institutional policy; at other times, it's up to each instructor. This allows you to log in, look around, and start getting familiar with the virtual classroom environment, without the pressure of learning the navigation with looming assignment deadlines.

REMEMBER

At first, learning the technology of online education takes time. However, over time and with repeated use, it gets easier and faster. Even learning newer technologies becomes easier and begins to take less time. After a while, you'll begin to notice similar features and navigational structures within like products. For example, it doesn't matter which web browser you use. You know when you open it that you'll see a place to type the URL, a Back button, and a Forward button. These functions may be placed in a different location on different browsers (Internet Explorer versus Chrome, for example), but you know that the functions are there somewhere and where to generally look for them.

Real-time meetings

Even though synchronous meetings have some great benefits, they're time consuming and can frustrate students if they're unaware of them ahead of time. Therefore, it's important to know up front whether the program or course you're considering requires live meetings, and if so, which day and time those meetings are held. Then you can determine whether your schedule would allow you to take the class, as well as what kind of work and/or childcare arrangements you'd need to make.

TIP

Confirm the time zone as well. Most synchronous sessions are in the evening, but 7 P.M. Eastern time is only 4 P.M. Pacific time, and that may pose a challenge with work and commuting schedules.

Coursework requirements

Finally, and most importantly, you must be sure that you have enough time in your schedule to complete the coursework. This includes tackling your reading assignments, reading and posting to peer discussions, and managing other important documents such as the syllabus and assignment details. It also includes the time it takes to actually complete assignments, quizzes, and group projects.

REMEMBER

In the face-to-face environment, the rule of thumb is for students to spend two or three hours working on schoolwork for every hour they spend in class. For a class that meets for three hours a week, the total time spent in class and studying would be 9 to 12 hours a week. In an online class, students should expect to spend approximately the same amount of total time. Time not spent in a physical classroom is spent participating in online discussions and completing other assignments.

REMEMBER

The preceding calculation assumes that the class is a standard 16-week course. In an accelerated program, the same amount of information is presented in half the time, dramatically increasing the amount of time required. Depending on the course, the workload can double, although that's not always the case. You might need to set aside 15 to 20 hours a week for a 3-credit course in an accelerated program. Now you know why we recommend taking only one course at a time when participating in an accelerated program.

Planning ahead: Figuring out whether your credits will transfer

It pays to think about the future when deciding to enroll in a college or university. Maybe you're going to start your degree online and finish it on campus, or maybe you plan to do the opposite — start on a physical campus and later transfer to an online program. Consider future possibilities and make sure the institution you choose supports those possibilities. For example, if you're a freshman and want to take your general education courses through a community college's online program, make sure your course credits will transfer to a 4-year institution when the time comes.

Bringing in credits from another institution

Many online programs accept credits from other accredited institutions. However, several variables are used to decide whether credits are transferrable. For example, some graduate programs simply require an undergraduate degree from an accredited school and individual course credit isn't a concern. However, other graduate programs require specific prerequisite courses that may or may not have been a part of your undergraduate curriculum.

Another variable is time. Coursework completed recently is more likely to be accepted for transfer. If several years have passed, the institution may ask that you retake certain courses. For example, science, technology, engineering, and math (STEM) classes often have a 10-year shelf life, whereas graduate courses often have a 7-year shelf life.

TIP

Whether you have taken classes recently or long ago, be sure to have your transcripts evaluated by the school before making your final decision about which school to enroll in. You may have to pay a nonrefundable application fee, but it's worth it to know up front whether your credits will transfer.

After you're told that credit is transferrable, be sure to get an official transcript of exactly which credits will transfer. This should be a formal document on the institution's letterhead with an official seal, signed by an administrator. This provides you with protection in case you need proof of transfer due to administrative staff changes within the organization.

Switching from one online school to another

If you want to switch from one online school to another, the process should be exactly the same as that described in the preceding section. Again, the fact that your credits were earned from an accredited institution doesn't guarantee that they'll fully transfer, but accreditation will definitely be a minimum qualification.

Down the road: Will institutions accept the online school's credits?

After taking courses or finishing a degree online, you may want to continue your education. Depending on which institution you decided to attend, many people reviewing your transcripts won't even know that the program or course you were last enrolled in was online. This is especially the case for institutions that have both on-campus and online course offerings. Therefore, transferring courses from an online institution to a campus-based institution should be no problem. However, the same concept of preparing early applies here.

If you're transferring credits from an entirely online program and you fear that your credits won't be as transferable, don't worry: As long as you do your homework when choosing an online institution, you should have no problems transferring credits — assuming that the credits are aligned with the program you want to transfer into.

If you know when you enroll in an online program that you plan to transfer to another institution in a couple of years, research both the online institution and the campus-based school or schools you have your sights set on, and find out whether the credits you earn will transfer from one to the other. Doing a little more research and legwork up front may save you several headaches down the road.

TIP

When conducting your research, don't hesitate to call and ask advisors or other staff for help. It may not be clear on an institution's website whether the specific credits you earned from another institution will transfer. For quick access to staff, you might see whether the institution's site offers a live chat feature where you can immediately be connected with someone who can answer questions on the fly, without the hassle of trying to figure out whom exactly to call.

Finding an Accredited School

Going back to school often means investing in your future. That investment isn't cheap, so you want to be sure you're getting your money's worth.

First and foremost, you should look for a school that's accredited. Accreditation is a process by which a school is determined to have met predetermined quality standards. These accreditation standards are determined and monitored by non-governmental agencies that have been authorized by the US secretary of education.

In this section, we discuss ways of determining an institution's credibility and quality.

Recognizing the two types of accreditation

Schools themselves can be accredited, and programs within schools can be accredited. (And yes, an accredited school can have accredited programs.)

The first type of accreditation is institutional accreditation, which means that all the parts of the institution work well together to meet its overall mission. There are both national and regional accreditation-granting organizations. Though national accreditation may sound like a higher level of accreditation, regional accreditation tends to be more credible. With respect to regional accreditation, the United States is divided into 6 regions. Those regions are served by 8 organizations. (See the nearby sidebar, "Regional institutional accrediting agencies," to find out which agencies cover which states.)

The second type of accreditation is called specialized, or programmatic, accreditation. This means that a specific program within the school has successfully completed the accreditation process relevant to its field. For example, if you look at Eastern Illinois University's education program, you find that it is accredited via the specialist level by the Commission on Institutions of the North Central Association of Colleges and Schools and by the National Council for Accreditation of Teacher Education for the preparation of elementary and secondary teachers and school service personnel. This means that this college meets general academic quality standards, plus standards specific to the education of future teachers. Most specialized accreditors confer the accreditation status only to programs within a regionally accredited institution. However, this isn't always the case. A few accredit institutions that aren't regionally accredited.

REMEMBER

When looking at colleges and universities, investigate whether the institution is accredited and, if so, at what level. Likewise, be sure the accrediting agency is a recognized body (use the list above). There are fake agencies operating! Don't be surprised if you find that community colleges are accredited at the institution level but not at the program level. It simply depends on the programs the institution offers and the level of program completion they provide. For example, most community colleges provide enough math courses to fulfill general studies prerequisites but do not offer a degree in mathematics. Therefore, they're not likely to have an accredited math program.

TECHNICAL STUFF

To earn and maintain accreditation status, an institution must participate in an ongoing process that reviews its resources, programs, assessments, and self-evaluation. The bottom line is that an accredited school has to document how it is meeting quality standards. The initial accreditation process can take upward of two years to complete. After that, the cycle repeats approximately every seven to ten years, depending on the guidelines set forth by the accrediting agency.

REGIONAL INSTITUTIONAL ACCREDITING AGENCIES

We present in this sidebar a list of the regional accreditors recognized by the US Department of Education as being qualified to confer accreditation status on institutions that meet their predetermined quality standards. Different agencies provide accreditation to different types of institutions. For example, one agency may accredit vocational institutions, whereas another agency may accredit postsecondary degree-granting institutions. For a complete list of regional and national agencies, and their scope of recognition, as recognized by the US Department of Education, you can visit the department's website at www2.ed.gov/admins/finaid/accred/accreditation_pg6.html.

Here's the list:

- **Middle States Association of Colleges and Schools, Middle States Commission on Higher Education (MSCHE):** Servicing Delaware, the District of Columbia, Maryland, New Jersey, New York, Pennsylvania, Puerto Rico, and the US Virgin Islands

  www.msche.org

- **New England Association of Schools and Colleges, Commission on Institutions of Higher Education (NEASC–CIHE):** Servicing Connecticut, Maine, Massachusetts, New Hampshire, Rhode Island, and Vermont

  https://neasc.org

  New England Association of Schools and Colleges, Commission on Technical and Career Institutions (NEASC–CTCI): Servicing secondary institutions with vocational-technical programs at the 13th and 14th grade levels as well as postsecondary institutions and institutions of higher education that provide primarily vocational/technical education at the certificate, associate, and baccalaureate degree levels in Connecticut, Maine, Massachusetts, New Hampshire, Rhode Island, and Vermont

  https://ctci.neasc.org

- **North Central Association of Colleges and Schools, The Higher Learning Commission (NCA–HLC):** Servicing Arizona, Arkansas, Colorado, Illinois, Indiana, Iowa, Kansas, Michigan, Minnesota, Missouri, Nebraska, New Mexico, North Dakota, Ohio, Oklahoma, South Dakota, West Virginia, Wisconsin, and Wyoming, including schools of the Navajo Nation `www.hlcommission.org`

- **Northwest Commission on Colleges and Universities (NWCCU):** Servicing Alaska, Idaho, Montana, Nevada, Oregon, Utah, and Washington

`www.nwccu.org`

- **Southern Association of Colleges and Schools, Commission on Colleges (SACS):** Servicing Alabama, Florida, Georgia, Kentucky, Louisiana, Mississippi, North Carolina, South Carolina, Tennessee, Texas, and Virginia

`https://sacscoc.org`

- **Western Association of Schools and Colleges, Accrediting Commission for Community and Junior Colleges (WASC-ACCJC):** Servicing community and junior colleges located in California, Hawaii, the United States territories of Guam and American Samoa, the Republic of Palau, the Federated States of Micronesia, the Commonwealth of the Northern Marianna Islands, and the Republic of the Marshall Islands

`https://accjc.org`

- **Western Association of Schools and Colleges, Accrediting Commission for Senior Colleges and Universities (WASC-ACSCU):** Servicing senior colleges and universities in California, Hawaii, the United States territories of Guam and American Samoa, the Republic of Palau, the Federated States of Micronesia, the Commonwealth of the Northern Mariana Islands, and the Republic of the Marshall Islands

`www.wscuc.org`

Seeing the benefits of accreditation

Accreditation status is important for both you and the institution. From the institution's perspective, it provides credibility and status within the academic community, and becomes an important marketing tool. Accredited schools also have the ability to attract more higher-qualified students, like you.

Included in the benefits from your perspective as a student are that you

>> Know that quality standards have been reviewed and met.

>> Can market yourself to prospective employers who look for applicants from accredited schools and programs.

>> Enhance your chances for graduate school. Having an existing undergraduate degree from an accredited institution is often a minimum requirement when applying for graduate school. Although it doesn't guarantee that your credits will transfer, it definitely helps.

>> Have an increased likelihood of receiving financial aid. Students attending nonaccredited institutions may be ineligible for student assistance such as federal/state aid and tuition reimbursement programs.

Determining whether an online program is accredited

Most institutions are proud of their accreditation status and want to show it off. Therefore, determining whether an institution is accredited usually isn't difficult. In most cases, you can find out by visiting the institution's website and clicking on the About Us or Academics link. If you can't find it on the site, your academic advisor can definitely share this information with you.

WARNING

The demand for alternative education delivery methods to meet the needs of busy adults has increased dramatically over the past decade. Unfortunately, as a result, several institutions have tried to quickly capitalize on this situation by creating diploma mills, which are nonaccredited institutions offering quick, online degrees without quality standards or properly trained faculty. Here are a few things to look for that may identify an organization as a diploma mill:

>> The institution has a name that is quite similar to a more well-known university.

>> The institution isn't accredited by an agency approved by the US department of education.

>> Students can earn degrees in very little time compared to other institutions. No one can earn a degree in 30 days. Trust us.

>> There are no admissions criteria. For example, if you're researching a Bachelor of Nursing program that doesn't require any clinical experience, be careful.

>> The cost to attend the institution is much less than at any other college or university offering the same program.

In response, an equally aggressive movement has arisen to establish quality standards for online courses. Organizations such as Quality Matters (www. qualitymatters.org) provide schools with benchmarks and a process they can use to ensure quality in the way they offer online courses. Schools may conduct other internal reviews. Because accreditation by one of the six regional agencies is institutional and includes traditional classroom education as well as online classes, be sure to ask every school you're interested in how they monitor the quality of their online programs.

Other factors that contribute to an institution's credibility

As you conduct your research regarding an institution's accreditation status, you should also look for other signs that the institution is a credible one. In this section, we provide you with some additional criteria for evaluating online programs and courses. These include the awards and recognition they've received, as well as the research conducted at the school. In most cases, institutions highlight this information on their websites as a way of enhancing their marketing efforts.

National awards and recognition

One of the best indicators of quality is recognition from nationally recognized professional organizations. Two types of awards are bestowed specifically to online academic programs or individual courses. The first type of award focuses on academic integrity and a program's overall curriculum, graduation rate, and/or contributions to the field. These awards are sponsored by leading professional organizations within the field of the program's subject matter.

Several awards may also be earned specific to the development and implementation of individual online courses based on quality design. To earn this award, a course instructor must demonstrate that their online course has met specific quality standards based on research and best practices within the field of online education.

Other awards that you may keep an eye out for are those bestowed on faculty. Faculty awards for work within the field or excellence in teaching are both indicators of quality.

TIP

Quality Matters is a leading organization in providing research-based, quality standards for the development of online courses. One question you can ask institutions is whether they subscribe to and train faculty around design standards such as Quality Matters. Because of the subscription costs to participate in Quality Matters, some institutions have created their own standards based on similar criteria. The most important piece is that the institution recognizes the need for such standards, provides professional opportunities around them, and acknowledges and promotes faculty whose courses meet the standards.

Leading research efforts in the field of distance education

Another indicator of quality is whether the faculty study the impact of online education — for example, Penn State World Campus in University Park, The University of Wisconsin in Madison, Nova Southeastern University in Fort Lauderdale, and Indiana University in Bloomington are all well-known for their research in online education. Although this research is usually conducted locally and within the College of Education, the results can be used to train faculty from other departments and institutions around the world. It can tell you a great deal about the school's attitude toward distance education: Those who research online education tend to support online education.

Consortium membership

One final consideration is membership in a consortium, or group of like-minded institutions. Membership doesn't guarantee quality or accreditation, but those who join are more likely to offer legitimate programs and services. By joining a consortium, schools have access to training, research in the field, and cutting-edge practices that help ensure quality.

Nationally, the best-known consortium is the Online Learning Consortium (https://onlinelearningconsortium.org), a community of institutions committed to enhancing their own understanding and practices related to quality online, blended, and digital learning.

Several institutions have pooled resources regionally as well. For example, California, Connecticut, and Florida all have statewide consortia.

Talking to the Right People to Find the Answers You Need

Now that we've given you some things to think about in choosing an academic institution, it's time to introduce you to some important people to talk to: your academic advisor, the faculty, and other students. In this section, we provide you with a list of questions you can pose to each of these people.

Communicating with a variety of people who have both an internal connection (faculty and staff paid by the institution) and an external connection (students) can help you gain multiple perspectives regarding the prospective program or a particular course. These discussions may happen over the phone or via email.

Either way, it always helps to be prepared and have your questions written ahead of time.

TIP

When discussing topics that impact your academic standing or financial status, request that any decisions made be documented in writing or document the conversation yourself. For example, after an advisor tells you that previous coursework will transfer, send an email summarizing your discussion and request a confirmation reply. This covers you in case you have a change in advisors and you need to justify your actions to someone else.

Talking to an academic advisor about the school

The first contact person you will have with any institution is an academic advisor. This person's role is twofold. Their first task is to serve as a liaison between the public and the institution. Recruitment of new students is usually a primary task of this person, although some institutions separate this role and have dedicated recruiters who point you to an academic advisor when you express further interest in attending the institution.

The second and more important task an academic advisor undertakes is helping you plan your academic adventures. The academic advisor answers questions, collects your application, and steps you through the enrollment process. The academic advisor should be available to help you not only during your initial application and enrollment process but also throughout your academic career when needed. Take advantage of this person's knowledge, and try to get as much information out of them as possible before deciding to enroll. Again, the more prepared you are before meeting your advisor, the better. So, here are some questions you should be ready to ask:

» **What courses are available?** This may seem like a simple question, but it's an important one. Knowing what courses are available, and when, helps you determine when you can start taking classes and in what order. For example, if you're required to take an introductory course as a prerequisite to all the other courses in a program, you must know when that course is offered next.

» **What prerequisites do I need?** Here comes that planning-ahead theme again. Determining each course's prerequisites tells you the order in which you need to take courses. Paying attention to these details helps you avoid missing a term because you have to wait for one of the prerequisite courses to be offered.

If you need additional prerequisites because some of your previous credits didn't transfer, you'll need to know whether they provide those courses. If not, you may have to take the courses somewhere else first.

» **What is your student retention rate — how many students return for the next term, in other words?** This question is telling. Having a small number of students drop out for one reason or another is fairly common for all academic programs. However, programs that have a retention rate of less than 85 percent should raise a red flag.

A good follow-up question to ask is whether the program documents why students drop out. If so, ask about the most common reasons for dropping out. This can tell you whether students are dropping out because of personal reasons or the program itself. If a large number of students drop out because the program is too difficult, because it requires more time than expected, or because the technology used is too difficult for students to learn on top of coursework, be cautious about enrolling in the program.

» **What kinds of student services are available?** This question is extremely important for students taking online courses. You want to be sure that the institution can provide you with a variety of resources at a distance. For example, you should ask whether the institution provides access to services such as the library, academic tutoring, and career development upon graduation.

Be sure to ask how these services are provided. Some institutions provide online students with the same services as their on-campus students only if they come to campus. Find out whether the institution is prepared to provide these services from a distance using a variety of technologies.

» **What kind of placement rate do graduates report?** Asking this question is a great way to find out how reputable the program is. It can also help you evaluate the job market in the field you're considering studying.

» What are the faculty's qualifications? Whether the courses are taught by full-time, tenured faculty or by adjunct is less important than the minimum qualifications for teaching in the program. Getting a feel for the faculty's qualifications helps you understand the skills and knowledge of those who will provide instruction.

» **When do I have to decide and register?** When asking this question, be sure to get an idea of multiple deadlines so that you don't feel pressured into making a decision immediately. Note that some institutions may offer a discount for starting earlier if their current enrollment is not as high as they want. Even so, be sure to take as much time as you need to make the right decision for you.

≫ How long is each term? Students commonly ask this question because they want to know whether school will interfere with an already scheduled vacation, a family wedding, or another event. The nice thing about online education is that as long as you have a computer with Internet access, you can still go to school. However, if you're planning a vacation where you won't have access to the Internet (or you really don't want to interrupt your honeymoon to study), don't be surprised if the institution or individual instructor asks you to take the class another time. Participation is such a large part of online education that if you're unable to participate, taking the class may not be worth it.

≫ When do classes begin? Some institutions provide only three start dates per year: one each for the fall, spring, and summer semesters. Other institutions, especially those offering accelerated programs, allow students to start classes more frequently. If you need to take advantage of financial aid, make sure the aid is available when you want to start. Timing can affect whether you can receive aid. (Flip to Chapter 6 for more about the financial facts of online education.)

≫ Are there any additional fees? It's important to know whether you'll be expected to pay additional fees beyond the application and tuition fees. These additional charges may include fees for hardware, software, or campus services. Campus services may include items such as a campus email address, server space for storing files, an ePortfolio subscription, or other similar services. They should not include standard fees for services provided only to campus students, such as healthcare or gym access — things you obviously won't be able to participate in.

≫ What is the cost for books or other required materials? Books are not cheap, and some people are surprised at how much a single textbook can cost. You'll be better able to budget if you know what the average cost of books and supplies will be per term. Textbooks and supplies are updated often, so you may not get an exact number, but you should be able to calculate a good estimate.

≫ How many students can be admitted per course? Do you remember our earlier discussion about the benefits and challenges of courses that are too small or too large? This question can help you determine whether your instructor may be inhibited from providing quality feedback because of the sheer number of students in the class.

≫ How long does it take to graduate? The answer to this question depends on how many classes you take at a time and whether the institution requires you to follow a prescribed sequence of courses. You may also want to find out whether there's a maximum time frame for earning your degree. Some programs require students to complete their degree within six years.

>> **What is the refund policy?** The answer to this question will let you know when you have to drop a course in order to receive a full refund. Most institutions give you a percent of your money back based on when you decided to drop a course. For example, you might have three days to drop a course for a full refund and be able to receive 50% of your money back if you drop before the end of the second week.

>> **What is your institution's complaint process for distant students?** Institutions that offer online courses to students should have a complaint process in place that provides clear steps students can take to file a complaint. The process should be completed and followed through from start to finish from a distance using technologies such as email, phone, and videoconferencing.

>> **What if I need to take a break?** Life happens, and sometimes students need to temporarily drop out of school due to other commitments. You should know what the institution's policy about this is and how it will affect events such as your graduation date and financial aid disbursement. You'll also want to know how long you can stop taking classes and when you can reenter. Understand that stopping and restarting your education may delay your graduation for several months, depending on how frequently the classes you need are offered.

TIP

The State Authorization Reciprocity Agreements, also known as SARA, is a consumer protection organization that states and institutions can voluntarily participate in. By participating in SARA, institutions agree to meet minimum standards around distance education, including maintaining clear, transparent guidelines around costs, refunds, licensure, and resolution processes. If the institution you're hoping to attend is in a different state from where you will reside as a student, you can ask whether the institution is SARA certified or check on the SARA website (https://nc-sara.org/directory).

Asking a faculty member about the program

When you talk to your academic advisor, ask to speak to a faculty member about the program you want to enroll in. Someone teaching within the program can give you a different perspective, specifically when it comes to the curriculum, assignment types, and time commitment necessary to successfully participate in the program. Here are some questions you might want to ask.

WARNING

If the institution doesn't want to let you talk to an instructor, consider research-ing other institutions. The availability of the instructional staff before you register can be indicative of their availability after you're enrolled. However, on the other hand, be patient and give your advisor enough time to locate an instructor who is available to speak to you.

REMEMBER

>> **What kind of training is required of faculty members who teach for this school?** This is a helpful question because it allows you to find out whether instructors are required to participate in professional development specific to online education.

Most programs require instructors to have subject matter expertise. However, not all of them require instructors to have any experience with teaching online. Institutions that require or provide additional training specific to this topic tend to have more well-rounded instructors that are better prepared to teach online.

>> **What can I expect in terms of workload?** This question may seem repeti-tive, but asking a faculty member within the program gives you an idea of the instructors' expectations regarding how much time you should plan to spend on classwork.

>> **What are the standards for faculty response time?** By asking a faculty member this question, you're kind of putting them on the spot to see how committed they are to responding quickly to questions via email or phone. You should receive an answer something like this: "The faculty at this institu-tion are required to respond to student inquiries within 48 hours. However, many faculty, including myself, are committed to student success and check our emails and log in to the course a couple times a day. This ensures a speedy response so that students can move forward with their studies." You may not receive quite that level of commitment, but you definitely don't want to hear that the faculty check their emails only a couple times a week, either.

>> **How do I get help when I need it?** This question is a helpful follow-up to the preceding question. It lets you see whether the program you want to enroll in has an established process for getting help. When asking this question, you want to hear something like this: "Within every course, students will find the necessary contact information for the instructor, technical support, and academic advising, including email addresses, phone numbers, and other important information needed to contact us for help. There's also a public discussion forum in the course where you can ask questions of your peers as well as your instructor. This way, students can participate in answering each other's questions, and they may be able to respond faster than the instructor simply because there are more of them."

Chatting with other students about their experiences

To gain a true understanding of what you may experience in the program, ask your advisor whether you can have the contact information of an existing student or a recent graduate of the program. This person can answer your questions in a manner that no one else will, and the information you get will most likely be the most valuable to you in your search. However, don't be surprised if some institutions are hesitant to do this. It's not necessarily because they don't want to share the information; they simply want to protect the privacy of their students. You'll want them to do the same for you if you enroll.

TIP

Many students share their experiences via social media sites like LinkedIn. You can look to see whether the school has a LinkedIn presence and whether individuals publicly identify as students. If so, you can politely message those who identify as current or past students with a message asking them about their experience.

You'll notice that the following questions are more open-ended than those we've had you ask previously — this is so that you can have a more informal conversation:

» **What has your experience been like?** Asking this question provides the student you're interviewing a wide range of options and allows them to think about what their most important experiences have been. By asking this question, you may find out about academics, time commitment, or even about the overall support network provided by the institution.

» **What has been the best part?** You really want to listen to the answer to this question and how enthusiastic the interviewee is about answering it. Someone who's excited to tell you all about the wonderful things the program has to offer can be quite encouraging.

» **What has frustrated you?** To paint a holistic picture of the program, you must ask what an individual sees as both the positive and negative aspects of the program. However, be careful with this question: Even though it's an important one, you don't want the interview to focus too much on the negative. You want open, honest answers that are direct and to the point. As human beings, we all have the capacity to find the negative in anything. Try to stay focused on the big picture and not the micro details, because every student's experiences are different.

» **How would you rate the quality?** Getting a student's perspective on the quality of a program is priceless. It lets you know whether that person would recommend the program to others, and why. Asking this question to a graduate who has recently entered the work field can also help you determine whether the information and skills learned in the program were transferrable to the workplace.

>> **What is the faculty like?** By asking this question, you get one person's perception of the qualifications and teaching abilities of the faculty. Again, remember to stay focused on the big picture. Try to steer clear of finding out every negative or positive aspect of every instructor (though it doesn't hurt to find out which instructor you should look forward to having).

Narrowing Your Options

Okay, so you've been introduced to a variety of people, asked questions, and documented the answers. Now what? It's time to decide which institution you'll attend. Consider the following list of items when making your final decision. Consider making a chart that helps you evaluate the pros and cons of each institution based on these items:

>> **Academics:** Does the program meet my academic goals?

>> **Cost:** Can I afford to attend the institution, or is financial aid available? If financial aid is required, what will my payments be when I have to start repaying my loans? Will I be able to afford them?

>> **Workload:** Is the workload feasible based on my current work/life situation, or can my schedule be rearranged to accommodate the program's anticipated workload?

>> **Time:** Is the length of the course or program something I'm able to sustain based on the anticipated workload? Can I graduate in a reasonable amount of time?

>> **Resources available:** What kind of resources are available if I need help (library, technical support, academic help, advising, and so on)? Are these resources adequate based on my anticipated needs?

>> **Independence:** How independent will I be within the program? Will there be group work? How involved are the instructors? Will I be able to work at my own pace?

>> **Overall match:** Overall, does this program match my personality and learning preferences?

IN THIS CHAPTER

» **Untangling the process of applying to school**

» **Gathering the forms and documents you need**

» **Estimating how much school costs**

» **Determining how to pay for classes**

» **Obtaining federal financial aid**

Chapter **6**

Applying to School and Securing the Cash

After you've decided which subject you want to study and where, the next step is to apply to a school. (Of course, some people apply to more than one school at a time, but Chapter 5 can help you narrow the selection.) In the first part of this chapter, we walk you through the application process. Then we introduce you to the forms you'll use as well as some strategies to make your application land on top of the applicant pool.

The rest of this chapter addresses the million dollar question: How much will your education cost, and how will you pay for it? (Okay, the tuition and other expenses may not actually cost you a million bucks, but when you're adding up all your expenses, it may feel like it.) We give you an overview of tuition costs as well as details about the federal financial aid program.

Applying to an Online Program

By the time you've decided which college or university to apply to, you've likely filled out a web-based information form in order to receive more details about the school's offerings. (See Chapter 4 for more details on this topic.) After you jump through those preliminary hoops and give schools your email address, they share the application process. You receive an email with links to forms and instructions, including fees that may be involved. Often, you have the opportunity to receive paper versions of the same material, too.

This process is similar to that of brick-and-mortar colleges: Fill out application forms, write an essay or two, and submit documents that show your achievements and education to-date. In the following sections, we describe a typical application process, one that isn't specific to any individual institution. This way, you can see the kinds of information most colleges ask for and then prepare accordingly.

REMEMBER

In the following sections, we're talking only about applying to online schools. If you want to enroll in an online program via your local 2-year college, you'll likely be asked to complete the on-campus application process, which may include testing for math or English placement.

REMEMBER

If you apply to more than one school at a time, you have to fill out specific forms for each institution. However, you may be able to send the same résumé or essay to more than one school.

The basic application forms

Your journey begins with paperwork. You'll find forms in both digital and paper format. Rather than work with paper-and-pencil versions, you may be asked to complete web based forms. The institutions that rely on paper applications may direct you to a site where you can download and print your own forms.

Preliminary demographic information

Every college you're applying to needs basic information about you, including the types described in this list:

>> **Contact information:** Your home address, email address (because now you live online as well as on the ground), and your most reliable telephone number

>> **Personal information:** Your ethnicity and citizenship as well as your military and marital status

>> **Academic plans:** The type of degree you plan to pursue

>> **Previous education:** High school data and any college credits you may have already earned

REMEMBER

If you're applying for early entry into college so that you can earn college credits while you're still in high school, the application process may be a bit different. It may require that you obtain permission from a parent or counselor (or both) and jump through a few additional hoops. Doing so is worth it if you're able to complete the process. Many students these days are graduating from high school with their diplomas and are only a few credits away from earning their associate's degree at the same time.

REMEMBER

If you apply to an on-campus school that happens to offer online degrees, this demographic information is identical to what you would provide in order to attend on-campus classes. Therefore, you may also be asked about extracurricular activities, honors, family background, and work experience. If you apply to an institution that specializes in online degrees, you're less likely to be asked about these extras.

Transcripts of your previous education

You need to provide transcripts of your educational experience to the schools where you're applying. Typically, this item needs to be sent directly from the institution to the college to which you're applying. In other words, self-made copies on your home inkjet won't suffice. The good news is that, in many cases, the college to which you're applying will accept an unofficial copy temporarily, as a way to keep the ball rolling. In this conditional enrollment, assuming that everything else is in order, you're accepted to start the program without delay. However, you're given a deadline for supplying the institution with an original copy of your transcript. To do this, contact the high school or other colleges directly and ask them to send these credentials electronically. Follow up to be sure they were sent. If the credentials aren't received in a timely fashion, you may be prohibited from enrolling for the next term. Also, during this waiting period, you won't receive financial aid.

REMEMBER

You must supply institutions with original transcripts that originate directly from the former school. Most institutions now offer an online service to request and pay for transcripts online, which lets you order multiple transcripts and send them off to different institutions. In some cases, the process is now digital versus paper-based, which helps expedite the application process.

A résumé

In many graduate programs, schools request a résumé to accompany your application. They want to see the connection between your work experience and your academic plans. Don't worry if these items don't exactly match up, especially if you're transitioning to a new career. If you're stuck on what to write or how to organize the résumé, we recommend checking out *Résumés For Dummies, 8th Edition*, by Laura DeCarlo (Wiley).

Financial aid paperwork

We list financial aid here as a type of document you may need, and we say much more about this topic in the section "Figuring Out How You'll Pay for Online Classes," later in this chapter.

Application fees

You didn't think you could apply to schools without paying application fees, did you? Yes, you must pay these fees even though it seems that you're doing all the work. Fees vary from school to school. Most range from $50 to $100.

Your personal essay

Some institutions require a personal essay as part of the application process. They can then not only find out more about their applicants but also see their writing skills and creativity, which is especially important for applicants to graduate programs. You can't earn a master's degree without having to write a significant amount of material, and by the time you progress that far in school, you're expected to know what you're doing.

Other institutions no longer require a personal essay. For instance, schools that offer bachelor's completion programs assume that students who apply have already learned to write in their first two years of college, which they would have completed before enrolling in the online program. Likewise, private schools that don't offer remedial courses expect students to already know how to write.

If you're required to put your thoughts to paper, take a look at the next few sections for a glimpse of topics you may be asked to write about, hints for creating a good essay, and excerpts from a couple of essays.

What you may be asked to write

If you're applying for an associate's or bachelor's program or anything at the undergraduate level, chances are good that you'll be asked to give a written statement describing your past work experience or extracurricular activities. This gives the school an opportunity to get to know you a little better.

Beyond that introductory information, you may be asked to develop a longer essay. The essay is typically a page or two long. Here are several common undergraduate essay topics:

>> Evaluate a significant experience in your life, and describe how it affected you.

>> Discuss an issue of personal significance, and explain why it is important.

>> Identify and describe a person who has had a significant influence on you, and explain that influence.

>> Choose your own topic.

WARNING

Choosing your own topic may allow for creativity, but it doesn't excuse bad writing. You still have to follow standard conventions and show good grammar and organization. Be careful not to get too abstract if you choose your own topic.

Graduate essays are completely different: The schools probe your motivation to continue your education as well as your professional experience. They want candidates with previous professional exposure because it enriches the classroom experience. Working gives you stories to share and insights to offer. For example, if you seek an advanced degree in education, you may be asked to provide a teaching philosophy statement that weaves together your personal beliefs about education with your work experience.

If you're going straight from college with an undergraduate degree into graduate school, write about volunteer or internship experience you can relate to your studies. After all, you must have *some* compelling reason to want to stay in school. Tell the reader what it is that has led you to love that field and how your experiences fit.

What the readers are looking for

Schools can tell a lot about your academic preparation and personal motivation from your written work. If your work is filled with grammatical errors or lacks basic organization, they'll know that you need remedial help. On the other hand, if your writing mechanics (grammar, punctuation, and spelling) are fine, readers can move on to how creatively you address the topic, your ability to analyze and think critically, and your overall written communication skills. That's good!

TIP

What other pointers should you remember? Check out this list of tips:

>> **Readers aren't looking for formulaic essays.** Following the 5-paragraph rule — with an introduction plus thesis statement, three supporting paragraphs, and a conclusion — is easy. Try to work a little beyond that. The people who read these essays read *a lot* of essays, so yours needs to be unique.

>> **Make sure your introduction and conclusion are strong.** Readers like pieces that start with a punch and end with a bang.

>> **Details count.** Be sure to support any opinions or assertions with details. Avoid vague, unsubstantiated comments. For example, if you say that a lot of people take online courses, back up your assertion with information from a

trusted source: "The Education Department reports that approximately 6.6 million students were enrolled in at least one online course in the fall of 2017."

>> **Reference research methodology and theory whenever possible.** Impress readers by sharing your knowledge of research in the field you're studying and how you apply it in your work now.

>> **Tell the truth.** Academic honesty starts with the application process. If you trust this school to give you a decent education and a degree, they should be able to trust you to do your own work and tell the truth. For example, don't write about how facing a catastrophic illness defined your personal views if you've enjoyed excellent health your whole life. It's these kinds of lies that snowball.

For much more detailed information about writing a college application essay, read *College Admission Essays For Dummies*, by Geraldine Woods (Wiley).

Samples of writing

Here's an excerpt of a writing sample for a graduate essay. The writer was asked to explain how obtaining a master's degree from that school would benefit a wide audience:

> "For the past seven years, I have supported faculty and subject matter experts in both academic and corporate settings. Currently, as our college's dean of instruction, I develop schedules for both students and faculty, provide faculty training, and supervise the faculty peer-coaching program. My highest priority is to assist faculty in developing quality courses based on research-based best practices in instructional design and instruction. To accomplish this goal, our organization emphasizes a systems approach to design and a variety of teaching methodologies to meet the needs of our diverse community. By accepting my application, you affect not only the lives of a single learner but also a community of educators and their students."

An excerpt of an essay for an undergraduate program in which the author explains her goals might look like this:

> "In North America, there is an unwritten rule that the senior year of high school is sacred. It is a time of morphing between childhood and young adulthood, of academic accomplishment and recognition, and of social development. So, when my parents announced two months before my senior year began that we were moving halfway across the world to serve in a relief agency, imagine my reaction. And yet, having to pull up stakes and establish a new identity in South Africa left an indelible impression on me. I not only found a new voice in myself, stronger than I had believed possible, but also learned that listening teaches more than talking. All these experiences and lessons have led me to want to earn degrees in cross-cultural communication and social justice."

Letters of recommendation

The application process includes having to supply letters of recommendation, which should come from people who are familiar with your academic work or who can vouch for your professional accomplishments. If you're a high school graduate, you can easily ask a teacher, school counselor, or coach to write a letter for you. If you're a working professional and have a good relationship with your boss, ask that person. They'll be not only alerted that you're returning to school but also likely flattered to know that you value their opinion. You may also want to ask a trusted colleague. It's good to see a variety of views. Be prepared to supply as many as three different letters.

WARNING

Be sure that your references understand your academic and professional abilities and accomplishments. Friends and relatives may not be the best choice for this task, unless they've had direct experiences working with you.

TIP

Check in with the people who write your recommendation letters, to make sure their letters are sent in a timely fashion. Even though they adore you, they might not follow through promptly. To help speed up the process, provide each person with a copy of your program description, application, résumé, essay, synopsis of the area to focus on — and a self-addressed envelope.

If someone asks what you want them to say, tell them that a letter typically includes this type of information:

>> **A description of your relationship:** For how long have they known you and in what capacity?

>> **An overview of your professional abilities and accomplishments:** You may want them to mention certain of your skills or abilities, and you may want to supply a résumé to work from.

>> **Your previous academic experience, if any:** Again, if your reference doesn't know this, supply your résumé.

>> **A general statement of why the program would benefit by accepting your application:** This is a nice way to close the letter.

Test scores

ACT, SAT, GRE, MCAT, PDQ, ASAP — acronyms like these invoke fear in most college applicants. Excluding the last two, these are the monikers of standardized academic tests sometimes used to predict a student's success. Some programs require these test scores as part of the application process. However, many online institutions have dropped the test requirement because they know that your high school GPA or the number of credit hours you're transferring into their program are better indicators of future success.

TIP

If you need to take these tests and submit the scores from them, make arrangements well in advance of when you want to start your academic program. It typically takes six to eight weeks to receive test results. When you take the test, you can indicate which schools you want to receive your scores, and the testing company will send your scores directly to them.

If English isn't your first language, you may be asked to submit English proficiency scores from either the TOEFL (Test of English as a Foreign Language) or TOEIC (Test of English for International Communication).

When it's all due

The due date for all this information about you depends on the school. If you apply to an on-campus school offering online courses that run on a typical semester schedule, you may face a deadline for admission. However, if you apply to a school that starts programs every few weeks, the deadline is (and your start date is) whenever you get your paperwork sent and are subsequently accepted and enrolled. You have to meet certain conditions related to financial aid, so if it isn't obvious, be sure to ask the academic advisor or admissions personnel about it when you first contact the school.

A helping hand to assist you: The recruiter, advisor, or counselor

To gather information about online schools, you sometimes have to complete online forms. (We cover this topic in Chapter 4.) After you submit your contact information, you may receive a phone call from recruiters — and their job is to hook you into the process by answering your questions, providing information, and then referring you to other helpful personnel. If you're applying to one of the well-known private online schools, you should know that these callers are highly trained in sales and marketing. Don't be put off by them, but do ask questions. We offer some suggested questions to ask in Chapter 5.

Sometimes, a recruiter works with you all the way through the application process, but more often, they refer you to an academic advisor or counselor. An academic advisor first helps you gather the necessary paperwork, by giving you a list of documents you need, such as the application, transcripts, and résumé.

When it comes to transcripts, you tell the institution where they should come from. As we discuss in the earlier section "Transcripts of your previous education," temporary copies can help keep the ball rolling. Your responsibility is to follow through to make sure transcripts are sent and received.

Though academic advisors have a lot of answers, some decisions have to be made by others. For example, the decision to transfer previous credits is most likely made by a dean or another administrator within the program you're applying to. However, the academic advisor serves as the facilitator by providing the dean with your transcripts and reporting any decisions to you. The academic advisor also helps facilitate introductions between you and other staff, such as the financial aid officer.

Calculating the Costs of Online Classes

There's no easy way to break the news: School isn't cheap. According to the National Center for Education Statistics, annual tuition in current dollars for 2-year institutions increased from $3,367 for the 1985-1986 school year to $10,598 for the 2016-2017 academic year.

It's impossible for us to tell you that a 2-year degree, for example, will cost you $15,000 because we don't know whether you want to attend a private college, a 4-year institution that awards associate's degrees, or a 2-year school. In addition, as soon as we give you a price tag, tuition will increase (it never decreases), making the number obsolete. Therefore, we look at the cost of one course in 2020.

For this baseline, consider the following costs for an undergraduate accounting course that awards three credit hours:

>> **At a well-known, private online institution:** $514 per credit hour ($1,542 total)

>> **At a public university that offers this course online:** $229.84 per credit hour in-state or $689.52 out-of-state

>> **At a 2-year community college in the Midwest that offers this course online:** $171 per credit hour in-district and in-state, $247.50 out-of-district but in-state, or $302.50 out-of-district and out-of-state ($513 to $907.50 total, depending on where you live)

In this example, you save money by taking the course by way of the local community college, though not everyone has that kind of option.

Now consider a graduate level course in education that awards three credit hours:

» **At a well-known, private online institution:** $776 per credit hour ($2,328 total)

» **At a public university that offers this course online:** $360.37 per credit hour for in-state residents; $808.46 for out-of-state residents and international students

REMEMBER

The more classes you take at one time, the more you owe at one time. And, the formula for determining tuition and total costs can vary based on the institution, program of study, fees, supplies, and location (online or on campus).

We can't provide exact numbers, but Table 6-1 shows some typical costs and specifies where you may see differences.

TABLE 6-1   On-Campus versus Online Costs

Cost	On-Campus	Online
Tuition	Costs vary depending on the type of institution (public or private, 2-year or 4-year).	Expect to pay the same amount as for on-campus education. Typically, schools charge by the credit hour or for the completion of an entire degree or certificate program.
Fees	You might pay fees for the college's technology, student activities, fitness center, on-campus labs, student health insurance, and other services. These vary greatly, depending on the type of institution.	You're less likely to have to pay the same fees online. Some schools charge for the services you use (for example, technology), and others charge no fees.
Books	Textbooks are *expensive*. Spending $100 or more on one textbook isn't uncommon.	The price of online textbooks is the same as for on campus. As with books for on-campus courses, you may be able to buy discounted or used books, but you might incur the additional cost of shipping and handling. Some sellers offer free shipping above a certain dollar amount.
Room and board	You might live at home and incur no additional charges for room and board. However, if you're an on-campus student enrolling in a residential college, you may be required to live on campus for at least the first year. In that case, you can add $6,000 or more to the price tag.	You can definitely live at home and incur no additional room-and-board charges.
Travel	If you're commuting to school, consider the cost of fuel and of wear-and-tear on your vehicle or the cost of public transportation.	No additional cost — you just work from the convenience of your home. However, some programs may require you to make an annual trip to their main campus (some doctoral programs and other graduate degrees, for example), so this trip would count as a cost.

TIP

Another way to save money is to look for courses that employ *open education resources (OER)*, which are resources created by people with the intention of making them available to others for free or at a dramatically discounted cost. Some states now have a way to flag these courses in the course catalog. For example, Washington state public institutions specify courses whose total materials-and-supplies costs are $50 or less.

REMEMBER

The result is that you might not save money in tuition and fees if you attend school online, but you may save money in room-and-board and travel costs, depending on how you run your own comparison. What you save on books depends on the seller and whether it offers free shipping.

Figuring Out How You'll Pay for Online Classes

Cash, check, or charge? Paying for school is never that easy. It's an expensive proposition and one that no one can afford to take lightly. After you determine what subject you want to study and where you want to go, you have to come up with the cash. This section introduces you to the idea of finding financial aid.

REMEMBER

Financial aid can pay for various expenses depending on the type of aid received. For the most part, aid can pay for tuition and fees, and possibly textbooks. If you're an online student, you can't use it to pay for your housing.

Every school has a financial aid officer who can help you throughout the financial aid process — and who may even approach you when you first inquire about the program. This person walks you through the various types of aid available at that specific institution and the steps you need to complete to possibly receive aid.

We should say from the beginning that every school has its own process. Therefore, we keep this discussion at a level that may be applicable to the majority of schools.

Do you need financial aid?

Though earning a degree or certificate at a 2-year college is affordable, graduate degrees and bachelor's completion programs at larger institutions carry a heftier price tag. If you're a working adult, imagine adding an additional $20,000 in debt! Few people have that kind of cash readily available, nor can they absorb those kinds of payments into their budget over the short term (the years you're studying online).

For that reason, you have to pursue the options. Further, many institutions ask you to complete financial aid paperwork when you apply, regardless of your expressed need. Why? The institution wants you to finish the degree. It tries to remove any barriers it can, including problems paying for school.

In all fairness, you may be able to afford the education without outside assistance. Good for you! In that case, just complete the required forms and relax.

What if you're not sure whether you need assistance? The federal paperwork helps determine this need. The government has a snazzy formula that considers all your expenses balanced against the amount you have saved, including money from a 529 savings account (the special one for education). Also, you can find an abundance of financial aid calculators and tools by making a simple web search, including resources on the Free Application for Federal Student Aid (FAFSA) site. And, the friendly financial aid counselor that the school assigns to you will have additional resources to offer.

REMEMBER

You need to fill out the financial aid paperwork only once, regardless of how many schools you're considering. However, if you receive aid, don't forget to reapply each year.

What types of financial aid are available?

Financial aid comes in a few varieties. In most cases, you use this aid for tuition and fees for online courses, assuming that you're attending an accredited institution. The financial aid counselor can advise you about any restrictions. In the following list, we look at some possibilities to see how they differ:

>> **Scholarships:** Gifts of a prescribed amount based on merit or circumstance. Scholarships are available for graduate and undergraduate study. You don't have to pay back scholarships. If the scholarship comes from the school or an outside agency, such as the Future Farmers of America (FFA) club, it may be restricted to a certain field of study or for use only at the school providing the scholarship. Federal aid may restrict whether the scholarship is available for graduate study.

>> **Grants:** Awards of a prescribed amount based on financial need. Some of these come from the US government, whereas others may come from the state. The two most common grants are federal programs: Pell and supplemental educational opportunity grants. Federal grants typically aren't available for graduate study. You don't have to repay a grant.

>> **Loans:** Money you borrow. Loans can be secured privately by way of your local bank or federally via Subsidized Federal Loans. These federal student loans don't accrue interest while you're in school. Obviously, these loans must be repaid. Any unsubsidized loans you secure accrue interest from the time they're disbursed. Therefore, if you're able to pay your tuition solely from the subsidized loans, consider declining unsubsidized loans.

Applying for Federal Financial Aid

Applying for financial aid requires diligence. You fill out the form and the government tells you how much government aid you're eligible for, based on financial need. Though the process requires attention to detail and a document search (old tax returns, for example) for the numbers you need, it's not *that* awful. The bright spot is that you need to apply only once each year to the government, and that information is then forwarded to the institutions you specify.

Knowing whether you're eligible for funds from Uncle Sam

To receive financial assistance from the federal government, you must meet certain criteria. The amount of assistance is based on a complicated formula based on anticipated need and expenses such as tuition, housing, and books.

Criteria for eligibility include US citizenship, a high school diploma or GED, and satisfactory grade performance. You should review other legal requirements as well, such as having a social security number (SSN), before completing the application.

Financial aid recipients are required to adhere to certain academic standards. Depending on the type of aid, students must attend at least half-time and be enrolled in a certificate or degree-seeking program. Performance standards set by the academic institution must also be met. Students failing to meet these standards can be denied federal assistance.

Filling out and submitting the FAFSA

Every financial aid application begins with the Free Application for Federal Student Aid (FAFSA). The FAFSA is not only required for federal financial aid but is also the benchmark for any other kind of aid consideration. Aside from basic demographic information, this form collects the details about your income or your parents' income and assets. How long it takes you to gather the information depends on how organized you are in general. Some people can find their tax returns at the snap of a finger, and others have to rummage through the entire basement. Leave yourself enough time to complete the task. Learners are required to complete the FAFSA form annually. The form is available online at `https://studentaid.gov` along with more information. Figure 6-1 familiarizes you with the look of the site. (Note that Federal Student Aid is an office of the US Department of Education.)

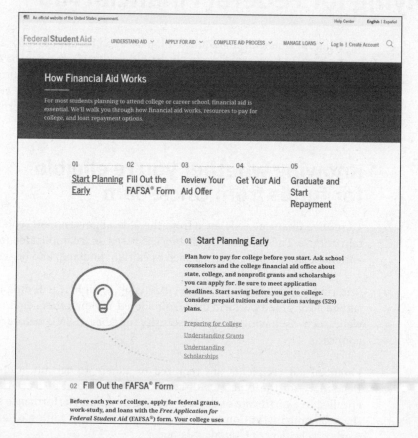

FIGURE 6-1:
The FAFSA portal.

Be wary of anyone trying to charge an application or service fee for any tasks associated with financial aid. Applying for financial aid should be *free*. Also, you should be able to find both answers to questions you may have about the process *and* help with filling out the application from the institution or the Federal Student Aid office.

The FAFSA is available online, and you can complete the application process digitally. It takes approximately four weeks for the government to process written applications, not counting the time your institution may need to process payments and so forth based on your application results. Completing the application digitally speeds up the process. Therefore, if you're applying shortly before classes begin, apply digitally.

After your FAFSA has been received and processed, you receive an email from the government indicating that your student aid report has been sent on to the school(s) you specified. The school takes over and administers the aid.

TIP

Start the process of looking for financial aid as early you can. January 1 is a crucial deadline because that's the date on which students applying for the next academic year can submit FAFSAs for consideration. Each institution has additional deadlines. Be sure to meet every deadline — if you don't, you may have to wait a full year before you can apply again.

TIP

On-campus institutions and online institutions follow the same processes, so it may be worth your while to pick up a few resources, such as the book *Getting Financial Aid 2018: Scholarships, Grants, Loans, and Jobs,* by The College Board. It's available from major booksellers or from https://store.collegeboard.org. You may also want to look at the Student Aid site at https://studentaid.gov.

Chapter 7

Getting Accepted and Prepping for Class

You've done your research, applied to an institution or three, and now you're waiting to hear back. What happens next? In this chapter, we discuss what to do after you're accepted. This process includes registering for classes, becoming familiar with the online environment, and purchasing your textbooks. Time to get started.

Finding Out Whether You've Been Accepted or Rejected

Many online institutions take less time to respond than a traditional academic institution does. When you apply to traditional institutions, sometimes you're required to wait at least two months to find out whether you've been accepted. Depending on whether the online institution accepts unofficial transcripts to admit you *conditionally* (admit you based on *copies* of your transcripts with the condition that you request original copies to be sent by a predetermined deadline), you may know within just a few days whether you've been accepted.

Institutions notify students of their acceptance in different ways. Some schools choose to notify their students via a phone call from the academic advisor. Others notify students via email. This not only speeds up the process but also reduces the need for paper. Few institutions choose to notify students via standard US mail. If the institution's website or application documentation didn't provide you with a timeline for notifying students of acceptance, contact your academic advisor. You can also contact your advisor after you've submitted your application, to receive a progress update.

TIP

You're such a smarty that we know you were accepted by multiple institutions — now what? How do you choose the program that is right for you? Refer to Chapter 5, where we talk about narrowing your options when searching for institutions. You should use the same checklist now for deciding which school is best for you.

Unfortunately, on the flip side of acceptance to a school is rejection. An application can be rejected for several reasons. Talking to your academic advisor can help you narrow down the reason that your application was rejected. Here are some causes of rejection:

>> **A simple data entry error occurred:** It happens.

>> **Previous academic history:** Your history failed to meet the prerequisites for the course or program.

>> **Previous academic grade point average (GPA):** Your GPA didn't meet the minimum standard for the course or program.

>> **Required deadlines:** You have to meet all deadlines within the application process.

>> **Lack of official transcripts:** Your transcripts from other academic institutions you attended weren't received.

>> **Enrollment limitation:** Program enrollment has reached its maximum for the current term.

TIP

If your application is rejected, avoid the assumption that this status is permanent. As you can see from the preceding list, many of the reasons that applications are rejected are easy to resolve quickly. Yes, you may have to delay your enrollment by one term, but don't let that deter you from accomplishing your academic goals. Here are a couple of steps you can take:

>> **Sharpen your academic prowess:** If your application has been rejected because of your past academic performance, you may be asked to take remedial courses or student success classes as a way to prove your

commitment and establish your academic abilities. These courses may be available at the institution for which you're applying, or you may be required to take these courses elsewhere. Also, in this situation, some institutions will place you on academic probation and conditionally accept your application. You're then required to maintain a specific GPA in order to enroll in future terms.

>> **Meet the necessary prerequisites: If** your application is rejected because you didn't take the prerequisite courses, you have to postpone your application until you have successfully met those requirements. Contact your academic advisor to find out who offers these courses and when classes begin. In this situation, be sure to ask your advisor whether your application will remain on file or you'll have to resubmit it after you have successfully met the prerequisite requirements.

Registering for Classes

Even if the physical task of registering for classes is an easy one, you want to be sure you're enrolling in the correct courses and taking them in the right order. This section helps you determine your academic path and provides strategies for staying on course during the registration process.

Creating a plan with your academic advisor (also known as Coach)

Your academic advisor's role is to guide you through the registration process, get you started, and keep you on track throughout your academic career. At some schools, this person is called the *academic coach*. The first task your advisor or coach should help you with is to create a roadmap of your academic career, in the form of a checklist of all the classes you must take within your program and the order in which you must take them. This list should also include other program requirements needed for graduation. Though each program is different, here are some examples:

>> **All courses in the program:** Listed sequentially in the order they should be taken by term

>> **Recommended electives:** Listed in sequential order by term

>> **Thesis, final project, and/or portfolio:** Deadline listed, if applicable

Who cares about the order in which you take courses, as long as you take them all — right? Well, not always. Some courses may not be offered every term. If you take courses out of order, you may find yourself in a position where the course you need as a prerequisite to the remaining courses in your program isn't available — which can force you to have to stop out for a term and delay your graduation date. It can also impact financial aid matters, because you may be required to take a minimum number of credits per term in order to receive financial aid. If you're forced to reduce your class load due to poor planning, you may not be able to receive your financial aid reimbursement for that term.

Even if communication with your advisor isn't required, and even if you have a detailed roadmap, touch base with that person after every term and before enrolling in the new term. This advice is especially important if you have failed a course or had to stop out for any reason and are ready to begin again. Touching base ensures that you're still on the right track and that program requirements haven't changed since your initial enrollment. A quick email exchange with your advisor should suffice.

For students who simply want to take a few classes for personal interest or professional development, the academic advisor still plays an important role. The academic advisor can serve as the first point of contact for administrative help such as registering for courses, paying for courses, and recommending other courses that meet your interests.

Picking your first classes

Most academic programs require students to take an introductory course before diving into more detailed topics. Online programs are no different. If you're enrolled in a degree program, you most likely have to take an introductory course as your first course. Students often complain that this is a waste of time and money if, in future classes, they'll simply focus in more detail on each topic discussed in the course. However, the introductory course serves several purposes, including helping students become familiar with the field and the institution — and with studying, in case it has been awhile since you last had homework or in case you need to develop college-level study habits. In the online environment, the introductory course also helps you become familiar with the technology used.

If you're not enrolled in a degree program or you have a choice regarding the order in which you take classes, think about possible learning curves and how much you can take on. For example, if you haven't been in school for a while, if this is your first college course, or if technology makes you nervous, you may want to take an introductory course or one with fewer credits that requires less time dedicated to coursework.

Choosing between traditional model and cohort model classes

Whether you'll be enrolling in courses that follow a traditional model or a cohort model is a factor to consider when you're looking at degree or certification program structures during the interviewing process that we describe in Chapter 5. The structure–model decision is determined by the institution and/or department sponsoring the program, and in most cases you don't have a choice of models.

Here are the differences between the two:

>> **Traditional:** In a traditional model, you may be required to take an introductory class as your first course, but then you break off from the pack and choose your own path. This is where it's important to pay attention to prerequisite requirements and details such as how often a course is offered throughout a year. Freedom is nice, but with it comes responsibility.

The traditional model is useful for students who want more control over their own destination. They can choose which classes to take and in which order. However, this model requires more planning. If you choose this model, *communicate with your academic advisor often* so that they can ensure that you're on the right track.

>> **Cohort:** In the cohort model (which we introduce in Chapter 4), you start and stop with the same people in every class. The only time students mix in this model is when the program allows students to choose elective courses throughout the program.

For example, you may want to earn a master of education degree. Jane Smith is in your first course with you — EDD101: Introduction to Education. Jane is in the next three courses with you as well. However, after taking the four core courses, it's time for you to take specialty courses. You may choose to focus on elementary education while Jane decides to take courses in special education. At this point, you part ways and see each other at graduation. In a cohort model, everyone who starts at the same time should finish at the same time, whether they take the same classes or not.

For many students, the cohort model works best for students whose entire academic careers are already planned out. Plus, it's not uncommon for students to become lifelong friends after "surviving" an entire degree program together. However, some students prefer diversity and would rather have different classmates from one course to the next.

Whether to participate in a traditional model or a cohort model is a concern only for those participating in a degree program. If you're taking classes for professional development or out of interest, you'll participate in a more traditional model where you choose what classes you take and when. However, you may still need to meet prerequisite requirements. If a course you want to take has a prerequisite you'd rather forgo, talk to your advisor, who may forward your request to the instructor. If the instructor is willing to consider your petition, that person may ask you to provide proof that you understand the concepts presented in the prerequisite course. For example, you may have to submit your résumé or pass a proficiency exam. Don't be surprised, though, if the instructor requires you to take the prerequisite course.

Deciding on other types of class structures

In Chapter 4, we introduce you to other course formats that you may want to consider when registering for courses. For example, if you're enrolled in a program that's geographically close, you may want to consider a blended program where you're provided some face-to-face opportunities with the instructor and your classmates. If distance is an issue but you like having voice interaction with others, a predominantly synchronous class may suit your learning style better. But, if your work/life schedule provides limited study time, you may be better off taking a self-paced course.

REMEMBER

As nice as it is to have choices, course formats can vary from class to class within the same program, depending on the program, course content, and instructor preference. Therefore, gain a sense of the entire program's expectations when conducting your research.

Gathering the information you need in order to register

TIP

Whether you register online, via postal mail, or over the phone with your academic advisor, keep the following information at your disposal for each class you want to take:

>> **Course term:** The term name and year, including start and stop dates — for example, Fall 2020, Aug. 10–Dec. 13, 2020.

>> **Course title:** The name of the course provided in the course catalog. It's often an abbreviated title due to the character restrictions of most catalog applications. An example of a full course title is English 101: Composition 1; a catalog may abbreviate it as ENG101 Comp1.

>> **Course ID/course reference number (CRN):** Usually, a letter representing the department followed by a course number. For example, E101 is the course ID for English 101: An Introduction to Writing. The CRN is an extension of the course ID that usually includes a cohort identification and section number.

For example, E100 OL1 002 might be the online version for English 101 and the second section offered to cohort 1. (We discuss cohorts in the earlier section "Choosing between traditional model and cohort model classes.")

>> **Instructor:** The name of the instructor teaching the section of the course you're enrolling in.

TIP

Most of this information can be found in your course catalog or the checklist/roadmap document you create with your academic advisor. However, you won't be able to find the CRN or specific instructor for the courses without visiting the institution's course schedule page. This page is usually connected with the registration site so that you can determine your desired course section and register right there. Contact your advisor and ask that person to show you where to find this information.

Navigating registration processes

Though your advisor helps you determine your academic path and is available for questions when needed, actually registering for classes is most likely your responsibility. Academic institutions use a variety of web-based applications and interfaces for registration. Many institutions send you information to establish an account on their student information system (like Banner or Peoplesoft). You use that system to register for classes.

Figure 7-1 illustrates what an online registration system might look like. In this example, you can see that all education (EDD) courses are about to be listed because all other fields are blank or have All chosen. If you know the course number or title, you may be able to search for those specific fields directly. After clicking Class Search, you see a list of all courses that match your search criteria, including each course's title, ID/CRN, instructor, start date, end date, and, possibly, more. Registering for a course is as simple as clicking on it.

REMEMBER

Each institution uses different registration technology, and it makes it look different from the one you see in Figure 7-1. However, the general information about each course is the same.

Taking action when a course you want is full

One advantage of a cohort model (which we describe earlier in this chapter) is that you're almost always guaranteed a seat in every course you need. When a cohort fills up, either a new cohort is started or students are asked to wait one term and start during the next rotation of courses.

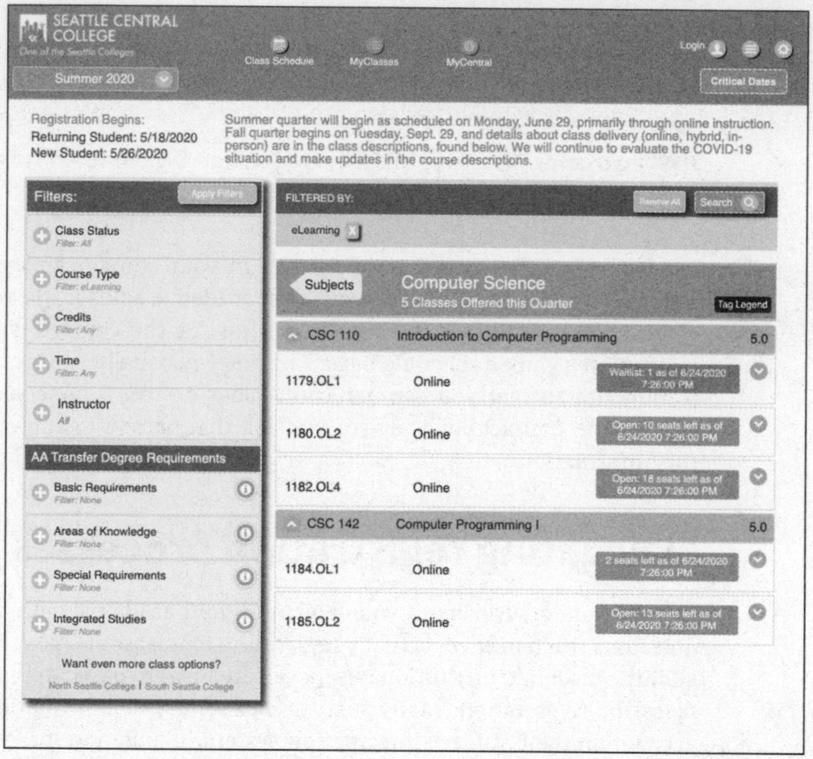

FIGURE 7-1:
An example of an online course registration system.

Courtesy of Nova Southeastern University

If you're in a traditional program and the course you want fills up, contact your academic advisor. Sometimes, that person can tell you whether enough other students need the course to justify opening another section. Also contact the instructor of the course. Instructors are often given the ability to admit additional students beyond the standard enrollment. If all else fails, work with your advisor to find another course in your program, and update your academic roadmap accordingly.

When in doubt: Talking to your academic advisor

How many times can we tell you to contact your advisor when you need something? Three, four, six, ten? We do so because this relationship is truly critical. Your advisor's job is to help you succeed. Take advantage of this and ask for help when you need it.

TIP

Though the assistance your advisor provides is priceless, never rely on one person blindly. All humans make mistakes. Be sure you understand what's going on at all times, and ask questions when they arise. One of the best ways to do this is to prepare everything yourself, such as your registration schedule, and ask your advisor simply to review it and provide feedback.

Getting Oriented

Institutions typically offer orientation sessions for new students enrolling in their first online course — whether it's in a degree program or a single course. These sessions are usually a one-time event with resources you can access as needed throughout your academic experience. Research shows that students who participate in an orientation program are more likely to succeed academically. Therefore, many online institutions provide orientation programs, even to those who are taking only a single online course. Some institutions require students to participate, whereas at other institutions, participation is voluntary.

REMEMBER

Trust us when we tell you that participating in an orientation program is worth your time and effort. It has been our experience that students who don't participate in an orientation program are often more confused and frustrated because they have to learn how to navigate within the environment while also focusing on academic deadlines.

To help you avoid becoming one of those frustrated and lost students, in the following sections we discuss how to determine what kind of orientation is available and how to participate in the process.

Determining whether an orientation is available and/or required

Hopefully, you asked about orientation during your initial interview when researching online programs. (See Chapter 5 for more about this process.) However, you may not have discussed the details needed to register for, and participate in, the orientation. This information should be provided with your acceptance information. If it isn't, contact your academic advisor immediately. The sooner you know, the sooner you can start planning.

If you didn't discuss this issue during the interview process, again, contact your academic advisor immediately. Knowing whether you're expected to participate in an orientation program and whether it's offered online is important. It's also important for you to know the timing of the orientation and whether missing it would delay you from starting your program.

WARNING

Some institutions require you to participate in an orientation program as a degree requirement. It would be a shame to skip orientation and not find out until you're ready to graduate that you're ineligible because you never took the orientation.

Distinguishing types of orientation programs

Orientation programs for online courses are provided via two delivery methods. Some institutions require students to attend an orientation at the campus, whereas others offer an online equivalent.

Face-to-face orientation

An institution may ask for you to attend an orientation on campus, for a number of reasons. Being onsite provides a secure way to confirm your identity and gives you the opportunity to meet some of your faculty and support staff face-to-face. You can confirm that your paperwork is in order (financial aid, registration, and other important documents) and get to know some of your peers. This experience also helps you feel more connected to the institution itself.

Here are a couple more benefits of face-to-face orientation:

>> **Live computer demonstrations:** Most likely, you get to learn about the online environment in a computer lab where someone actually demonstrates how to log in, navigate within the system, and perform other tasks needed to successfully participate in the institution's online classes. For example, you need to know how to access the library's online database. This experience is priceless! It's a good thing, too, because in this situation, you're responsible for travel, lodging, and food expenses — you may as well make the most of your orientation experience.

>> **Q&A opportunities:** You're introduced to policies and procedures in an environment where you can ask questions and receive immediate answers. You also get to hear the questions asked by your peers and the answers to those questions as well.

Online orientation

In contrast to a face-to-face orientation, you may be offered an orientation that is completely online. Online orientation programs are usually delivered in one of four ways:

>> **Web pages on the institution's website:** Institutions that don't require students to participate in an orientation program may simply develop web pages and provide students with links to those pages in their acceptance documentation. These pages may be compiled on one site (usually, the technology support department's website) with a navigation system, or they may be randomly scattered and referenced as needed within your course. For example, separate links to technical information may lead you to a different site than links to library resources, which may lead you to a separate set of resources maintained by library staff. In this form of orientation, no one knows your progress.

>> **Self-paced orientation inside the course management system:** This method is similar to the preceding one in that the materials are available immediately and 24/7, but it's a little more authentic in that you get to work within the course management system you'll use for coursework. The institution can track student completion by way of the course management system.

>> **Instructor-led orientation inside the course management system:** Some institutions require a more formal orientation program. These institutions hire an instructor to facilitate an online orientation similar to the other online sessions of the academic courses you enroll in. The orientation lasts a couple weeks, at most. The advantage to this structure is having an instructor available to answer questions when needed. The disadvantage to this structure is that you may not have access to the materials after the course is complete. Another disadvantage is that these orientations have specific start and stop dates. If your acceptance to the institution came after the orientation class began, you may have to wait until the course is offered again before enrolling in courses required by your degree program, unless the institution allows you to concurrently enroll in both the orientation and program courses.

>> **Synchronous web conference facilitated by an instructor:** Synchronous web conferencing tools may be used by institutions to hold live sessions where the facilitator can take participants on a virtual tour of a course management system, a virtual library, and other utilized instructional tools. The advantage of this method is that you have a live person you can ask questions of, and orientation is accomplished quickly and expediently. The obvious disadvantage is working with scheduling challenges.

Figure 7-2 illustrates what an online orientation program may look like. In this example, students are provided with a class-like experience that welcomes them to the program and provides resources to policies/procedures, technical support, and academic services. It is delivered in the same LMS they use for courses.

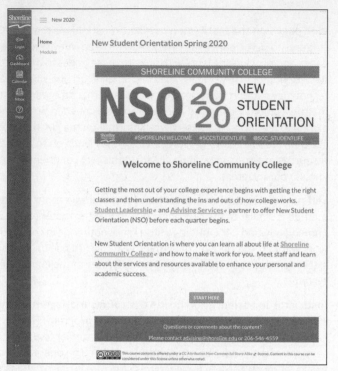

FIGURE 7-2:
An example of an online orientation program.

Courtesy of University of Illinois Global Campus

Participating in orientation

No matter what type of orientation program your institution offers, be sure to play an active role. We can't stress enough how beneficial participating in an orientation program can be. This is a great time to learn how to navigate and use your institution's technology in a safe environment without the pressures of homework and assignment deadlines. In the following sections, we explain how to register for orientation (if needed), and we provide pointers on how to make the most of your session.

Registering for the orientation (if necessary)

To track which students have participated in the orientation, you may be asked to register for it as though you were registering for a class — your school will provide instructions on how to do so. As a matter of fact, institutions that require this component track it on your transcript as a way of easily determining whether you've successfully met graduation requirements. Other institutions, especially those where the orientation program isn't required, may not have a registration system.

Don't get too excited about the thought of the orientation program being listed on your transcript. It doesn't boost your GPA. Most orientation programs, even those that are required, are *zero-credit* requirements: They can keep you from graduating, but they don't affect your academic standing.

Taking a virtual tour and noting important information

Most orientations, whether they're face-to-face or online, provide students with some kind of virtual tour of the learning environment. These tours can be developed using still screen shots of a sample course or video, or by demonstrating application sharing in a live environment.

During a virtual tour, students are provided with a visual demonstration of how to log in, navigate within the course management system, and perform common, daily tasks. These may include reading new announcements from the instructor, checking for new posts within the discussion forum, replying to a peer's post, checking internal email, submitting assignments, and using other software required by your academic program.

As you participate in the orientation program, note important information and keep it close to you for future reference when studying. Here are a few vital pieces of information to write down:

>> Contact information for technical support, including email and phone number. (See Chapter 10 for more about technical support.)

>> The URL to the institution's course management system where your classes will be housed.

>> Steps for logging in and navigating to your virtual classroom. (See Chapter 9 for general tips.)

>> How to navigate and log in to the library. (See Chapter 12 for basic guidelines.)

>> How to start a new discussion post inside your course's discussion forum. (See Chapter 11 for an introduction.)

>> Any additional tips provided for student success.

This tour is one of the most valuable assets of the orientation program. If this resource is something you can get to at any time, be sure to note its location for future reference. You should also bookmark important external resources linked to from within the orientation. Finally, don't forget to bookmark other important sites, such as your institution's home page, the course management system login page, the library, and the technical support home page.

TIP

Add a bookmark to the login page on your browser's toolbar so that you can find the bookmark easily. Most browsers let you specify bookmarked pages to be displayed on the toolbar, where you see them whenever you open the browser, or on the regular list of bookmarks.

Buying Books

After registering for your courses, you need to find out what textbooks and other supplies are required for your courses. This section helps you determine how to find out which supplies you need and how to purchase them.

Knowing which textbooks you need

Most brick-and-mortar schools have switched to an electronic registration system. As a result, institutions have also connected their registration systems to electronic bookstores. Therefore, after completing your course registration process, you see a button labeled Buy Your Books Now that links to the institution's online bookstore. Clicking on this link not only takes you to the virtual bookstore — it also creates a list of textbooks and supplies you need based on the courses you're enrolled in. Clicking this button doesn't obligate you to purchase your books from this site. It's just the best way to find out what books and supplies are required for your courses. Some institutions may provide a syllabus link in their course listings, which often includes required materials. However, you must check the date on which the syllabus was updated before using it as a reference for purchasing books and supplies.

Deciding where to buy your textbooks

Just because your institution's registration system is connected to an online bookstore doesn't mean that's where you have to purchase your gear. You have choices! Granted, purchasing textbooks and supplies from your institution's online bookstore can be quick and convenient — for a few reasons:

>> **Accuracy:** You know you're getting the right books and supplies.

>> **Speed:** The process for purchasing the books and supplies is integrated with or linked to the registration system, making the purchase a quick one.

>> **Convenience**: The books and supplies are delivered right to your door (with a shipping fee, of course).

But, are you getting the best deal, especially when it comes to textbooks? Sometimes, purchasing textbooks via the institution's bookstore is more expensive. Determining where you can purchase textbooks at the best price takes some legwork. First, you need an accurate list of all the required textbooks. You can find this information in the institution's registration system or at the online bookstore. Be sure to write down the following information about the textbook before searching elsewhere:

>> Title

>> Edition (some newer editions are much different from their older editions)

>> Year of publication

>> Author(s)

>> ISBN

Take this information to online bookstores, such as Amazon.com or Campusbooks. com. Because online bookstores have a larger market to cater to, they often purchase items in large quantities, allowing them to discount the price to consumers. Another advantage of online bookstores is that they deliver the books right to your door. Depending on the amount of your purchase, you may qualify to have the books shipped for free.

TIP

Shop around for the best deal before automatically purchasing a textbook from the institution. You may even want to purchase your textbooks for the same term from multiple vendors. When doing this, though, be sure to pay attention to taxes and shipping costs to make sure you're truly getting the best deal.

TIP

Consider *renting* textbooks. If your biology book costs $300 and you're a computer science major, you won't want to keep the book after the class. In that case, renting might be a smarter choice. Look to vendors like Chegg.com or Campusbooks. com for rental information.

TIP

Whenever you're looking for textbooks outside the institution, mention that you're a student — some bookstores provide educational discounts to students. If your institution doesn't provide you with an ID (some online institutions don't), see whether the vendor will accept a copy of your registration as proof, or contact your advisor.

TIP

Double-check to see if your textbook comes as a bundle, including access to online components. Components may include additional study guides, slides, or self-quizzes. These books usually require an additional access code. If you are purchasing used books, this code might be expired, so make sure you know in advance.

Buying new or used — that is the question

Most academic and online bookstores give you the option to purchase either new or used textbooks. Whether a textbook is available as a used book is based on whether the same book has been used in the past and whether students sold the book back to the bookstore at the end of the term.

Should you purchase new or used books? New books are for you if you want to

>> Be the first to highlight and write comments in the margins

>> Avoid reading what others thought was important (in the form of old highlighting and notes)

>> Spend lots of money — new books are more expensive

>> Enjoy the smell of a new book (like a new car)

Of course, every issue has two sides. Buying a used book is better for you if you

>> **Want to save money:** You can save upward of 40 percent of your total costs by purchasing used textbooks.

>> **Recognize the value of others' contributions:** You might see value in reading what others have written in the margins, for example.

>> **Care little about reselling:** It's hard to resell a used book. Buyers are more reluctant to purchase a book with more than one previous owner.

Buying used books offers some obvious benefits. But, do you know what you're getting when you buy them online?

Sites like Amazon.com (www.amazon.com) and Sellbackyourbook.com (http://www.sellbackyourbook.com/) provide a venue for people to sell books they no longer need. To sell on these sites, a seller must first create a profile. Each of a seller's items is described by providing the book's overall condition and any special conditions or damages endured by the book. For example, you may read an ad that says something like this: "Book in great condition with highlighted text in 3 of the 13 chapters. No writings in the margin and no bent pages. This book is a steal." Some ads even have pictures of the book, which allow you to see proof of its condition. This feature is useful for ensuring that you're buying from the right person.

Another way you can determine whether you're purchasing from an honest person is to check the seller's ratings. Attached to each seller's profile is a rating system that allows buyers to rate their purchasing experiences with that seller. These ratings are public for other prospective buyers to see. They allow you to see whether the seller has provided honest information about their products, shipped them in a timely manner, and provided quality customer service. A positive rating may look something like this: "Overall rating 99%;" a buyer's comments accompanying this seller's rating might look like this: "Great customer service, and product was in excellent shape. Fast shipping, too. A+ seller."

TIP

Before purchasing a used book online, check the seller's overall rating and read the comments left by other buyers. This saves you a lot of future headaches and helps guarantee a positive purchasing experience. Also, make sure you know whether your book is bundled and requires an access code for additional content.

THE WAVE OF THE FUTURE: DIGITAL TEXTBOOKS

Digital textbooks are available for permanent download to your computer or temporary use by logging in to a website. Sites such as Amazon (www.amazon.com) and ebooks (www.ebook.com) sell electronic books that you can download and access from your computer, cellphone, or personal digital assistant (PDA). These downloads, which are usually permanent, are often a few dollars cheaper than the print version.

Some institutions have switched to digital textbooks. You purchase the book as a computer file and read it on your computer or a digital reader such as the Amazon Kindle. These devices store hundreds of books in digital format and are the size of a standard notepad. Programs and individual courses that use digitally formatted textbooks will give you additional information during the application or enrollment process on how to purchase the books and the required reader when registering. In fact, some schools provide the ebooks as part of your enrollment.

Chapter **8**

Mentally Preparing and Having a Technology Mindset

Have you heard of the author Bob Bitchin, creator of *Latitudes & Attitudes* magazine? Bob says that "the difference between an adventure and an ordeal is attitude." This couldn't be more true when it comes to online learning. This chapter addresses the kind of mindset you need in order to succeed. In addition to describing the right attitude, we'll dig into how you can be flexible and learn new things using the tools you already have at hand.

Taking On the Right Attitude

Remember *The Little Engine That Could*? "I think I can, I think I can. . . ." The relationship between persistence and success is real. As you prepare for this new way of learning, your attitude sets the stage for success.

TIP

Personality inventories can be a lot of fun when they give you meaningful information about yourself — if you want to try to test yourself, search online using the term *growth mindset quiz*.

Understanding growth and fixed mindsets

A good deal has been published about growth-versus-fixed mindsets. The best-known author in this area is Carol S. Dweck, PhD, and we recommend her book *Mindset: The New Psychology of Success*. We paraphrase the main points in this section.

A *growth mindset* is one that is open to continuous learning and improvement. It assumes the attitude that anything is possible, and that you can learn anything if you supply enough effort and persistence. In a growth mindset, failure isn't a bad thing. Rather, it's a tool for learning. When we fail, if we pay attention to the feedback about *why* we failed, we have an opportunity to do better the next time.

In contrast, a fixed mindset is one that assumes we have limits. "I can't possibly be a nuclear scientist if I didn't pass algebra."

To focus on the positive, let's stay with the growth mindset. And that, in fact, is one characteristic of someone with a growth mindset — focusing on the positive. Telling yourself that it's possible and intentionally sending affirmative messages reinforces the growth mindset.

TIP

If you find yourself engaging in negative self-talk, such as "I can't do this" or "I'm so dumb," stop, take a deep breath, and take a break. Do something you enjoy for a little bit and come back to learning when you feel more positive.

REMEMBER

Technology changes! Just in the course of writing this book, a couple of major vendors changed how users can best work with their tools. By having a growth mindset, you'll keep looking for other methods and take on a problem-solving attitude.

Effort and persistence are huge in a growth mindset. In the world of online learning, this might mean retaking the practice tests several times until you fully master their ideas. It might mean submitting a paper and having to rework it after receiving comments from the instructor. It might also mean asking for help, but not giving up on yourself. (We talk about finding a tutor in Chapter 10, and effort and persistence might lead you there.)

Susan's mother taught piano. The old saying "Practice makes perfect" was slightly altered to "Perfect practice makes perfect," so Susan learned to break things down slowly and practice until she mastered those smaller pieces. This idea applies to music, reading, biology — you name it. With a growth mindset, you hang in there, little by little, until you have learned the material.

TIP

Don't hesitate to start out small: Little by little, your practice sessions (or the amount of time you can persist at studying) will grow over time. If you can handle 15 minutes of repetition to learn a language, for example, that's good. Maybe in the beginning you can read only 20 minutes of world history. That's okay — you'll improve. Some experts recommend setting a timer for study sessions so that you don't feel overwhelmed when a break is forthcoming. This method — the *Pomodoro* method — works.

Your intellect is not a fixed amount. In fact, the more you learn, the more you grow your capacity to learn more. Going into a new experience with that attitude will set you on the right path.

Feedback plays a powerful role in learning. Think about something new you may have tried recently. During the beginning months of the COVID-19 pandemic, Kevin decided to try his hand at photography. Some of his earlier shots weren't framed well or had less-than-adequate lighting. However, he shared some of his work on social media and asked for feedback from his friends who are well-versed in the subject. From their feedback, he was able to make adjustments and improve.

In a classroom experience, feedback comes from many different courses. Of course, a test score is a form of feedback, but if you can drill into specific questions and see where you went astray, that's helpful, too. Feedback from your instructor on written work is feedback. Likewise, feedback from peers is extremely helpful.

REMEMBER

The trick is to look at feedback as an opportunity to learn, and not as a wholesale personal attack or a reflection of your intelligence. Rarely do people give critical feedback in order to hurt you.

Recognizing that age is just a number

We don't know how old you are, nor do we care. Age is only a number and has little to do with your ability to learn. Quite a bit has been written about generational differences, but it's not helpful to stereotype in a learning environment. Again, if you have a growth mindset, it doesn't matter if you're 60 years old and learning a new technology. You *can* do it if you're willing to persist.

Likewise, if you're 18 years old, the world unfairly expects you to be technologically adept. That may not describe you, and you may need to work just as hard as the 60-year-old to master a topic. Hang in there.

Kevin's grandmother was a telephone operator by trade. Her desire to learn and her open mind helped her manage several major technological changes in her lifetime. In her early career, she physically connected phone lines so that people could talk; later, she learned to have FaceTime conversations with family members from her tablet.

Knowing the Tools You Might Use

In the online environment, you're asked to work with different types of technologies. In this section, we discuss some of the more common terms and technologies you can expect to master.

Learning management system: LMS

In both higher education and corporate learning contexts, a learning management system is the primary tool for organizing and delivering content for learners. Common LMS names are Canvas, Bridge, Blackboard, Moodle, Docebo, and Litmos. (Figure 8-1 shows a typical home page on the Canvas system.)

FIGURE 8-1:
The home page of a course taught on Canvas.

Almost all LMSes have a few qualities in common:

>> **You need an account, and you log in to do the work.** In higher education, the institution assigns you an account, often when you're accepted to the school. In business, it's also likely that you'll be assigned your own account. If you're taking a course for personal enrichment or on your own, you may need to sign yourself up.

>> **Your "lessons," or whatever you need to learn, are organized by modules or folders.** (We cover this topic more in Chapter 9.) The beauty of a learning management system is that it keeps resources organized. The instructor or designer can break up content by week, theme, or level.

>> **Your activity is tracked.** A learning management system has the ability to track your participation. The system knows whether you spent 5 minutes or 50 minutes on a page. It knows whether you aced the latest exam and might need more challenging content. Don't be alarmed! Some of this information is used to make suggestions or open additional content based on need.

TIP

Use a password tool to help you generate (and remember) a strong password for any application you use, including the LMS.

Self-paced learning

We cover instructor-led versus self-paced learning in Chapter 4, but this is a good place to mention it again with respect to the learning management system. If you're enrolled in a self-paced course, the setup might be linear and you may see fewer navigational options. (See Figure 8-2 for an example.) Especially for compliance training, a self-paced course may require you to click through, page by page.

Another major difference with a self-paced course has to do with interactivity — you might feel like you're the only person in the course. There may be no requirements for you to engage in discussion, for example. To some learners, this is great! To others, it's hard to stay motivated. Again, your attitude is everything.

The system can still track your movement, and it knows whether you pass a quiz easily or struggle with it.

Taking screen shots

Screen shots might seem like a silly topic to cover, but more and more instructors are requesting proof, by way of a screen shot, that you've completed a task. A *screen shot* is literally an image of your computer screen.

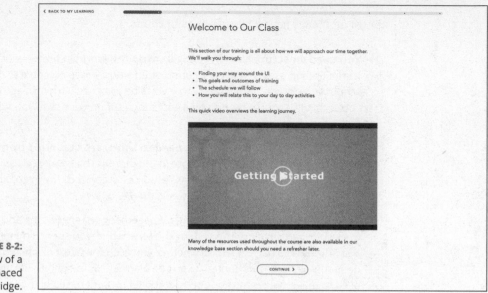

FIGURE 8-2:
A view of a
self-paced
course in Bridge.

We take a few minutes to coach you through taking a screen shot. How you do it depends on the type of machine you use — Windows, Chromebook, or Mac.

On a Windows machine

If you're on a Windows machine, press Win+Shift+S to take the screen shot. That is, hold down the Windows key and press Shift+S — what you might also think of as capital *S*. (Figure 8-3 shows the keyboard combination you need.) This action brings up a window that allows you to decide whether you want to drag over a specific area or save the entire screen.

FIGURE 8-3:
The Windows
keyboard, with
highlighted keys.

After you determine the area you want to capture, you need to save the screen shot. The Save command takes you to your normal folders area so that you can decide whether you want to save the image to the Documents folder, the desktop, or the Pictures folder.

On a Chromebook

If you use a Chromebook, hold down the Control (Ctrl) key and press the Switch key, as shown in Figure 8-4. The screen shot displays in the lower right corner. If you click on the small image, it gets saved to the Downloads folder.

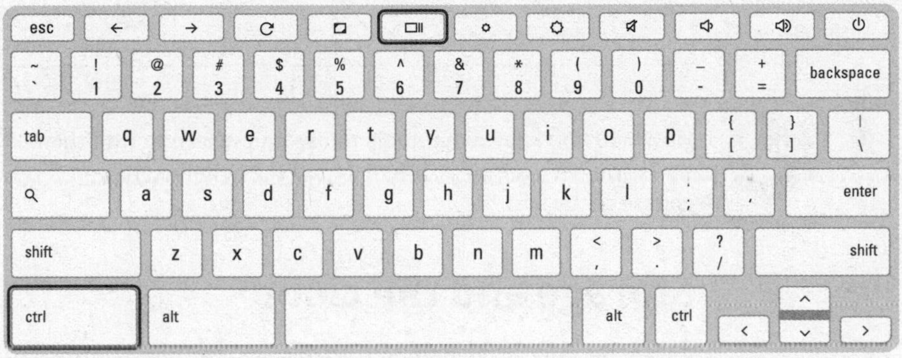

FIGURE 8-4:
The Chromebook keyboard, with highlighted keys.

On a Mac

If you use a Mac, hold down the Command key, the Shift key, and then the number 3 (in that order) for the entire screen. If you want to capture only a small area, press Command+Shift+4, as shown in Figure 8-5, and then drag across the screen to select the area you want to capture. Your screen shots are saved to the desktop.

FIGURE 8-5:
The Mac keyboard, with highlighted keys.

Additional tools

It's possible that your school will ask you to use additional tools. For example, in Washington state, all online learners have access to Panopto, a video recorder and editor. (See Figure 8-6.) Learners can make a short video using a webcam and upload it for review. Imagine how helpful that would be for a language class!

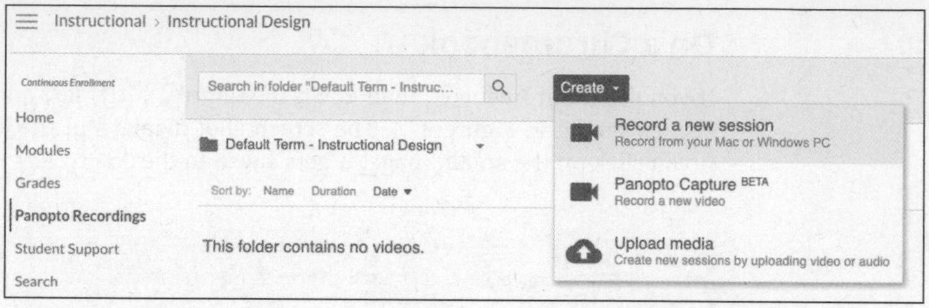

Continuous Enrollment

Home

Modules

Grades

Panopto Recordings

Student Support

Search

Search in folder "Default Term - Instruc...   🔍

📁 Default Term - Instructional Design   ▾

Sort by: Name   Duration   Date ▾

This folder contains no videos.

Create ▾

🎥 **Record a new session**
Record from your Mac or Windows PC

🎥 **Panopto Capture** ᴮᴱᵀᴬ
Record a new video

☁ **Upload media**
Create new sessions by uploading video or audio

FIGURE 8-6:
An LMS with
Record sessions
using Panopto
software.

REMEMBER

How will you know what tools to use and where to find them? Not a problem. Any tools you need are sure to be listed in the syllabus, or you'll see a direct link in the course materials.

Storage and the cloud

As you become an adept online learner, you'll soon acquire quite a few documents and files — meaning you'll soon need a place to store all this new stuff. Sure, you can print everything and build a pile of paper, but we don't recommend that method. Instead, think about saving everything in digital form — for example, when you locate the document that has your instructor's contact information. What do you do with that?

You *can* store everything on your computer's hard drive. In Chapter 3, we show you how to set up folders to be organized for this task. If you don't want to store everything on the computer, though, a reliable and free option is cloud-based storage.

REMEMBER

Cloud-based applications and storage are often free and solve the problem of taking up space and resources on your computer. More and more software is cloud based these days.

If you have an account with Microsoft 365, your cloud-based storage is called OneDrive. You store documents and files there, and you can access them from any computer as long as you're logged in to Microsoft 365. You can also share these documents with others, if you give them a link.

If you don't use Microsoft 365, you can have a similar experience with Google Drive. After you sign up for an account with Google (even if it's just for email), you have access to a drive where you can create and store Word and Google documents, spreadsheets, presentations, and all kinds of files. And it's *free*.

Other products, like Dropbox and Box, provide similar services. Do some research about which product sounds easiest and won't charge for their services.

Saving what you need

Sometimes within a learning management system, you can download documents you want to save, like the syllabus or the instructor's contact information. How to do this varies based on the particular LMS and how your instructor uses it. So let's consider a few scenarios inside of Canvas to use as examples of how you might download documents shared by your instructor:

>> **Document embedded on a page in Canvas:** Your instructor might embed a document directly on a page. When this happens, Canvas provides the Download button, as shown in Figure 8-7. Clicking this button automatically downloads the file to your Downloads folder.

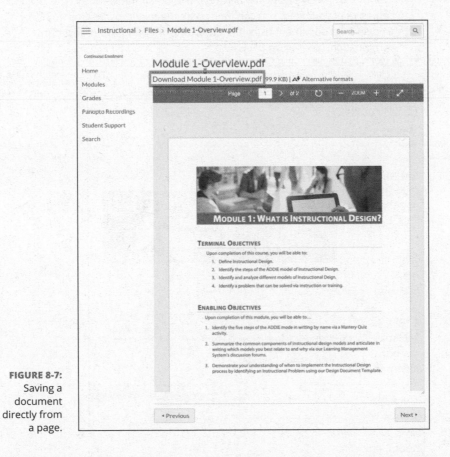

FIGURE 8-7:
Saving a
document
directly from
a page.

>> **Direct link to a file within the text of an HTML page:** Sometimes, the linked document is supplemental to other information. For example, an instructor might provide a link to an assignment's template document in the middle of the assignment's instruction. When this happens, the title of the document is most likely displayed in blue and is underlined, to indicate that it's a link. Try left-clicking on the link to see whether it automatically downloads. If not, you can also right-click on the link and choose the Save Link As option, as shown in Figure 8-8. This action brings up a dialog box in which to save the file and most likely defaults to the Downloads folder again. Click on Save or OK in the pop-up box to save the file.

>> **Text copied from the screen:** If you want to copy only the displayed text, try this strategy: Click on the page and then hold down the Control key (or Command, if you're using a Mac) and the C key simultaneously. This action copies what you need. You can then paste the text into a Microsoft 365 or Google Docs document using the Control+V or Command+V keyboard combination. (See Figure 8-9.)

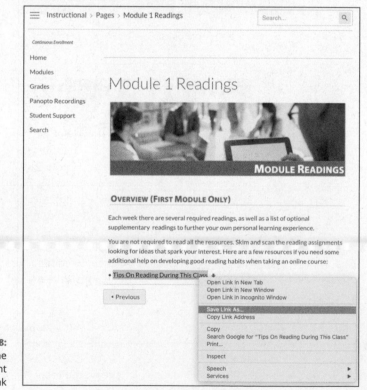

FIGURE 8-8:
Saving the document from a link

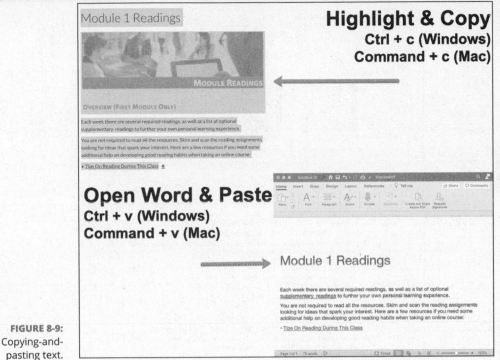

Highlight & Copy
Ctrl + c (Windows)
Command + c (Mac)

Open Word & Paste
Ctrl + v (Windows)
Command + v (Mac)

FIGURE 8-9:
Copying-and-pasting text.

You Don't Have to Know Everything

That's a fine heading to read in a how-to book, right? Yet we are serious. Because the shelf life of information is rather short these days, it's more important to know *where* to look for information than to already know it all. Notice how this concept ties in with the growth mindset we mention earlier in this chapter? You can't know it all — you have to look at yourself as a lifelong learner who is capable of learning new subjects. You have to persist and keep looking — and yes, you may need to ask for assistance now and then.

Help is as close as whatever search engine you use. Need help figuring out how to create pivot tables using Excel 2010? "Google it," just like we did in Figure 8-10. (Fun fact: *Google* was not a verb ten years ago.)

TIP

If you have a solution you've tried elsewhere, try it again in a new context. Recently, Susan's sister was trying to make an alarm system stop beeping. Her sister is a nurse, not an alarm system technician (and this was not a life-or-death alarm). She decided to reboot the alarm, like she would reboot a computer, so she powered off the device, counted to 30, and restarted it. Guess what? It worked!

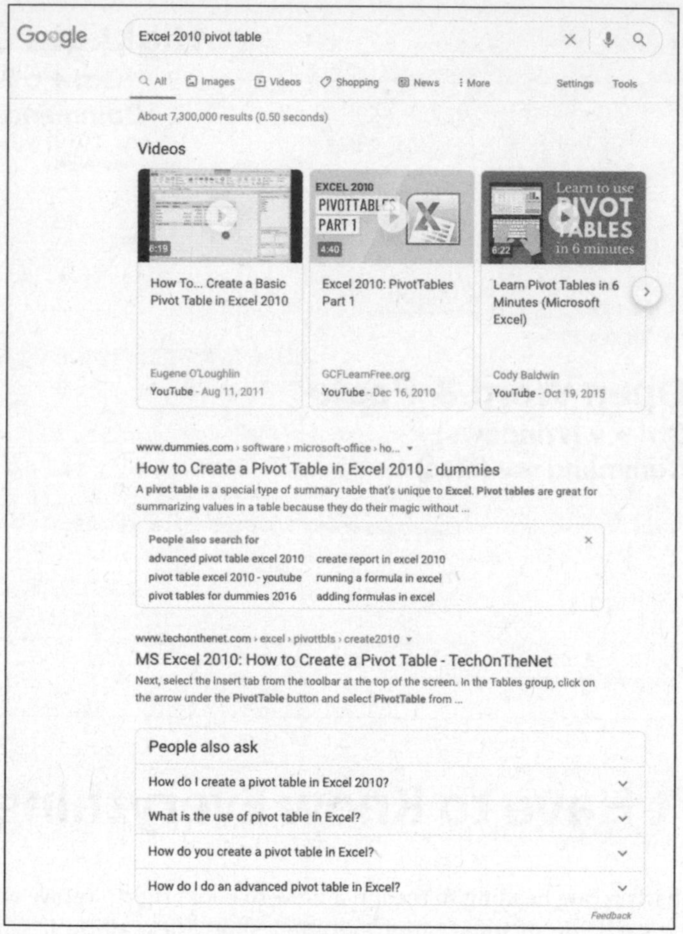

FIGURE 8-10:
An Internet search using Google.

We cannot overstate the importance of having a growth mindset.

Mastering New Tools Quickly

In writing this book, Susan didn't know how to take a screen shot on a Chromebook. In addition to searching on Google, she searched on YouTube. Did you know that YouTube is the second most frequently used search engine? The advantage of YouTube is that longer processes can be documented: You can play, pause, do it yourself, and keep repeating until you understand the process. The disadvantage is that you may have to watch ads before you get to the good stuff.

That said, if you're looking for software assistance, be certain that you're viewing the same version. (Figure 8-11, for example, shows that we're interested in the 2010 version of Excel.) If you watch a video on how to use Excel, and the recording uses Excel on Windows 365 but you're still on Excel 2010, you'll see something different.

TIP

When you search on YouTube, be *specific*.

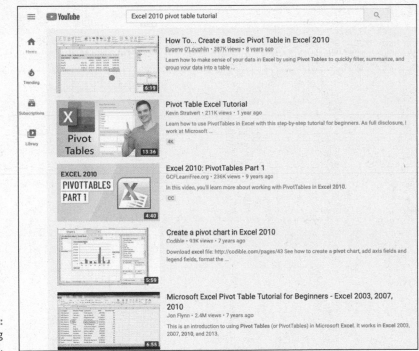

FIGURE 8-11:
Searching
YouTube for help.

3

The Virtual Classroom: Being an A+ Student

IN THIS PART . . .

Explore your virtual classroom

Get to know your instructors and classmates

Work on your communication skills

Develop the study habits you need to succeed

Become a global learner

Build a portfolio to showcase your best work

Chapter **9**

Navigating the Learning Environment

On the first day of an in-person class, the instructor usually passes out papers, explains the class, reviews grading, and talks a little about what the class entails. In online learning, the same kinds of resources are available, but you receive them in a different fashion. After you register for one or more online classes (see Chapter 7), you're ready to log in and find your way around the virtual learning environment, which is where learners and faculty gather together. The beauty of this virtual classroom is that you don't have to dress up, you don't have to fight for parking, and most of the time you can attend school whenever it's convenient.

This chapter walks you through a typical login experience and helps you become familiar with some of the materials and activities your instructor may distribute.

Reaching Your Virtual Learning Environment

Your calendar tells you that class starts today. What does that mean? Do you need to log in at 8 A.M. to complete a task? We assume that you're excited to get started with online learning but a little anxious about what to do first. It's not as easy as showing up to the right building or room, and this way of learning is new for you. In the following sections, we explain how to use the right web address, set some Internet options, log in to the interface, and find the link for each course you're taking.

TIP

Some organizations let you log in a day or two early, just to start looking around — if you're given this opportunity, take advantage of it. If you don't have time to log in early, at least log in on the first day so that your instructor knows you're present.

Using the right address and setting some Internet options

Sometime before the start of a course, the school sends information about how to log in to your virtual space. In some cases, you may receive this notice a week in advance; in other cases, it may arrive hours before the course begins. It all depends on the organization. This communication includes a specific URL (web address), a username, and a password or the option to set a password. You type the URL (for example, **myschool.edu**) on the address bar of the browser, in place of whatever URL shows up there when you open your browser. Press the Enter key, and the web page should change to wherever you need to be.

The correspondence from your organization should include instructions explaining which browser to use and how to set it for optimal performance. (See Chapter 3 for the basics on browsers.) For example, Instructure, the company that owns the Canvas learning management system (LMS), recommends that you use the Chrome browser. You should know how to display content that might pop up in another window — some browsers are set to block these by default. (This feature is affectionately known as "the pop-up blocker.") In most cases, when viewing course content inside your LMS — Canvas, for example — you'll want to keep pop-up windows from being blocked. Figure 9-1 illustrates a situation where content has been blocked and then shows you how you can tell Chrome to allow blocked content from that site so that it doesn't happen again when you're browsing in your course.

Every browser and operating system works differently. What you do in Chrome to control pop-ups differs from what you do in Safari. In Figure 9-1, we show you how Google Chrome displays an icon in the address bar to indicate that a pop-up must be enabled.

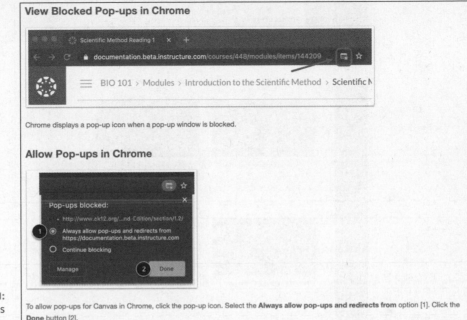

View Blocked Pop-ups in Chrome

Chrome displays a pop-up icon when a pop-up window is blocked.

Allow Pop-ups in Chrome

FIGURE 9-1:
Enabling pop-ups
in Chrome.

To allow pop-ups for Canvas in Chrome, click the pop-up icon. Select the **Always allow pop-ups and redirects from** option [1]. Click the **Done** button [2].

Logging in and checking out the interface

REMEMBER

After you find your way to your virtual learning space, log in for the first time by using the username and password provided by the school. These words or codes are *case sensitive,* so you cannot capitalize at will. Type the information exactly as it is on the paper (or on the screen if it was emailed to you).

Generally, your login doesn't take you directly to your course — rather, it takes you to a home page that includes additional information and a link to your course. (If you're taking more than one course, you see a link for each one.) This first home page, sometimes called the portal, may include information like announcements to all students, links to the library, or tutorials for common processes. It may even be the same page you used to register for classes. Figure 9-2 shows a sample of a portal from which a student would access their course(s).

REMEMBER

If your portal looks nothing like the one in Figure 9-2, don't worry: What you see when you log in depends on the LMS software your school uses. (In Chapter 8, we introduce the concept of the learning management system [LMS].) Whether you know which system your school or organization uses may make for interesting cocktail party conversation with other online learners, but it doesn't matter much in terms of getting your work done. If your organization doesn't blatantly tell you the LMS in its correspondence, you see the logo when you log on to the course. Vendors *love* to let you know who they are.

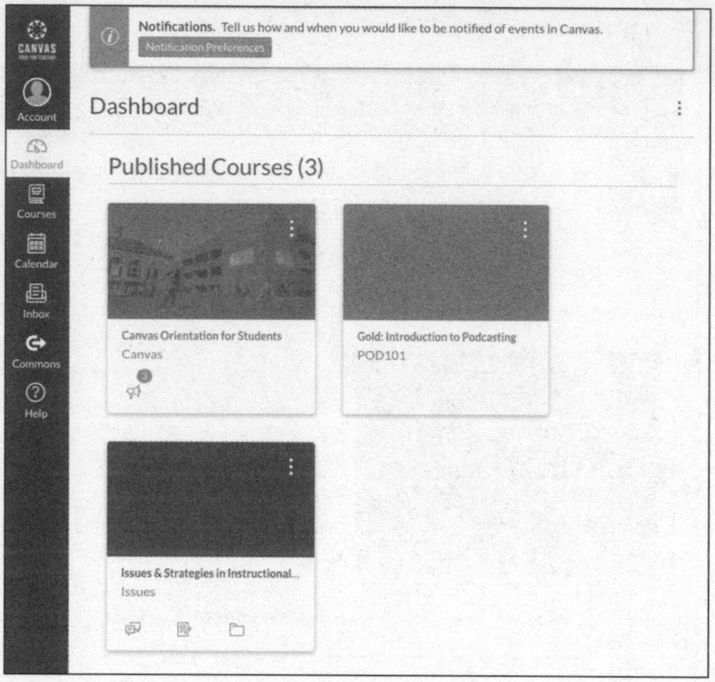

FIGURE 9-2:
Canvas: A portal you might see when first logging in.

If you're taking courses strictly for business purposes or personal enrichment, the LMS might be an Enterprise version. (It is custom branded to look like it is part of the business.) How you navigate — looking for course links and announcements, for example — still works the same in principle.

TIP Many organizations ask learners to change their passwords as soon as they log in (typically, from the home page) for their own security — if you're assigned a password, we recommend changing it, but not immediately. First, take some time to look around your new environment — specifically, finding and printing your technical support info and your instructor's contact info before changing your password. That way, if for some reason you get locked out of the system, you know who and where to call. (Flip to Chapter 3 for the basics on passwords.)

Finding your course's home page

As we note in the preceding section, the LMS software determines exactly what you see on the application's home page when you log in. Despite all the possible variations, however, you're sure to see a link to your course, most often identified by the course name and catalog number. (Refer to Figure 9-2.) After you find the link to your course, click on it to go to the main page, or *home page,* of your course.

You may not be able to see the entire course at once. Some instructors like to show only the material that's needed in the beginning so that students don't become overwhelmed. The process is new, after all. However, your interface probably has links to some standard materials, such as a welcome message from your instructor, the syllabus, the calendar, and other information we look at more specifically later in this chapter. So that you know you're in the right place, Figures 9-3 and 9-4 show what you might see when logging on to two different systems for the first time:

» **Figure 9-3 shows the home page of a course taught on Canvas.** Notice that you see courses you have access to along with groups and announcements. Announcements might be reminders of deadlines, notes about additional resources, or basic processes that relate to everyone. This kind of opening page lets you choose to go where you need with the information that will help you succeed.

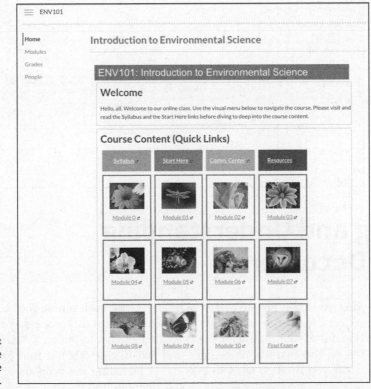

FIGURE 9-3:
The home page
of a course
taught on Canvas.

>> **Figure 9-4 shows the home page of a course taught on Moodle.** In this case, you see links to content right away. You can jump directly to the lessons of the course and information about assignments. Announcements may be off to the side or contained within a special forum.

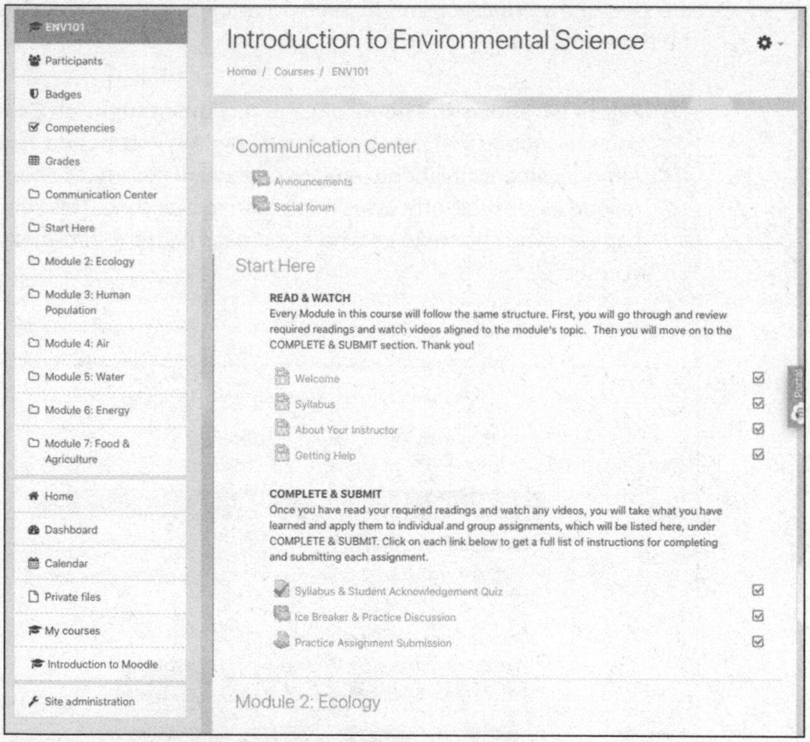

FIGURE 9-4:
The home page
of a course
taught on
Moodle.

Figure showing the Moodle home page for "Introduction to Environmental Science" (ENV101), with a left navigation menu (Participants, Badges, Competencies, Grades, Communication Center, Start Here, Module 2: Ecology, Module 3: Human Population, Module 4: Air, Module 5: Water, Module 6: Energy, Module 7: Food & Agriculture, Home, Dashboard, Calendar, Private files, My courses, Introduction to Moodle, Site administration) and a main content area with Communication Center, Start Here, READ & WATCH, and COMPLETE & SUBMIT sections.

Locating and Understanding Critical Documents

After you know how to reach the right page for each course you're taking, you can collect a few major documents you need. (Think of this process as a treasure hunt.) Hopefully, your instructor has been kind enough to put an X Marks the Spot button on the course's home page, but just in case it's not that easy, this section walks you through what to look for — including the syllabus or course outline, calendar, and grading details — and where to find it.

TIP

Start a folder for each online course you take. Find the documents in the following sections and keep copies in a folder, either on your computer's hard drive or in cloud storage. (We talk about the cloud storage option in Chapter 3.) You may want to print copies of your documents, but if you're worried about what happens if your computer crashes, cloud storage is the way to go.

The syllabus, or course outline

To teach this particular course, your instructor has to determine its goals, objectives, assignments, and much more. By putting these in writing, the instructor creates a syllabus, or *course outline*. Every course needs a plan. The syllabus communicates that plan and is therefore one of the most important documents in your course. You can think of this document as a general map of where you're headed in a course.

A link to the syllabus is often front and center on the home page. It may be a button to the left or an icon in the middle of the page, but it's generally visible. A typical syllabus includes information about these areas:

>> **Course basics:** The name of the course, credit hours, goals and objectives, and required textbooks

>> **Instructor contact information:** Name, biography (possibly), address, phone, email, and other contact information, such as time zone and availability

>> **Course content:** Topics to be covered and, possibly, a schedule or calendar (as described in the next section)

>> **Grading:** How you'll be evaluated, the kinds of assignments you'll be assigned, the rationale for those assignments, and the distribution of points (as we detail in the later section "The grading system")

>> **Policies:** Academic honesty, the general expectations of logging in and participating, whether late work is acceptable, netiquette expectations, and other policies that help you understand how the instructor runs the class

>> **Resources:** Links to technical support, the library, and the bookstore; academic advising or tutoring; disability services; and other resources students may need

REMEMBER

Think of the syllabus as an informal contract between you and the instructor. The instructor has the responsibility to teach you as planned, and you have the responsibility to follow through on expectations. To use the syllabus to your advantage, read it and become familiar with what is expected of you. Pay special attention to how you'll be graded and the general expectations of logging in and participating.

The calendar

Even though a course might be advertised as "anywhere and anytime," you still have to complete assignments according to a calendar. Even self-paced courses have deadlines.

Most LMSes have a built-in calendar feature that tracks your assignment deadlines based on your instructor's input. If you're taking multiple classes, these calendars combine all your course deadlines in one place and allow you to display one or multiple classes at a time. You can typically find a link to the calendar on a more global navigation bar immediately after logging on to your LMS. The calendar feature often lets you view your calendar in multiple ways: by week or month or as a list:

>> **Month view:** This calendar, found on the home page, is in a traditional chart format that almost anyone can recognize. (See Figure 9-5.)

>> **List view:** This form, which lists the assignments in a linear fashion, may be found on the home page or as a link elsewhere. (See Figure 9-6.)

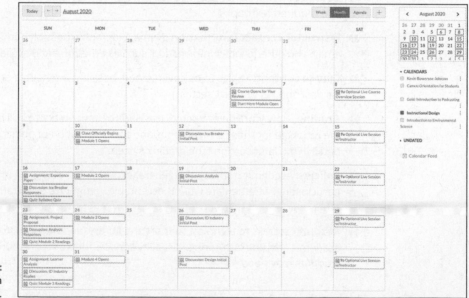

FIGURE 9-5:
A calendar with a monthly view.

FIGURE 9-6:
A calendar view listing assignments.

The figure shows a Canvas calendar in Agenda view:

Today Aug 2, 2020 – Sep 5, 2020   Week Month Agenda +   < August 2020 >

Thu, Aug 6
- Course Opens for Your Review
- Start Here Module Open

Sat, Aug 8
- 9:00am Optional Live Course Overview Session

Mon, Aug 10
- Class Officially Begins
- Module 1 Opens

Wed, Aug 12
- Discussion: Ice Breaker Initial Post

Sat, Aug 15
- 9:00am Optional Live Session w/Instructor

Sun, Aug 16
- Discussion: Ice Breaker Responses
- Quiz: Syllabus Quiz
- Assignment: Experience Paper

Sidebar calendar for August 2020, and:

▾ CALENDARS
- Kevin Bowersox-Johnson
- Canvas Orientation for Students
- Gold: Introduction to Podcasting
- **Instructional Design**
- Introduction to Environmental Science

▸ UNDATED

- Calendar Feed

TIP

Coordinate all your calendars so that you know when major assignments are due and how they intersect with business and family obligations. Most people keep multiple calendars and rarely synchronize them. The calendar in the kitchen doesn't include the business trip you have planned, and your office calendar says nothing about needing cookies for the PTA. For example, look ahead to see whether a group project is coming up in your class, and make sure you don't plan a family weekend getaway in the middle of it.

TIP

Consider transferring all calendar items into your favorite calendaring program, such as Microsoft Outlook or Google Calendar. When you do this, you can set up reminders to alert you whenever assignments are due or synchronous sessions are scheduled. If you already use an electronic calendar for home and work, you might be able to automatically add your assignments calendar to it. Most calendar features nowadays help you do this by providing an RSS (really simple syndication) feed, which lets you synch and view your assignments calendar using the same calendar you use for home and work. Figure 9-7 shows an example of where the RSS feed is located in a Canvas calendar, and Figure 9-8 shows that feed added to the iCal application on Kevin's Mac computer.

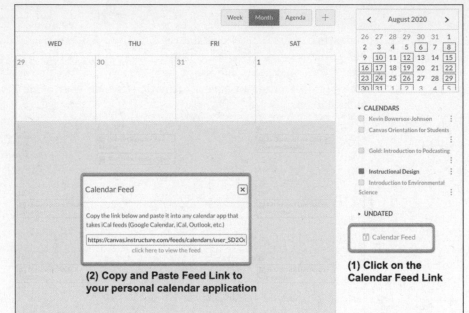

FIGURE 9-7:
A calendar
RSS feed.

FIGURE 9-8:
A calendar
with an added
RSS feed.

When coordinating your calendars and figuring out deadlines, pay attention to the *time* when something is due and the *time zone* the course calendar refers to. The LMS time-stamps all your submitted assignments for the instructor's record. For example, assignments due at midnight Eastern time are due at 9 P.M. Pacific time. This big difference can have a dramatic effect on your grade if assignments are turned in late.

As you're coordinating dates, consider whether you need a calendar in digital or paper form. Though coauthor Susan keeps an electronic calendar on Google Calendar, she also has several paper versions printed and hanging in front of her monitor. There's no shame in printing!

Keep track of due dates, and don't depend on your instructor to remind you. Similarly, don't assume that the instructor uses the calendar feature within the course software. Instead, take responsibility for writing down and coordinating dates.

The grading system

If you're going to invest a major portion of your free time in studying, we assume that you want to be rewarded with a good grade. In the following sections, we describe a few key documents related to grading: the grading scale, any rubric used for your course, and the late policy.

The grading scale

You undoubtedly want to identify how you'll be graded and what you need to do to earn the highest score possible. Somewhere in your course — possibly in the syllabus but also as a separate link on the home page — you should see a grading scale. Figure 9-9 shows its vital components: a list of general assignments, the available number of points for each assignment, and the grade distribution based on the total number of points you earn. Notice that the example lacks grades D and F. We were thinking of a graduate level course, where typically anything lower than a C is considered failing.

When you first examine a grading scale, focus on the types of assignments, how much each assignment is worth, and any projects or assignments that seem to be worth a lot more than others. Also pay attention to the proportion of points assigned to ongoing or routine activities, such as weekly discussion sessions or chapter tests.

Grading & Assessment

Your grade will be based on:

Activities	Total Points	% of Final Grade
Weekly Discussions (8 @ 25 pts ea)	200 points	20%
Weekly Quizzes (points differ each week)	100 points	10%
Final Project Assignments (5 @ 100 pts ea)	500 points	50%
ePortfolio	150 points	15%
Reflection Paper	50 points	5%
Total	**1,000 points**	**100%**

Grading Scale

Letter Grade	Percent	Points
A	94 to 100%	935 to 1000 points
A-	91 to 93%	905 to 934 points
B+	88 to 90%	875 to 904 points
B	84 to 87%	835 to 874 points
B-	81 to 83%	805 to 834 points
C+	78 to 80%	775 to 804 points
C	74 to 77%	735 to 774 points

FIGURE 9-9: A view of a typical grading scale.

You can learn a lot from the example in Figure 9-9. If you read this document carefully, you can make these conclusions:

>> **Discussion is important in this course — worth 20 percent of the grade.** Elsewhere the instructor should describe the expectations and how your post will be evaluated.

>> **Quizzes are twice as important as weekly reflections, but only half as important as discussion.** The instructor may use quizzes as a way to make sure you keep up-to-date with the facts of the course and don't fall behind. This way, you can also test yourself so that you know where to focus your energy.

>> **The final project is worth half of your grade, but there's no final exam.** It is likely that the five assignments making up the final project are evaluated using a rubric, so you should start looking for the rubric. If you cannot readily find it, ask the instructor! You should also start organizing your time by breaking this large project into smaller pieces.

>> **Earning an A doesn't come easily.** You need 94 percent to earn an A.

Rubrics

A rubric is an evaluation plan or a scoring tool that helps the instructor determine how well your paper, project, or participation lines up with the ideal. A rubric, typically found in the assignment's instructions or linked to them, usually includes several categories that are deemed important to the final product. For example, in written work, the quality of your ideas is assessed along with your ability to think critically and write in a grammatically acceptable form. The rubric communicates what's important by the relative weights given to the categories. Look at the sample rubric in Table 9-1, which is for the discussion portion of a course.

When you look at a rubric, you should determine what's important and where the instructor will turn their attention. Most rubrics have categories that organize the evaluation. Then, within each category, you see details about what an excellent paper or project would include. The rubric in Table 9-1 tells you that

>> The development of ideas is twice as important as mechanics (5 points versus 2 points).

>> Proper citation is expected, according to the Content description.

>> You must respond to at least two peers in order to receive full credit.

TIP You can earn higher grades by reading and following the rubric — we guarantee it. Reading the rubric in detail before completing the assignment can help you prepare and self-check your assignments before turning them in for grades. (For more information about rubrics, see Chapter 16.)

TABLE 9-1 ### A Typical Discussion Rubric

Categories	Exceptional
Content	The content is complete and accurate and offers new ideas for application by way of clear evidence of critical thinking. The discussion is well supported with details from the readings, which are cited properly. Postings are characterized by originality and relevance to the topic and encourage further discussion on the topic. (5 points)
Interaction	The student routinely responds to other students (at least twice) and offers additional insights and considerations that extend collective understanding. Communication encourages further responses, raises questions, or politely offers alternative perspectives. (3 points)
Mechanics	The writing is free of grammatical errors and follows acceptable standard English conventions (spelling and punctuation, for example). Posting is submitted before the deadline. (2 points)

The late policy

As much as you plan to be on time with all your assignments, occasionally life gets in the way. Be sure that you understand the implications or penalties of the late policy for your online course. The late policy may be included in the syllabus or with each assignment. Some instructors accept work past the deadline; others don't. In every case, if you know that you won't meet the deadline and you have an acceptable reason, contact your instructor. Explain the circumstances and politely ask for an extension.

WARNING

Notice that we say "and you have an acceptable reason" for missing the deadline. An acceptable reason is a serious illness in your family, the earlier-than-expected birth of a baby, a death in the family, or a natural disaster, such as flooding. Acceptable reasons are not the NASCAR race you attended, that impromptu trip to the beach, or Mother's Day. In those situations, you could have planned in advance to complete your work on time.

Modules and More: Understanding a Course's Content Organization

Take a look at any standard textbook and you'll see that it's divided into chapters. Each chapter covers a different topic. In some cases, Chapter 4 makes sense only if you've read Chapters 1, 2, and 3. In other textbooks, you can jump around from chapter to chapter and the content still makes sense.

Online courses are organized in a similar fashion. They're also broken down into smaller pieces, or "chapters." Your instructor probably organizes what you're going to do in the class according to weeks or topics. This way, you focus on one chunk of information at a time. Some instructors, though, organize content for a class by different functions: discussions, assignments, quizzes, tests, and the like.

You can see evidence of how the course is organized by checking out the course's home page:

>> Figure 9-10 shows the organizational pattern for one online course on the screen. The navigation suggests that the information has been chunked into smaller units, called modules. Each module probably contains just enough data for one or two weeks. In many courses, everything you need to complete the module can be found within the week or topic heading.

>> In other courses, materials and assignments may be provided according to function. This situation requires a little more clicking on your part. For example, if there's no obvious link to modules organized by week or topic on the course's home page, you may have to click on a Discussions link and then another link, labeled Week 2 Discussions, in order to participate in Week 2's class discussion. Next, you may need to go back to the course's home page and click the Assignments link to locate Week 2's assignments. In most cases, this structure is determined by the LMS, not by the instructor.

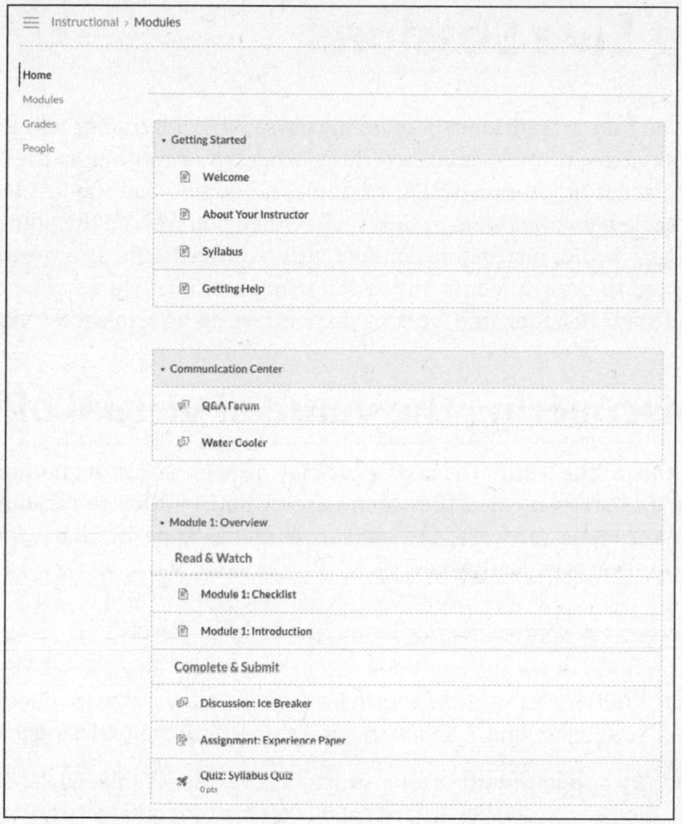

FIGURE 9-10:
A sample home page that shows module organization.

The following is a representation of the screenshot in Figure 9-10:

> ☰ Instructional › Modules
>
> **Home**
> Modules
> Grades
> People
>
> ▾ Getting Started
> 📄 Welcome
> 📄 About Your Instructor
> 📄 Syllabus
> 📄 Getting Help
>
> ▾ Communication Center
> 💬 Q&A Forum
> 💬 Water Cooler
>
> ▾ Module 1: Overview
> Read & Watch
> 📄 Module 1: Checklist
> 📄 Module 1: Introduction
> Complete & Submit
> 💬 Discussion: Ice Breaker
> 📝 Assignment: Experience Paper
> ✎ Quiz: Syllabus Quiz
> 0 pts

The way a course is organized affects the placement of certain documents related to assignments and testing — especially rubrics, handouts, and resources. Your instructor may store handouts and resources in a couple of different locations:

» **The instructor may place all resources within the module for which they're needed.** For example, the Module 1 handouts are placed in the Module 1 folder, including the instructions for an upcoming assignment and the details on grading, including the rubric.

» **The instructor may put all rubrics and related documents together in one location.** It is then named Grading or Assessment.

REMEMBER No two instructors are the same, and you may need to look around to find the materials you need. Your instructor should be consistent so you can find info quickly after spending a little time becoming familiar with your virtual classroom. We would like to promise that, but we cannot. If you feel lost, ask the instructor: Just say that "the *For Dummies* people" got you thinking that you might be missing something.

Attending Live Sessions

If you take a traditional in-person course, your instructor will tell you about their *office hours,* or the established times when you can drop by the instructor's office to discuss any concerns. For example, if you bombed the last test, you may want to review your answers or talk about where you missed the point. Similarly, in the virtual world, instructors conduct virtual office hours as a means of staying connected to their students. In the following sections, we describe these office hours and their benefits, and we provide pointers on how to access virtual offices.

Discovering the value of virtual office hours

In the online world, the instructor may have an office in another state or country. For that reason, the office hours are virtual — they're conducted online. Using synchronous software, the instructor makes time available for conversation or communication with you.

Instructors approach office hours in a couple of ways:

>> **Walk-in:** Some instructors make themselves available for questions and comments, and if no one shows up, they busy themselves with other work.

>> **By appointment:** Other instructors have a specific agenda and use the time to provide additional information that may not otherwise be covered in class. For example, coauthor Kevin regularly previews technology tools that students may find helpful.

TIP

In many cases, these virtual office hours are recorded, so if you can't attend the live meeting, watch the recording later, if possible, and gather the same information. The instructor posts a link after the meeting so that you know where and how to access the recording. However, even if your instructor's office hours are recorded, nothing beats live interaction — so attend if you can. You won't regret it.

You may need a few private moments with the instructor to ask a question about a grade, comment on a personal situation, or talk about a classroom situation. If that's the case, let the instructor know in advance by way of an email. You can then schedule a private conversation.

Lots of learners and instructors enjoy virtual office hours because they afford a kind of real-person connection that the asynchronous environment doesn't. Office hours provide you with the opportunity to interact with live voices. Yes, using a simple microphone/headset device (available at any office supply store — see Chapter 3 for details), participants can talk to one another. The instant gratification of communication during virtual office hours is quite powerful in reinforcing a sense of belonging and presence within the class. It gives both faculty and learners an opportunity to strengthen the learning community bonds.

Virtual office hours are also useful for reinforcing course content. Coauthor Susan is able to demonstrate new technologies by sharing her screen with learners. They get to see a live demonstration of how to use the technology and follow step-by-step instructions for doing so.

REMEMBER

In addition to providing virtual office space for instructors, your institution may provide students with real-time tools for students who want to meet with other students in order to complete group projects or discuss content, for example. Access to these tools are often restricted by course enrollment and recorded for security purposes. They provide a vehicle for collaborating on assignments in an interactive environment. We discuss group work in more detail in Chapter 13.

Accessing the virtual office

If your college provides virtual office space to instructors and/or students, you see a special login place within your course — typically, on the home page. Often, the software needed for office hours is different from the LMS, though they should be integrated. For example, you might have a course offered in Moodle with office hours occurring in Zoom, but a link in your course should take you seamlessly to your new destination.

Figure 9-11 shows a typical virtual office space. Notice, in the center, the space for sharing slides or images. To the right is a list of participants as well as a place for chatting using text. At the bottom are additional controls, including a Mute button that controls audio and a Video button for sharing your webcam so that attendees can see you. These features are fairly standard in web conferencing software.

No matter what technology is used for virtual office space, the institution should also provide links to tutorials on how to navigate to, and interact within, the synchronous environment. These tutorials may be a part of your institution's orientation materials, which you are, we hope, able to refer to at any time. (Check out Chapter 7 for more about orientation programs.)

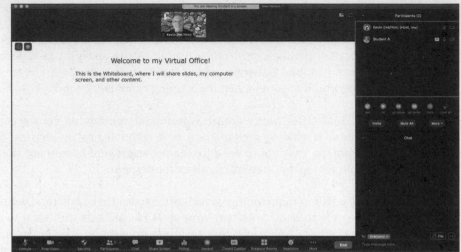

FIGURE 9-11:
A sample
interface for an
online office
hour.

IN THIS CHAPTER

» **Working well with your instructor and classmates**

» **Introducing the folks behind the scenes**

Chapter **10**

Meeting the People in (and Around) Your Classroom

Remember the first day of school when you couldn't wait to find out who your teacher was and who was in your class? In the online classroom, that same kind of excitement (or nervousness) exists. Unless you're enrolled in a self-paced course with no interaction with anyone but your professor, you want to figure out who else is in (and around) your classroom and how they relate to you.

People in the online classroom tend to fall into two camps: those who are quite visible and those who work behind the scenes:

» **The visible people — your instructor and the other students:** You want to identify how your instructor works and the ways in which they communicate with you. You also want to get to know the other students and see how you work with them as a member of the community.

» **The people behind the scenes:** Not everyone in the online classroom works front and center. You may encounter guest speakers, administrative staff monitoring how the class is progressing, or technical support staff. All these people help make sure the system works and that you get the best educational experience for your money. Plus, your personal support system of family and friends cannot be discounted.

This chapter helps you sort out all the people you meet in your online experience.

Getting to Know the Folks Who Are Front and Center

During your time in class, the people you interact with most frequently are your instructor and the other students. They're the folks who shape your overall online experience the most, so knowing what to expect from them and how to conduct yourself around them is important. We explain in the following sections what you need to know.

Acquainting yourself with your instructor

An *instructor*, simply stated, is the person who's in charge of your online classroom — they run the show. In the following sections, we explain the credentials and training that instructors need, describe where to find your instructor in the online classroom, and provide pointers on communicating effectively with your instructor.

REMEMBER

What you call your instructor may vary from course to course or from school to school. Typically, professor denotes full-time, tenured faculty, whereas instructor or adjunct instructor signifies that the individual may not have full-time employment. A facilitator is another term some schools use to describe the instructor role, especially within adult and online learning environments. If the titles of instructor or facilitator have any significance (they don't always), it's to denote that the students have a lot more responsibility in making connections in the learning, and the facilitator helps this happen. Throughout this book, we use the terms *instructor* and *facilitator* interchangeably to describe the role, regardless of title or rank.

Necessary credentials and training for instructors

The same requirements and qualifications for teaching in a face-to-face class apply to teaching online. In the 2-year or community college system, that may mean having a master's degree in the discipline; in a 4-year university, institutions may require an instructor to have a doctorate degree in order to teach graduate level courses. In a virtual high school, the instructor needs to meet the state's requirements for certification or licensure, which begin with a bachelor's degree.

Online institutions also request that instructors complete some kind of online training in order to teach. The best schools go beyond showing instructors what buttons to push and include more information about how online learning is different from face-to-face classroom education. By exploring what makes online learning unique, your instructor can better manage the virtual classroom and teach more effectively. In fact, most higher education faculty aren't hired for their teaching skills; they're hired for their subject matter expertise. (For instance, if an institution needs a geology professor, it finds someone with knowledge in geology.) Therefore, if your online instructor has additional training in "how to teach," they're probably more advanced in understanding how to help students learn than they might be if they were teaching in a traditional classroom. As a student, you win.

TIP

How do you find out about your instructor's credentials? Typically, you can find a listing of faculty somewhere on the institution's website — often referred to as the organization's *faculty directory*. It may be organized by program or discipline. Each instructor probably has a web page that welcomes students and lists credentials. When in doubt, this is a helpful question to ask as you search for the right school. We talk a little more about this topic in Chapter 5.

Where you "see" your instructor

Rather than stand in front of a face-to-face class, lecturing and directing students' behavior, the person in charge of your online classroom makes information available and creatively gets students involved in thinking about and working with those concepts. The instructor guides students toward understanding the material.

In the virtual world, you don't have the advantage of looking at your instructor live and in person. Yet a good online instructor lets their presence be "seen" in several ways:

>> **Announcement area for posting news:** Your instructor may communicate with the whole class by posting ongoing announcements and news. You can typically find these postings on the main page when you log in (see Chapter 9 for details on logging in and navigating your classroom), but some instructors communicate this kind of information via email or the course's internal Inbox feature, which acts like email. Instructors make announcements to keep students on task, remind them of deadlines, or enrich their understanding with additional resources and links.

>> **Discussion area:** You may see your instructor busy in the discussion area. Many online courses require students to interact with each other by posting answers to discussion questions and extending the conversations by way of replies to one another. Often, instructors facilitate these discussions by raising additional considerations, asking for clarification, or extending questions that probe deeper into the material.

>> **Synchronous or virtual office hours:** As mentioned in Chapter 9, some instructors offer synchronous sessions where they can conduct discussions in real time. Attending these sessions is another way to get to know your instructor and peers.

REMEMBER

How much your instructor gets involved in discussions depends on the nature of the class and their own style. If you're a graduate student in an advanced seminar, chances are good that you and your classmates will need very little guidance to explore course themes. However, if you're taking an entry level psychology course, your instructor may be much more active in guiding the discussion.

>> **Grades and feedback:** Ultimately, you see your instructor through the grades and feedback *they* provide. As assignments are scored, instructors comment and leave notes in grade books. This feedback helps you close the loop so that you understand not only what you know but also what you still need to figure out.

TIP

Giving quality feedback takes a great deal of time, so be sure to read the comments your instructor leaves for you. For example, if your instructor tells you to be more careful in citing research (or suggests that you *start* citing), check your course for tutorials and additional links to citation resources. If you want to earn points, send back a sample citation and tell the instructor where you learned to format it. That shows that you're paying attention and that you value the input. Don't be afraid to reach out and ask additional questions if feedback is unclear.

Communicating effectively with your instructor

Your instructor communicates with you as a member of the class and privately, but how should you communicate with the instructor? To start, find out how they prefer to be addressed. Some instructors expect you to address all correspondence with their title, such as Professor Manning. Some prefer Dr. Manning, but check to see that you have the correct title. Others are more casual and ask you to call them by their first name.

WHAT'S IN A DOCTORATE TITLE?

What's the difference between a PhD and an EdD when you read academic titles?

- *PhD,* which is short for doctor of philosophy, is a *terminal* degree (meaning you can't get higher than this). It generally requires two to four years of coursework beyond a master's degree as well as original research in the field of specialty. People in the hard sciences (such as chemistry and computer science) earn PhDs. PhDs are also conferred on those in the social sciences, such as sociology, psychology, and education. These fields are often referred to as the soft sciences.

- *EdD* stands for doctor of education. This degree is similar to a PhD in that it's a terminal degree requiring two to four years of coursework beyond a master's degree and original research in the field of specialty. Some argue that the EdD is more practice based, whereas the PhD is more research based. In addition, as you might expect, the EdD is specific to educators.

Other fields have their own terminal degrees. For example, the terminal law degree for professionals is the JD, which stands for *juris doctor.* Another example is the MFA, which is the terminal degree for those in the applied arts. A third example is the MLS or MLIS for librarians, which stands for *m*aster's degree in *li*brary *s*cience or *li*brary and *i*nformation *s*ciences.

TIP

Follow the instructor's lead to gain a sense of how they prefer to be addressed, based on email they may send you before the class begins, on course documents such as a welcome page, or in course announcements. Most instructors will even create an About Your Instructor page to provide biographical information, preferred methods of communication, and office hours. Look at how they sign those pieces of correspondence. Do they refer to themselves as Professor, or do they sign their first name?

REMEMBER

Figure out whether your communication should be public or private, as described in this list:

>> **Public:** If you have a question about how the course works or where you can find some information, initiate communication in a public forum such as your discussion area. Be sure to read any FAQs or announcements before you ask, however, because many times teachers answer questions in advance. One advantage to asking appropriate questions publicly is that your peers might know the answer and then read and respond to your post before your instructor can. This provides a lot more opportunity for building a community of learning and support.

TIP

If you choose to initiate communication publicly, be sure to ask — and avoid immediately jumping to the conclusion that the information isn't available. To avoid making instructors sound fickle, diplomacy goes a long way. For example, rather than read, "You haven't included instructions on this assignment," an instructor would much rather read, "I can't seem to locate the instructions on this assignment, although I'm sure you included them."

>> **Private:** If your question deals with grades or personal issues, initiate a private email. By all means, if you have a criticism or you find something in the course that isn't working, use diplomacy and communicate privately. Examples may include typographical errors or hyperlinks that don't work. For example, you might write, "I realize you have no control over websites that aren't part of this class, but I just wanted to let you know that one of the links appears to be broken." That's much better than, "Hey, you're sending me on a wild goose chase!"

REMEMBER

Instructors like to maintain contact with students; otherwise, they wouldn't be teaching. You don't need to send a daily email, but in some situations you should definitely communicate with your instructor:

>> **If you'll be away:** Let your instructor know when you have an emergency that will take you away from the course for more than a couple of days. Be sure to let the instructor know how you plan to make up for lost time or keep up with the course. This often works for emergencies, but don't expect instructors to necessarily be so forgiving for vacations that take you away from coursework. Online learning is flexible to a point, but students should expect to be engaged for the entire time the course is scheduled.

>> **If you experience technical difficulties:** Tell your instructor when your computer has crashed and you're operating from a different venue, or when you've experienced a technical issue and have reported it to technical support personnel. (We discuss technical support in more detail later in this chapter.)

>> **If you get major feedback:** When you receive individualized feedback from the instructor on a major project, consider acknowledging it and addressing any follow-up questions they may have asked. You don't have to do this for typical weekly assignments.

>> **If you're an overachiever:** If you're one of those students who excels and wants to work beyond course requirements, contact your instructor and ask for some additional resources and guidance. Obviously, teachers love these kinds of questions.

> » **If you're having trouble:** On the other hand, if you're struggling with the course, either because the content is too difficult or life is getting in the way, let your instructor know at the first warning signs. This may be a situation in which the instructor diplomatically suggests that you take the course at another time, but you save face by letting them know in advance and not failing without warning.

Interacting with fellow students

In the online education environment, you deal with your fellow classmates daily. Learning online is rarely an isolated, independent event and can be quite social! In the following sections, we explain how to get to know the other students and how to get along.

Introducing yourself and getting to know your peers

Most online courses have an icebreaker activity, like their face-to-face counterparts. The only difference is that the online introduction is often text based, with the option to introduce yourself using audio or video as well. This is a perfect opportunity for you to share a little bit about yourself, your previous experience, and what you hope to gain from the course. It's up to you how much personal information you want to share.

Always sign your work and begin to build your online persona under your identification name. For example, at the end of all posts by coauthor Kevin, he signs with this name, his pronouns, his geographic location (city, state), and his signature smiley face. He also links to www.mypronouns.org to emphasize the importance of respectful pronoun use.

It's easy to make assumptions about cultural and academic backgrounds. It's true that your peers will come from diverse backgrounds and will be spread out around the world, but stay away from assuming stereotypical information such as gender, race, socioeconomic status, and intelligence. A lot of Pats, Chrises, and Ryans have had their gender identities switched mistakenly because of stereotyping. These stereotypes can damage the dynamics of an online classroom. As a matter of fact, it's this diversity and the sharing of different perspectives that, when appreciated and celebrated, enrich the learning experience for everyone.

To ensure that your gender identity is respected, consider disclosing your gender pronouns directly in your introduction so that you reduce the possibility of letting your instructor and classmates embarrass themselves by using assumptive language when referencing you and your work. You may also want to make this info a part of your signature, as Kevin does. With that said, it is *vital* to respect your peers' pronouns, whether you understand them or not. You can also simply refer to your peers by name.

Another element of identity that your peers may or may not choose to share with you is a picture of themselves. Some of your peers may choose to share photos of themselves at work, with family, or even swimming with dolphins during their last vacation. Having a picture to go along with a name can provide an element of connection. You may even be amazed at how you imagine your peers' pictures in your mind when you read their posts and emails. You might even get an audio or video introduction as well, because these features are often built into discussion forums.

Knowing your peers can help you understand more about who they are and what amazing contributions they can add to the learning experience. If your class requires a biography-type assignment, take the time to read the introductions of your peers and get to know them better. You'll notice that some students can log in three times a day because of their lifestyles (for example, they're retired or temporarily unemployed), whereas others may barely make it to class three times a week. The biographies help explain that and allow you to be a little more compassionate toward your classmates' circumstances.

TIP

When it comes to writing your own profile, focus on making a good impression in a small amount of space. Provide your instructor and classmates with an overview of who you are without boring them with all the microdetails. For formal profiles, we recommend that you write in third person. However, for most classroom introductions, writing in first person is acceptable and comes across as being less formal. Consider adding some of the following information:

>> **Name and geographic location:** Provide your full name and where you reside. You don't have to give your full address — your city and state are fine if you live in the United States, and your country/territory is sufficient if you live outside the US.

>> **Professional background:** Provide your readers with a brief understanding of what you do and your professional history, if appropriate. Remember to keep it brief. Summarize your experiences into only one or two sentences, even if you've been in the field for 25 years.

>> **Academic background:** Let your peers know where you are in your education and why you've chosen the program or course you're enrolled in.

>> **Personal information:** Feel free to share personal information such as whether you're married, whether you have children or pets, or what your favorite hobbies are. It reminds others that they're in class with other human beings who have outside interests and responsibilities.

Playing well with others

View your online classroom as a community of peers you don't get to see every day — like co-workers, if you will. Just like at work, sometimes you need to use a professional voice, and other times you can goof around.

Communicate formally when you submit assignments that will be read by the whole group. If you're required to write a summary of the main points of the unit, for example, write in a scholarly manner, with appropriate references and correct grammar, and without unsubstantiated opinion. Your classmates will figure out quickly that you're an A student and take this seriously. If you don't, you'll quickly be read as someone who either lacks polish or just doesn't care. We say more about writing style in Chapter 16, but for now, recognize that people will judge you based on written communication.

On the other hand, there are plenty of times when you can lighten up. For example, when you respond to someone else's work, you may not need to be as formal. A sample comment is, "Hey, Molly, you're my idol. You brought up some excellent examples. I really appreciated how you. . .."

Finally, you can just relax and shoot the breeze at times. Many online classes have a place where you can share information that isn't related to the course. It might be called the student lounge or café. Don't be afraid to help build community by sharing work examples, personal stories, and even social happenings such as a conference you attended. These experiences directly benefit learning in that they connect what you're learning to real life, and anytime you make those connections, the concepts are reinforced. Just remember to keep these conversations in the designated areas so as not to disrupt the flow in content-related discussions.

WARNING

Since texting came along, we've seen a lot of learners resort to shorthand in their online classroom as if they were sending a text message versus submitting a formal assignment. At all costs, avoid writing comments like "i no what ur saying." Also avoid abbreviations like *atm.* Instead, write out the entire phrase *at the moment* and use complete thoughts to convey your message. This shows professionalism and a sense of caring about the quality of your own work.

REMEMBER

Students who take the time to get to know their peers, communicate often, and consistently participate go a long way toward building community. The group begins to trust one another when they realize those are real people on the other end of the computer screen. That trust comes in handy when you need to work together collaboratively. If one of your classmates needs some special consideration in a group assignment, for instance, the group is more likely to grant it to someone who has pulled their weight and contributed previously versus someone who has only been sitting in the background and hasn't cared to interact. The same human dynamics you find in a face-to-face classroom play out online.

Seeing Who's Behind the Scenes

We predict you'll spend so much time interacting with your fellow students and instructor that you won't notice the following groups of people. But they're present and working behind the scenes to ensure your success. These people include guests, technical and academic support staff, and friends and family. This section helps you understand who they are and the differences they can make in your educational experience.

Noting classroom guests and observers

Much like in the face-to-face classroom, you may or may not notice several outside guests visiting the virtual classroom. Outsiders can include guest speakers, support staff, and administrators. The following list describes some of the people you may see:

>> **Teaching assistants:** Some online classes are large enough that the instructor needs help facilitating the course. In this situation, teaching assistants may be employed to help with tasks such as facilitating discussion, answering questions, and grading assignments. Students should interact with teaching assistants in the same manner they do with their instructor.

>> **Librarians:** Gone are the days of thinking about librarians as the people who peer over their glasses and shush you for being too loud in the library. Besides, how can you be too noisy in a virtual library? There are several instances in which you may "run into" a librarian from your institution. Your instructor may invite a librarian to guest-lecture in your classroom as a way to encourage library use and help you learn how to conduct research for a specific assignment. Or, you may get the chance to chat live with a librarian when you need help navigating the virtual library. No matter the situation, your institution's librarian is a useful resource. Communication with librarians can be more casual, but you should still keep it professional.

>> **Guest speakers:** Hearing about different experiences from professionals within the field is important for students. After all, one major benefit of online learning is that your instructor can connect you with professionals around the world that you may not normally get to learn from. For this purpose, your instructor may ask a practitioner to join the class to share their experiences and answer student questions. This can be done using discussion boards or a live event such as a conference call or a web conference over the Internet. In any case, do what you can to actively participate in these opportunities. Thank the guest for sharing time and talents, and then ask a question that shows a real interest in the work.

>> **Administrative staff:** Have you ever taken a class where the instructor asks you to ignore the person in the back of the room taking notes, explaining that the person is there to observe the instructor's teaching abilities? The same thing happens in the online environment; you just may not know it. Because online education is rather new, institutions often set quality standards specific to an instructor's ability to teach online. The only way to know whether the instructor is meeting these standards is to log in and observe. Administrative staff may log in to your course and take note of the instructor's language use, frequency of communication, and response time to student questions. Again, you may or may not know this is going on. Either way, the process helps ensure that you're receiving the best education possible.

Administrative staff: These folks also interact with students when they need to resolve a conflict between the instructor and a student, when there's a question regarding a final grade that was assigned, or when they're seeking feedback regarding the quality of the overall program. It's important to know who your administrative staff are and to always interact with them in a professional manner. Administrative staff include the department chairperson of your program, the dean of the college, the institution's dean of academic affairs, and the department's administrative assistant.

REMEMBER

All the personnel described in this section are required to follow a set of federal guidelines to protect and respect your privacy. None of them is permitted to share contact information or change your grade. Learning management systems (LMSs) such as Canvas have roles and permission settings that restrict access. For example, a guest speaker shouldn't even be able to access or see the grade book.

Calling on technical support

The purpose of technical support is to support and complement the learning process of both instructors and students. They usually don't appear in your course roster like your peers, but they are there to help you succeed. In fact, technical support is so important that you'll most likely be given that contact information even before you log on to your course. In the following sections, we explain how technical support staff can help you and how to ask for that help. We also tell you when tech support can't be of service — and how to find solutions on your own.

Most institutions have information about how to contact technical support somewhere on their websites so that it's quick and easy to find. Most learning management systems provide a Help link on their main navigation bar for quick and easy access. Contact information may include a phone number, an email address, or even a link to chat with a live person via the Internet.

Write down the technical support contact information and store it in your wallet or purse in case you need it at work, while traveling, or when the Internet connection is down and you can't get to your virtual classroom.

What technical support can fix

Technical support staff focus strictly on the technology they provide for interacting with their products and services. For example, institutions provide technical support when you've lost your password for logging on to your course or when you're unable to physically access the registration website.

Before calling technical support, ask yourself: "Who owns the technology that I can't get to work?" For example, if you're writing a paper for your class and your word processing program keeps crashing, you have to contact the company that created the word processing application.

You should definitely contact your institution's technical support staff whenever you experience one of these problems:

>> You can't log on to your course.

>> You can log in to your course, but pages don't load.

>> You can't get a synchronous tool to load (like a chat window).

>> You try to post an assignment and nothing happens, or you see an error message.

>> You can't access other necessary websites, such as the library.

>> You can't remember your password, or your account has been locked after too many failed attempts.

If the technology required by a class is working but you're simply having trouble learning how to use it, contact your instructor first. Your instructor is responsible for facilitating the learning process, including the use of instructional technology. If your instructor can't help you, they will forward you to the appropriate training tutorials or support staff.

If, for some reason, technical support staff can't resolve a problem immediately or you've attempted to contact them several times without success, *contact your instructor*. In fact, some instructors like to know anytime you contact technical support — not because they want to get involved but because they care about whether you're having difficulty. Letting your instructor know that you're having a problem and what you're doing about it tells the instructor you're responsible and committed. It also allows the instructor to inform your peers in the class if the problem is universal. (If the specific problem pertains to submission of homework, go ahead and submit your assignment to your instructor via email when possible, to provide you and your instructor with a time-stamped submission of the completed assignment.)

Asking for help appropriately

If you need immediate help, don't use email to contact technical support. You may not receive a response for up to 24 hours, and it can take even longer if additional information is needed.

What is "immediate?" Your idea of immediate and technical support's idea may not coincide. If you find at 11:59 P.M. that you can't post an assignment that's due by midnight, that's probably not the best time to call technical support and expect an immediate response. If at all possible, call during normal working hours. You may also want to see whether live chat support is available and what hours you can use that service.

Anytime you contact technical support, provide them with as much information as possible. The more information you can provide, the more likely your problem can be solved immediately. Here's a checklist of information you should be prepared to provide when something goes wrong:

>> Your full name

>> Your student ID

>> The course ID and full course title

>> Your instructor's name

>> The web page you were on when the problem occurred

>> A description of what you were doing immediately before the problem occurred

>> Your computer's operating system (OS), such as Mac OS, Windows, or Linux

TIP

Knowing which version number of your operating system you have installed is extremely helpful. Version numbers are used to help indicate minor updates. For example, you may have MacOS Catalina (10) as your operating system and version 10.15.6. This tells technical support when you last updated your machine and if you missed any important updates that might be contributing to your problems. After you know the version number of your operating system, write it down for future reference. Most people know which OS they have, but they may not know which version they're using. Finding the version you're using is different for each operating system, so check your manual or ask a technical support staff member to help you find it when needed.

>> The Internet browser you were using, such as Internet Explorer, Firefox, or Safari.

Windows-based machines come with Internet Edge preinstalled, and Mac-based machines come with Safari by default, but you can add other browsers on your computer. As with the operating system, if you need to know which version of a particular browser you're using and you don't know how to find it, ask technical support to tell you how and then document the information for later use.

>> The names of other programs or applications that were running when the error occurred.

>> Include a screen shot if you're able to take one that clearly illustrates the problem. (We walk you through taking screen shots in Chapter 8.)

If you don't know how to find some of this information about your computer, that's okay — the technical support staff can help you figure it out. But be sure to take notes and learn how to find the answers for yourself in the future. This not only helps you learn more about your computer but also speeds up future technical support calls.

What technical support can't do (and what you can do about it)

The technical support staff consists of amazing people with a wealth of technical knowledge. However, it's not uncommon for institutions to hire one technical support staff to support several thousand faculty and students. Therefore, don't be surprised or disappointed if they have to send you elsewhere for help. Most likely, technical staff won't provide assistance with teaching you how to use your computer or train you on individual applications such as Microsoft Word or PowerPoint.

If your institution offers training sessions via webinars, take full advantage of them. These online workshops use synchronous technology that allows presenters to share content with participants in real time. These sessions can provide you with new skills, such as using advanced features of common applications like Microsoft Word or PowerPoint.

If your institution doesn't offer this type of training, you can check out the product's website or other training sites for tutorials and support tips. Here are some ideas to get you started:

>> **Training home page for Microsoft:** Check out the numerous tutorials at

```
https://support.microsoft.com/en-us/training?ui=en-us&rs=en-us&ad=us
```

>> **Lynda.com:** This site is another one that hosts a variety of tutorials, which you can often get free access to from your local library, including online access from home with your library ID and password.

>> **YouTube:** You would be surprised how many organizations have made their workshops available. Just be certain they use the same version of software you need help with.

Let me "Google that" for you

When all else fails, or technical support is closed but you need help now, you always have another option: Google. How often are you hanging out with friends and family and you collectively can't solve a problem or someone says something that doesn't seem completely true? What do you do in that situation? In our experience, today's culture is not to go to the library and look up the answer, but rather to pull out our phones and look it up at www.google.com. This same strategy can also be used for solving your technical problems. You can open Google and easily conduct a web search for training sources available online by product. For example, if you're trying to figure out how to create a table of contents in Microsoft Word, you can open your Internet browser and type **Tutorial table of contents Microsoft Word** into the Google search engine. Often, videos and step-by-step tutorials for learning how to use a variety of applications are instantly available at your fingertips.

Taking this approach does require a problem-solver mindset, knowing that you might have to look through a few videos to see which one most aligns with your situation. However, becoming a problem-solver provides you with a level of independence that can save you the time spent waiting on others and makes you more marketable. As a matter of fact, one of the most common questions Kevin uses when interviewing instructional designers is, "What was the last tool you learned by teaching yourself, and can you explain your process for doing it?"

Receiving academic support

For many online students, enrolling in an online class signifies returning to school after a period of academic inactivity. In other words, as a learner, you may feel rusty. It may have been awhile since you tested your study skills. Even if you've been an active learner in some context, you'll probably feel a little awkward in the online environment at first. After all, this is new to you. What if you attend a class and find that you need additional academic support? Academic support staff can help you through any transitional difficulties you're experiencing, including those with writing, course material, and basic student skills.

Obtaining assistance with writing

If you ask experienced online students, they will probably tell you that they were surprised at first by how much writing they had to do in an online class. But when you think about it, this is how students and faculty communicate — with their fingers. Writing skills take on increased importance in the online world. A typical course involves writing responses to discussion questions, and usually a few papers on the side. We talk more about those specifics in Chapter 11 and 12.

TIP

If you find that you're not earning the scores you want or if you receive direct feedback from the instructor about your writing skills, take action! Here are a few suggestions:

>> **Check with your instructor or academic advisor to see whether your school offers writing services.** Some institutions are prepared to offer writing assistance to their virtual students. If this service is offered, you may have access to online tutors with whom you can schedule appointments. For distance students, tutoring is usually done using synchronous tools where you can share your document with the tutor in real time. The tutor can then give you immediate feedback and make suggestions for where you might find additional resources specific to the areas you need help with.

>> **Look for assistance online.** Run a quick Internet search on *writing assistance* to find a multitude of websites that provide good advice on organizing your writing. Look for a site that's specifically hosted by a college or a library. A couple of excellent examples are the Guide to Grammar and Writing at https://guidetogrammar.org/grammar and the Purdue Online Writing Lab at https://owl.purdue.edu. GrammarBook.com offers free online guides with supplemental quizzes to support understanding: www.grammarbook.com.

>> **Find assistance by using in-person services.** Good writing is good writing, regardless of whether you're online. Visit an educational services provider in your area, such as Sylvan Learning (www.sylvanlearning.com), Kumon (www.kumon.com), or any similar business, and see what services they offer. They work with people other than young children.

WARNING

Plagiarism is never acceptable. Don't get sucked into a site that provides free research papers — this is the fastest way to end your academic career.

Finding a tutor for your topic or basic student skills

Online courses sometimes move fast, and you're expected to keep up the pace. If you find that you're falling behind because you're struggling to understand course material, you may decide you need a tutor. A *tutor* is a personalized teacher who helps you with specific subject matter. Finding a tutor for a specific subject is relatively easy because that person doesn't have to be online. For example, if you need help in college-level math, you can probably find someone who tutors specifically at your institution through student services or you can search online. Just don't forget to check references and ask questions about qualifications. On the other hand, if you find that what you need is a refresher on time management or note-taking while reading, academic tutors can provide help with these general student skills as well. Except for dealing with the online technology, reading, note-taking, and studying for exams don't differ much between traditional and online courses.

Tutors vary in terms of their credentials, experience, and fees. How do you know what you need? Here are a few questions to consider:

>> **Do you need a brush-up or major instruction?** If you just need to review, a family friend with a degree in the subject area may be willing to pitch in. But if you feel you need serious instruction or more attention than a volunteer has time for, look for a tutor with teaching experience and advanced coursework in the subject matter.

>> **Are you an international student who needs help with North American writing conventions?** Students who need more extensive grammar and mechanics help than subject matter knowledge may want to look for an ESL tutoring service that is familiar with strategies for teaching English as a second language. You might even find this at the institution you're attending.

>> **How much can you afford?** A tutor associated with a corporate agency (for example, Sylvan) costs more than a former licensed schoolteacher who now works from home. In all cases, ask about credentials and experience. Don't be afraid to ask for and check references, either. After all, you're paying for this service.

In some cases, online students need someone to sit beside them to help with learning the basic tasks of understanding their computers or navigation. Most likely, you can find a computer tutor at your local BestBuy (Geek Squad) or Apple Store (Apple Genius), but that person won't be able to coach you through processes specific to your LMS. For that kind of help, you need to call your institution's technical support staff. See the earlier section "What technical support can fix" for more details.

Developing your personal support system

Attending school is a *commitment*. It takes, time, energy, thought, and the attitude to succeed. Though you may feel this is your adventure to own, you must remember that every decision you make affects those around you. Therefore, involving your family and friends in your decision-making process helps them understand the role they play in supporting your decision to go to school.

Because you won't be leaving to go to a physical classroom, your family and friends may mistakenly perceive you as being available. For example, your kids may want you to play with them outdoors, or your friends may want you to host movie night. They see you physically home and may not understand that you need to study. These temptations are hard to say no to. As a matter of fact, you may feel a little guilty saying no, which can cause you to fall behind in your coursework. That's why it's important for you to set boundaries for yourself and others. Many families experienced this situation intensely, and had to adjust appropriately, at the beginning of the COVID-19 pandemic — trying to study while kids who are out of school are home, trying to learn or begging for attention.

TIP

One good way to set boundaries? Establish specific days and times for studying. During those times, go into your study space and put a note on the door that says something like this: "Studying in progress. Please do not interrupt." If you have young children, make time to explain your situation in terms they understand, and let them help make the Do Not Disturb sign. This may give them a feeling of ownership and pride in helping you achieve your academic goals. When they feel good about helping you, you feel less guilty for soliciting their help. A good pair of noise canceling headphones is also helpful — expensive, but worth investing in if you can.

The most valuable thing that family and friends can do to help you succeed is to respect your time and space when studying. Some beneficial ways they can do this include babysitting the kids, refraining from temptations that take you away from studying, and making dinner on study nights. It's also nice if your supporters can be flexible during times when your workload increases.

Supporters can also help you academically. By reading rough drafts and providing you with constructive feedback, supporters help you identify areas of your work that need polishing before you turn it in. To help them provide constructive feedback, provide the assignment's description so that they know what the instructor expects. You can also ask your supporters open-ended questions after they review your assignment, to see whether they're able to answer the questions in a manner that reflects what you're trying to convey in the assignment.

Chapter **11**

Communicating Clearly Online

I n a face-to-face classroom, hashing out new concepts and debating the merits of various ideas are hallmarks of good learning. The same is true in online education. The amount of communication that occurs between students and faculty and the quality of those messages set a quality online course apart from a mediocre one.

In the world of online learning, people communicate through a variety of tools, including email, messaging, and discussion forums. This chapter examines how people communicate online and how important communication is to your success as a learner. We consider the persona you create and present to others through your communication, and we examine the details of discussion and the influence of social networks in facilitating conversation.

Checking Out Methods of Communicating Online

In a robust online course, you can expect to see communication occurring on several different levels. Messages are directed toward the class as a whole from the instructor, individually from the instructor to single learners (and from learners to the instructor), and from learner to learner. If you were to visually plot that network of messages, a good course would look messy because there would be so many connections between learners. This section examines some of the primary ways people communicate in an online course.

Instructor-to-class communication in news and announcements

Think about the first day of school at a face-to-face school. Assuming that Security remembers to unlock the classroom door, the instructor stands at the front of the class and welcomes learners. Entering the virtual classroom isn't much different. Typically, a welcome message or some kind of greeting from the instructor awaits you. This communication is intended to be read by every member of the class. It may be posted on the course's home page in a News and Announcements area or within a specially designated discussion forum. (We describe discussions later in this chapter.) This kind of introductory message lets you know that you're in the right place. It may also tell you what to do next. Figure 11-1 shows the Recent Announcements tab on the course's home page, which has a link to a Welcome to Class message. Figure 11-1 also shows the announcement itself.

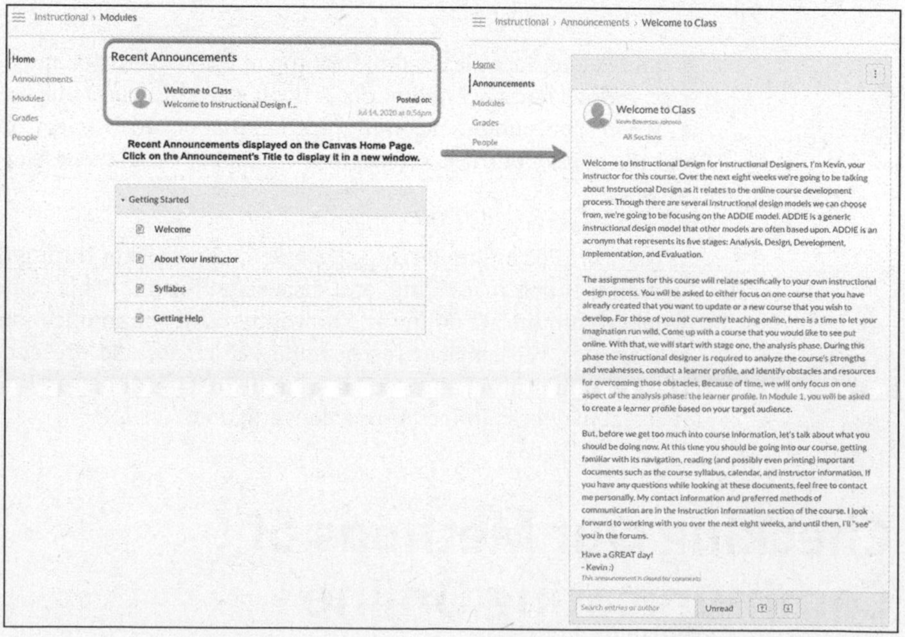

FIGURE 11-1: A sample announcement from an instructor on a course's home page.

After that initial announcement, your instructor may use the same public method for several different purposes. They may use announcements to

>> **Keep everyone on task.** For example, if you're three days into the course and no one has been brave enough to post the first assignment, the instructor may post an announcement to reinforce the procedures and help students feel more comfortable trying the assignment. Again, this announcement may appear on the course's home page or in a discussion forum.

>> **Summarize the last unit and preview what's to come.** The instructor may review the material the class examined in the previous unit and connect it to what's to come in the next unit. Read these kinds of summaries with the idea of mentally testing yourself. Do you know what the instructor is talking about? If not, go back and review!

>> **Reinforce news from the institution that you should know about.** For example, occasionally the school needs to shut down its servers for maintenance. Someone may email you and post a message on the portal or the first page you log in to, but chances are good that your instructor will remind you again.

REMEMBER

Read all messages posted by your instructor, even if you're tempted to bypass lengthy messages in favor of getting to your next task. Instructors include pertinent information in their messages. Plus, you spare yourself the embarrassment of asking a question that was already addressed in an announcement.

Learner-to-learner communication in discussions

We hope the kind of communication you find most common within your course is learner-to-learner discussion about the subject matter. Why? Because a course in which learners actively discuss and debate is a course where the learners are interested! It's also a course that demonstrates active, engaged learning at its best.

Many online courses follow a social-constructivist format of presenting information and then asking learners to discuss and add to the concept. By writing about how the materials fit into the world or one's profession, everyone in the class gains a clear picture of the subject matter. Collectively, they "construct" their understanding. For that reason, instructors ask students to engage in discussions with one another.

PORTAL, SCHMORTAL

In some cases, the page from which you log in to the school's system is called the *portal*. In addition to accessing your courses, you can link to the library or bookstore or other services. Sometimes, this is built into your learning management system, and at other times it's a separate website created by your institution. In other cases, the first page you see after you log in to your learning management system may be referred to as the portal. This page usually displays links to your individual courses and summarizes announcements and calendar events in one place — particularly important if you're taking more than one course at a time. Not every school uses the term *portal* to mean the same thing. However, use of the term *home page* to represent the main page of your course is fairly consistent.

Discussing means having a conversation. This is a little different online than in person because your fingers often do the talking. We describe online discussions in the later section "Participating in Discussions." For now, recognize that learner-to-learner communication should dominate your online experience.

One-on-one communication via private email or messaging

Private, one-on-one communication is meant for your eyes only and may come via your email or an internal messaging feature if your learning management system supports it.

TIP

Whenever possible, use the tools that are available within the learning management system (LMS) to communicate. For example, your system may have built-in "messenger"-type tools — these systems act like instant messaging when the other person is online. If the person isn't online when you send the message, they receive it when they next log in. Your school may assign you an internal email that doesn't require you to give out your personal email address. The advantage of sending and receiving messages within the system is that your academic work is all recorded in one place. You don't have to sort through your Aunt Tilda's forwarded jokes to find the instructor's note.

In this section, we describe several types of private communication: instructor-to-learner, learner-to-instructor, and learner-to-learner.

Instructor-to-learner communication

Instructors communicate with learners privately for several reasons:

>> **They send feedback.** Many instructors like to follow longer assignments, such as papers, with comments. Though these can be posted in an electronic grade book, there usually isn't sufficient space. Therefore, instructors email their comments and feedback.

>> **They nudge.** Occasionally, you may have an attentive instructor who notices you're not meeting the deadlines. They may send you a little note to remind you to stay on task.

>> **They praise and send additional resources.** Sometimes an instructor wants to acknowledge excellent work from an individual and perhaps provide additional resources that the rest of the class wouldn't be interested in. This may be a case for private communication.

>> **They communicate grades to you.** Thank goodness! Actually, your instructor must communicate grades privately, by law. Your grades and feedback can't be posted publicly.

Figure 11-2 is an example of a private communication your instructor may send. This one was sent via an internal messaging feature. The same result can be accomplished via email.

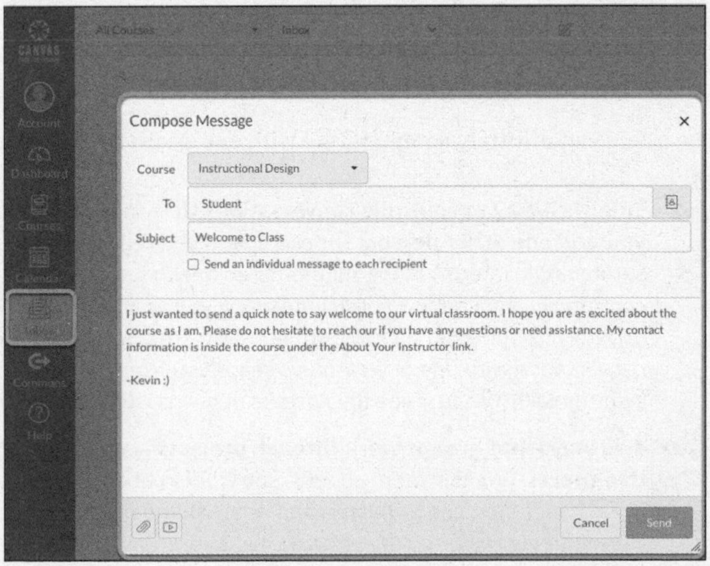

FIGURE 11-2: An example of internal private communication.

Learner-to-instructor communication

Not only can instructors send learners private communication but learners may also need to communicate privately with instructors. Why would you want to communicate with your instructor privately? Here are some reasons:

>> **You're in distress.** Something is going on in your life that requires your attention and is preventing you from focusing on school or completing your assignments. The whole class doesn't need to know about this, but your instructor does. This is a case for private email.

>> **You're experiencing technological difficulties.** Whenever you have a problem with your computer, the software, or the system and need to work with technical support, it's a good idea to also inform your instructor. They may not be able to remedy the situation, but you're at least alerting them to the problem.

>> **You want to ask a question specifically about your academic work.** Instructors cannot discuss your work publicly — it's the law! Therefore, if you ask a question in a public forum about your performance, your instructor can't answer it. On the other hand, you can discreetly email the instructor to ask about your work.

REMEMBER

When it comes to communicating with your instructor, diplomacy is the best policy. In other words, try not to push the instructor beyond reasonable expectations. Most institutions have faculty guidelines related to how quickly instructors should respond to emails — usually, within 24 to 48 hours. If you send an SOS at midnight, don't expect a response right away!

Learner-to-learner communication

Learners can privately communicate with one another, too, as in these examples:

>> **Email is a way to continue conversations that may be of interest to only you and one other person.** For example, if you read that your classmate Sarah has an interest in the culture-based health issues specific to the Polish community and you're a Polish immigrant, you may want to email her privately to share some family stories. Having the opportunity to continue a conversation with one of your peers keeps you from overposting on discussions as well. (We describe the dangers of overposting later in this chapter.)

>> **Two ways that groups work through projects is via email and collaborative spaces.** (We talk more about group work in Chapter 13.) Email allows you to exchange files, send updates, and establish meetings. Plus, it's easy to copy your instructor on the email so that they know your group's progress. Collaborative spaces allow you to store documents that you can all get to and

work on. For example, if you have a Google Docs document stored in a folder on Google Drive, anyone in the group can add their comments and continue working.

» **Sometimes, students exchange contact information such as cellphone numbers, but there's not a lot of work you can do on your phone.** At best, this is a way to say, "Hey, did you see the new edits?"

Creating and Putting Forward an Online Persona

A country song that was popular a few years ago told the story of a man who presented himself online as a suave ladies' man, when in fact he was a bit of a nerd offline. Online, you can be anyone you want to be. Though we don't recommend misrepresenting yourself, you may want to carefully consider the persona you put forward since it's the tool you will use to cultivate lasting relationships with your peers online. We explain what you need to know in the following sections.

Depicting positive personality traits online

Written text is void of the nonverbal cues people often rely on to fill in communication gaps. Absent eye contact, facial expressions, and voice intonation, people have only the written word from which to judge the person on the other end of the computer connection. The persona you put forth online comes through in your writing style. How you write, the words you choose, and the frequency with which you post all say something about who you are.

Are you shy? Online, you can be as forward and confident as anyone else. Remember that the nature of asynchronous communication means that nothing happens immediately, so what you say by way of posting becomes as important as what the next student says. It's not like a typical classroom, where the more aggressive students attract the most attention by raising their hands or talking out loud first.

Being judged by words alone may be a wonderful feature of online communication because it means you're less likely to be judged on characteristics like your physical appearance or voice. Your ideas stand on their own. We say more about writing in Chapter 16, but for now remember that the "voice" you use — casual or academic — says a lot about how you're perceived. If you write like a scholar, you'll be viewed as a scholar.

A few personality traits that come through in written communication are the key to your success as an online learner. The following sections explain how to depict yourself as a serious-yet-warm person who shows leadership skills and avoids being high maintenance.

TIP

Heed these tips as you develop your online persona:

>> **Understand the impact of photos.** When introducing yourself to your class for the first time, you may consider attaching a casual photograph. Photos are a way of sharing who you are, but they have drawbacks, too. A photo reveals your age, weight, race, and gender — all possibilities for bias. You should never feel pressured to reveal your identity if you don't want to! If your instructor asks for a photo and you don't want to share it, email it privately but request that it not be shared with the rest of the class.

>> **Substitute stickers, bitmoji, and avatars.** Wildly popular these days are graphical versions of who you are. If you don't want a photo to show who you are, one of these items might be an option. The drawback is that you might look like anyone else. True story: Kevin and Susan have essentially the same avatar; only their eyeglasses are different and her skin is darker.

>> **Use emoticons appropriately.** We want to add a final word about *emoticons* — the symbolic smiley faces that pepper today's communication. As long as you use them sparingly, a wink or a frown can say a great deal. However, emoticons don't belong in the text of your academic papers. Save them for back-and-forth discussion among peers.

Finding a mix of serious and funny

The serious learner posts full-bodied, articulate responses to questions. The responses are well researched and reference some of the assigned readings to demonstrate the connection between theory and practice. The serious learner asks direct questions that demonstrate critical thinking as a follow-up to their peers' work. The rest of the class quickly identifies who the serious learners are, based on the quality of their work. (We wrote that with our serious voice.)

You may think that we're going to contrast the serious learner with the class clown. Not so! In fact, it's possible to be genuinely funny, insightful, and serious all at the same time. If you see a play on words or detect a pun, go ahead and write it. This doesn't really make you a class clown.

TIP

If you think of the class clown as a goof-off and wonder where that person is in online education, you may not find them. Why not? Because students who goof off don't last in online education! But that doesn't necessarily mean there's no place to clown around in the online learning environment. If your instructor sets up a "student lounge" for posting off-topic, you can safely post the latest hilarious viral video or clean joke of the day there.

WARNING

Humor should never be insulting, sarcastic, racist, sexist, homophobic, or directed toward any single individual or group. Because it can be easily misconstrued, be careful if you have a twisted sense of humor — keep it to yourself.

Also, don't post political memes or jokes. You run the risk of offending others and being labeled one way or the other. It just doesn't work in online learning.

Adding warmth to your words

Establishing the right amount of "presence" online can be a challenge, especially when you're balancing multiple roles and have limited time. We acknowledge this! You don't have to be a social butterfly and respond to everyone when interacting with your class. However, being a social recluse and posting only the bare minimum probably isn't the way to go, either.

TIP

What sets a recluse apart from a social butterfly isn't just the amount of posting but also a lack of warmth. Even if you can't respond to many of your peers because of time limitations, a few warm messages go a long way toward establishing you as a friendly classmate and not a recluse. To warm up your communication, you may want to try these tips:

>> **Always address the person by name.** "Jane, that is an intriguing point you brought up."

>> **Introduce just a touch of personal information.** "Your analysis reminds me of the time we vacationed in New Jersey."

>> **Compliment freely.** "I love how you wove the reference to Mac*b*eth into your description of the current conflict."

>> **Show gratitude.** "Thanks for asking me about that assignment."

Showing off leadership qualities

Leadership is a quality you might not expect to see online, but it definitely shows! Leaders are learners who

>> **Post early (or at least on time):** If you have several days to submit a public assignment, see whether you can be one of the first posters. The others will follow your lead.

>> **Volunteer to be leaders when assigned to groups:** Just be sure you have the time and skills to follow through. That generally means coming up with a plan; it shouldn't mean doing all the work.

>> **Present themselves as serious students:** Our earlier discussion of serious students explains that they post thoughtfully and back up their ideas with research. They set examples for the rest of the class.

Avoiding a reputation as a high-maintenance person

WARNING

No one wants to be remembered as high maintenance. How can you avoid this? Try these strategies:

>> **Report problems, but save the drama for another setting.** Everyone has problems. You might be experiencing computer issues, a life event, or a broken link in the course. High-maintenance learners tend to describe each of these problems as if they had equal weight. They also tend to post these problems publicly, when sometimes a private message to the instructor is a better choice. (We explain earlier in this chapter when to properly use private messaging.)

>> **Try a few things on your own before calling a full-blown SOS.** Try to find your own resolution before posting publicly that you can't do something. For example, if you're assigned to read an article online and the link doesn't work but you know the title, try running a quick search for it on your own. Then you can score points with the instructor by posting that the original link didn't work, but you found an alternative.

TIP

When it comes to pointing out typos or instructions that don't work, send those notes privately to the instructor. Just as you wouldn't want everyone in the class reading the feedback your instructor gives you on assignments, your instructor doesn't want the feedback you give them shared with everyone else, either.

>> **Establish boundaries regarding what and how much you share.** The public forum isn't the place to explain your messy divorce. Your classmates came to learn, not counsel. The educational experience you share should be the basis of your interpersonal relationships.

>> **Have a backup plan or a personal technician if you start to experience a computer issue every week.** Everyone has computer issues periodically. However, we observe that high-maintenance students tend to have them weekly. If that's you, and you tell everyone within shouting distance, your classmates will begin to question your competency. Though you can't see people rolling their eyes online, we believe it happens!

Developing relationships

Think about the nature of work in the 21st century. Many people routinely collaborate with colleagues in other cities, towns, and countries. We send emails, attach files, and make phone calls. We depend on each other to get work done. No one says these relationships aren't real!

The same is true for online education. Learners interact by way of technology and come to depend on one another to get work done. In the process, very real and lasting relationships form.

When you present your ideas to the class, your intellect shines, not your gray hair, thick glasses, or skinny legs. Friendships develop based on the quality of your ideas, as well as some of the characteristics we describe earlier in this chapter. The serious students tend to hang together, while the ones with active senses of humor banter among themselves. Birds of a feather flock together.

This is not to say that the online classroom is polarizing! Putting aside some of the biases that may creep into a traditional classroom, learners form online relationships based on what and how they think. It's not uncommon to see a young learner who is technologically comfortable befriend an older learner when they have the same academic goals and share similar insights.

A special bond forms with cohort groups. Cohorts are groups of students who start a degree or certificate program together and stay in the same group for their entire time online. These learners may be together for a year or more. Our observation is that they disclose more personal information as time passes and therefore provide more support and understanding when trouble arises. (Flip to Chapters 4 and 7 for more about cohorts.)

TIP

You may question whether these online academic relationships are real and lasting. They are very real as long as both parties make an effort to maintain the relationship, and it can easily move from academic cohort to friendship. As your friend discloses information in posts or emails, take the time to send a private message to commemorate a birthday or a child's T-ball success. Or, send a good-luck e-card right before you all hunker down for finals. Touch base after class if you wind up in different courses, and keep up-to-date on professional accomplishments. Most people agree that it's nice to be remembered!

Participating in Discussions

Some instructors describe discussion as the heart and soul of online learning. For academic courses that require participation, there's little doubt that discussion is a cornerstone. In this section, we look at why discussion is important, how discussions are organized, and how you can determine what's expected of you to succeed in online discussions.

Understanding why you're asked to discuss

No doubt you've heard the expression "Practice makes perfect." It makes perfect sense if you're studying keyboarding skills or French pronunciation, but seeing how this works is a little more difficult when you're studying a subject like economics or world literature. Furthermore, in an online course, it's impossible for the instructor to see learners practicing, right?

REMEMBER

Not so! Online discussion is one of the methods instructors use to witness your learning. Here's why:

>> **Discussion shows you are reading.** When you answer a discussion question and refer to your assigned readings or textbook, you demonstrate to the instructor that you're actually reading the material.

>> **Discussion shows your ability to think critically.** Many instructors want you to take the content and break it down, analyze it, put it back together in a way that is meaningful, and add an interpretation of how this works in the real world. This is critical thinking! When you participate in discussion, you show your ability to think critically.

>> **Discussion helps you learn better. It's** not enough to read, cite, and move on. Instructors want you to personalize and internalize the information. In fact, this is one of the ways adults learn better and faster.

>> **Others benefit from discussion, too.** In the constructivist classroom, everyone wins when you take a topic and develop it fully. When you add your insights and interpretations, the rest of the class is able to consider whether they agree or disagree and, most importantly, why.

Organizing discussions in different ways

Discussion is a conversation that occurs online and requires more than one person. For example, John puts forth an idea to which Chris responds with an example supporting his idea. Others join in the conversation, too. Sally suggests an alternative view to what John has written with an additional reference to the literature. Pat asks a question for clarification, forcing John to find another way to explain his original idea. All of this gets rolled together for a more complete understanding of the content. By the time the discussion runs its course, the readers and authors have looked at the subject matter more thoroughly because of the diversity of views.

Depending on the learning management software, you may see your conversations displayed as small pieces connected to one another in a couple of ways: chronologically or threaded. Each piece comes from an individual speaker and is a piece of written text, or post:

>> **Chronological posts:** The posts may be connected in a linear fashion, following one another in chronological order. Figure 11-3 shows what this looks like.

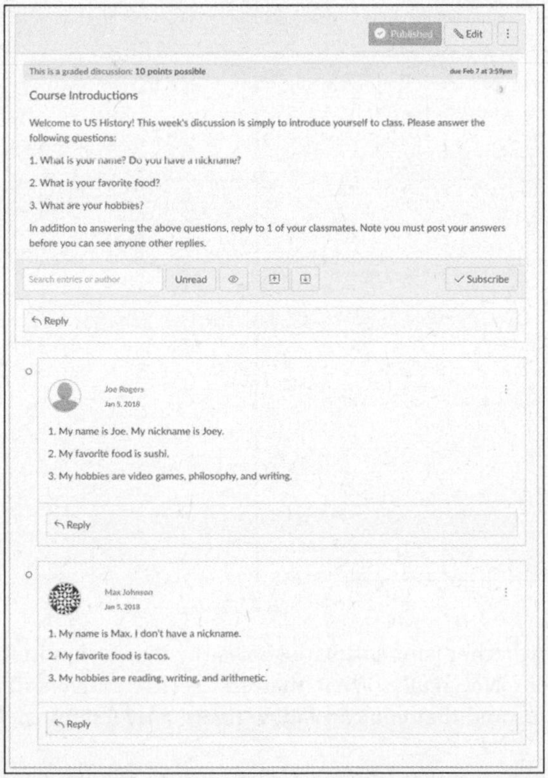

FIGURE 11-3:
Canvas
discussions:
A discussion in
chronological
order.

>> **Threaded posts:** A threaded discussion displays the conversation in a different graphical fashion: When you look at the display, you're better able to see how ideas connect to one another. The dates may seem out of order, but not if you follow the conversation as if it were in outline form. Text that's indented is directly related to the post above it. Figure 11-4 shows a threaded discussion.

Threaded Discussions

Published | Edit | ⋮

This is a graded discussion: **10 points possible**   due Jun 7

Course Introductions

Welcome to US History! This week's discussion is simply to introduce yourself to class. Please answer the following questions:

1. What is your name? Do you have a nickname?

2. What is your favorite food?

3. What are your hobbies?

In addition to answering the above questions, reply to 1 of your classmates. Note you must post your answers before you can see anyone other replies.

Search entries or author | Unread | 👁 | ⊞ | ⊟ | ✓ Subscribe

↩ Reply

> **Jessica Doe**
> Jun 7, 2019
>
> My name is Jessica. I don't really have a nickname. My favorite food is pizza. In my spare time I like to play guitar (acoustic or electric), play volleyball, and read.
> Edited by Jessica Doe on Jun 7 at 2:50pm

>> **Emily Boone**
>> Jun 7, 2019
>>
>> Hi Jessica,
>>
>> I love pizza! What are your favorite toppings? Do you have a favorite place to order from? What kind of books do you like to read?
>> ↩ Reply 👍

>>> **Jessica Doe**
>>> 10:23am
>>>
>>> I love pepperoni, sausage, and peppers on my pizza. I go to a local pizza place in my neighborhood. It's super yummy! What toppings do you like? I love reading science fiction series.
>>> ↩ Reply 👍

>>>> **Emily Boone**
>>>> 10:27am
>>>>
>>>> Awesome, those toppings all sound great. I like pepperoni or usually just plain cheese. What are some of your favorite sci-fi series?
>>>> ↩ Reply 👍

FIGURE 11-4: Canvas discussions: A discussion displayed in threaded fashion.

Does it matter whether your software shows the discussion in threaded or chronological fashion? Not really. What matters is that conversations are occurring between learners and that you can follow these conversations.

REMEMBER

Many learning management systems allow you to change how you view discussions. You control whether you see them in threaded or unthreaded fashion according to your settings. If you have this option, play around with the settings until you find the system that works best for you.

Figuring out discussion requirements

Each instructor has their own expectations regarding discussion and participation. You may find these expectations in several places:

» **The syllabus:** Chances are good that the instructor lists discussion as a component of your grade in the syllabus. They may say something like this: "Participates in discussion by posting an initial statement and responding to two other peers each week." Read those statements carefully to determine what is expected. (Chapter 9 describes a course syllabus in detail.)

» **The instructions:** You most likely have a page in your course that describes what you should do in the discussion area; you should be able to find a link to this page from the course's main page. The questions you're expected to answer may be listed there. Often this is where the instructor reminds you of how much to write and how to post. For example, you may read, "Answer one of the following questions in 300 to 500 words. Be sure to reference one of our assigned readings. Before the close of the module, respond to two of your fellow students' posts."

» **The grading scheme and rubric:** These items may be on a separate page within your course, or they may be woven into either the syllabus or the instructions. The *grading scheme* is the overall plan for how you are graded. A *rubric* spells out what counts in an individual assignment. For example, a rubric may state that you need an on-time post of 300 to 500 words with proper citation, and you must respond to two peers. See Chapters 9 and 16 for the details on rubrics.

Avoiding overposting

Overposting can occur in two manners: writing too much and responding too frequently. Both have consequences.

» **Writing too much:** When your instructor asks for 300 to 500 words and you submit a three-page essay, you have overposted! The result is that your classmates won't read through your ideas, and no one will want to discuss them. You may be penalized for overwriting, too.

TIP

Before posting, count your words. You can do this in Microsoft Word by looking at the bottom of the document. Toward the left side you will see page x of y and then the number of words. You can also find this information by choosing File ⇨ Info (or Properties) from the menu at the top. You may need to isolate (highlight) the paragraph you want counted. In Google Docs, choose Tools ⇨ Word Count from the top menu bar.

>> **Responding too frequently:** You don't need to respond to everyone's posts. When your instructor asks for a minimum of 2 responses to others, they may be hoping for 4 or 5, but not 15 or 20!

Think of this in terms of the face-to-face classroom. How do you react to a student who has something to say to everyone's comments? Doesn't that person seem to be an attention-seeker? After a while, aren't the ideas a little self-serving? Do learners begin to roll their eyes when the commenter opens their mouth?

The same happens when learners overpost. However, in the world of online education, you can choose to avoid reading what those who overpost have to say. This is not always a good thing.

We like to encourage good discussion with quality posts. Think of contributing 10 percent of the comments. Discussions can grow exponentially, and you don't want to be the person whose posts no one reads because you're too prolific.

Tapping into Social Networks

What's popular online waxes and wanes. However, one idea that has passed the test of time is the notion that people like to connect socially with technology.

A social network starts with a website — like Facebook (www.facebook.com), Instagram, (www.instagram.com), or LinkedIn (www.linkedin.com) — that allows users to find other people like them, send messages to each other, and share bits and pieces of information. Say you're interested in artificial intelligence. A social network connection on LinkedIn could result in sharing articles or self-study programs, which could lead to a new career! This section addresses how to use social networks to your advantage academically and what to avoid.

Benefitting from communicating outside the virtual classroom

Because social networks are built on the principle of connecting people and because learning is largely social in the online classroom, using a social network in connection with your online education has several advantages:

>> **Supporting schoolwork:** If you organize a social network around the topic you're studying, you'll connect with people and resources that can help. Within that group, you can talk about how your coursework applies to the real world. You can look for people to follow and additional sources to read. Figure 11-5 shows a social network in action.

>> **Help after graduation:** Several social networking sites focus on professional connections more than personal ones. For example, LinkedIn (www.linkedin.com) promotes itself as a network for professionals seeking to maintain job-related contacts. The site organizes information by company so that you can find other people who may be helpful in job searches. After you complete your program or degree, you can ask classmates to become part of your network so that you can exchange ideas about job seeking, new prospects, and other topics. Your academic program might also support a group on LinkedIn so that you can meet alumni.

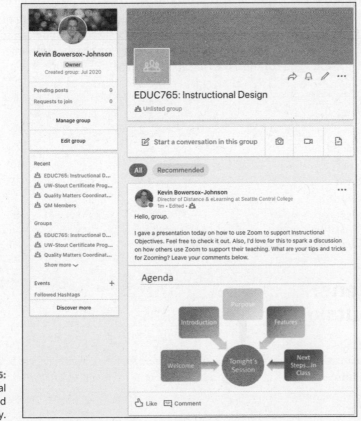

FIGURE 11-5:
A social network, used academically.

Avoiding distractions

TIP

Social networks can be distracting. Isn't it always more fun to talk socially than to study? If you think you want to use a social network to embellish your online education, consider these ideas to limit distractions:

>> **Keep your profile private.** Let only your immediate classmates know your username and contact information. That way, strangers won't seek you out.

>> **Don't add extra widgets and tools.** For example, you can add an application that allows you to save the rainforest or play trivia games, but these probably aren't related to what you're studying.

>> **Create separate accounts.** If you already use a social network and your class suggests establishing a group, consider signing up with a different email address and username. Keep your personal account and your school account separate so that you won't be tempted to jump from school to personal issues.

If you do commingle personal and academic accounts, be aware of how to set privacy limits within the tool. For example, on Facebook, you can control who sees your timeline, whether they can post to it, and who your other friends are. It's good to know how to set those limits.

IN THIS CHAPTER

» Scheduling time to study

» Surfing the Web with ease

» Reading course materials efficiently

» Using the virtual library

» Studying offline

Chapter **12**

Developing Good Study Habits for Online Courses

Many students taking an online class for the first time are not accustomed to the amount of self-discipline it takes to succeed. The most important habits you must establish when taking an online course are setting aside time to study and developing patterns of good studying behavior. In this chapter, we provide strategies for organizing and using your time wisely.

Setting Aside Time to Learn

When taking a face-to-face course, having class in a physical building on a specific day and time each week forces you to prioritize class time in your schedule. Friends and family understand why you're unavailable to hang out, make dinner, or go to the movies.

Other than the occasional synchronous (real-time) session, in the online environment, you're responsible for determining the days and times you will participate in class by logging in, reading and responding to discussion, and performing other academic tasks. As long as you meet deadlines, your schedule is really up to you. Therefore, you must have good time management skills to succeed.

Once your class begins, take time to review the workload and assignment deadlines; you can typically find this information in the documents we describe in Chapter 9, such as the course syllabus. Use this information to help you set a weekly schedule and make a commitment to stick to it. This section focuses on strategies to consider when you're determining how to plan your weekly study schedule.

On the other side of the coin, during the COVID-19 pandemic, both learners and instructors needed to use time management skills as a way to set boundaries. People were stuck in their homes and school was one escape people used to cope. As instructors, we saw dramatic increases in the number of posts students submitted. For example, Kevin's icebreaker activity for a class with 25 students went from an average of 75 total posts to nearly 300 posts. Schedules and boundaries can help prevent you from burning out. Schedules and boundaries also help you mentally prepare for the tasks ahead, even if you're still in the exact same physical space.

REMEMBER

Regardless of what you're working on, your study time should be scheduled (not incidental) and uninterrupted. See Chapter 8 for recommended strategies on this, even if you share space.

Working at your peak times

REMEMBER

Knowing when you're the most productive is important when scheduling study time. Studying when you're tired can lead to frustration and poor performance. For some, peak times are mornings, before the kids get up. When teaching, coauthor Susan started many of her mornings writing and grading student papers a few hours before her family woke and the school-prep frenzy began. Coauthor Kevin, on the other hand, takes time during his lunch hour or immediately after work before going home to complete his academic tasks. Whether you're an early bird or a night owl, set aside time that fits your schedule and lifestyle.

Checking in every day for a short time

TIP

To help you stay on top of classroom discussions, instructor announcements, and other basic course activities, set time aside to log in several times a week — daily, if possible. Sometimes you only need to set aside 15 to 30 minutes to keep up with what's going on. During these quick check-ins, you should

>> Check for new announcements from the instructor.

>> Check the course calendar to confirm that you're on track.

>> Read new discussion posts from peers. Respond only to posts that you have time for. If you need to take longer to think about a response, make note of the post so that you can return later. Most learning management systems (LMSs) have a way to flag (mark) a post so that you can come back to it easily.

>> Note any assignments that you plan to work on soon for reference purposes. See if there's a version you can download. (Sometimes, the instructions to a longer assignment may be stored as a PDF file.)

Calculating how much time you need to finish longer tasks

Some tasks require the allotment of a significant amount of time. For example, it may take longer to compose an original response to a discussion question (not a reply to what someone else wrote), complete assignments like projects or presentations, or take online quizzes.

REMEMBER

When we talk about estimating study time, we're not referring only to computer time. The fact that you're taking an online class doesn't mean you'll be learning only when you're in front of a computer. You'll complete many tasks offline as well. What you do offline is just as important as what you do online when scheduling your study time. (We discuss offline activities in more detail later in this chapter.)

Be sure not to make too many assumptions when estimating study time. For example, when calculating how much time it takes to complete an essay assignment, don't forget to count the time it takes to research the subject before sitting down in front of your computer to write it. Learners often overlook these details and scramble to complete their assignments at the last minute.

Though no two learners require the same amount of time to complete any one assignment, here's a list of tasks to consider when calculating the time it will take to complete an assignment:

>> **Understanding the assignment:** It takes time to read the assignment description and absorb what's being asked of you. More time may be needed if you have questions that need to be answered by the instructor. We recommend skimming all assignments provided to you within a unit or a module as soon as the instructor provides it to you. This explains what's expected of you and gives you plenty of time to ask clarifying questions if parts of an assignment are unclear.

>> **Prep time:** This refers to the time it takes you to lay the groundwork for the assignment. For example, some instructors require that all essays be completed using a specific document structure. Therefore, you have to set up a document with specific margin settings, a title page, page numbers, and a reference page. Those less familiar with these word processing features may take longer to do this before even focusing on the assignment details.

TIP

If your instructor requires you to use a specific document format for each assignment, create a template that you can use over and over again. For example, during his studies, coauthor Kevin was required to turn in all assignments using the institution's standard document structure — including a title page with the assignment's title, course ID, course title, instructor name, student name, institution name, and assignment due date. The document was also required to have 1-inch margins and page numbers in the upper right corner, be double-spaced, and have a references page at the end. So Kevin created a document with all this information, leaving the assignment title, course ID, course name, instructor, and due date blank. For each new assignment, he opened the document and immediately chose File ➪ Save As from the menu bar and saved the file in the appropriate course folder on his computer with an obvious filename. It took approximately 30 minutes to an hour to create the original template, but only one minute to customize it for every assignment.

>> **Research time:** For most assignments, you can't just sit down and write without having some background information. This involves doing research — reading chapters within your assigned textbook, conducting interviews with professionals in the field, watching a video, or conducting database searches at your virtual library. Graduate programs, especially, require you to write about more than just your opinions and experiences. You're required to back up your thoughts with theory and research analysis conducted within the field being discussed.

>> **Editing:** Editing refers to checking spelling, grammar, document formatting, and editorial style. *Editorial style* refers to the technical formatting in documents, including reference citations, punctuation, abbreviations, numbers, and more. Two common editorial styles are Modern Language Association (MLA) and American Psychological Association (APA). Becoming familiar with these styles can be time-consuming and can require a true attention to detail; flip to Chapter 15 for more about these styles.

>> **Learning new technology:** Some assignments may require you to use a technology you're unfamiliar with. Therefore, it takes additional time to learn how to use that technology. You may have to set time aside to watch tutorial videos, practice using the technology, or read any associated documentation.

Blocking off enough study time each week

Within the first week or so of an online class, you should establish a routine for studying. At first, set aside as much time as you can to read the syllabus, review the course calendar, and complete the first set of assignments. Make a mental note of how long it takes you to log in, navigate the virtual classroom, and complete assignments.

After the first week of class, plan out your weekly schedule, taking into account both daily check-ins and the larger blocks of time you'll need for finishing longer tasks. In Chapter 9 we talk about synchronizing your course, work, and personal calendars. Here, we ask you to take it a step further by adding specific tasks to your calendar. For example, if you set aside study time on Friday night from 7 to 9 P.M. in your calendar, you can divide that time into parts. From 7 to 7:30 you can check in with your course, read new posts, and confirm assignments. From 7:30 to 8:30 you can conduct research for the essay assignment that's due next week. And from 8:30 to 9 you can develop an outline for the essay based on your earlier research.

TIP

One way to help you determine how long it takes to complete a task is to simply jot down the start and stop times when studying. This is especially helpful during the first few weeks of a course. By doing this, you can better estimate how much time you really need to set aside on your calendar. It's amazing how little time most people think tasks will take.

Navigating the Web Efficiently

As you become more familiar with your virtual learning environment, you begin to spend less time focusing on navigation and more time actually completing assignments. This section provides some timesaving tips on navigating the web.

Keeping multiple browser windows open

When you're quickly checking in with new course happenings and responding to peers' posts, you may want to conduct some quick searches for resources to share. Keeping the course page open in your Internet browser tab while going off and searching for those resources in another browser window or tab can help you to quickly search for and then copy-and-paste information from one window to another.

On most Internet browser applications, new windows can be opened in either a new, floating window or in a tab within the existing window. Both methods are helpful:

» Figure 12-1 shows multiple floating windows. To open multiple windows in most Windows-based browsers and Chromebooks, hold down the Ctrl key and press n for *new* (Ctrl+n). Mac users, hold down the Command key and press n (Command+n).

» Figure 12-2 shows a single window open with multiple tabs. To open a new tab within a window in most Windows-based browsers and Chromebooks, hold down the Ctrl key and press t for *tab* (Ctrl+t). Mac users, hold down the Command key and press t (Command+t). We feel that the tabs are more organized and easier to keep track of.

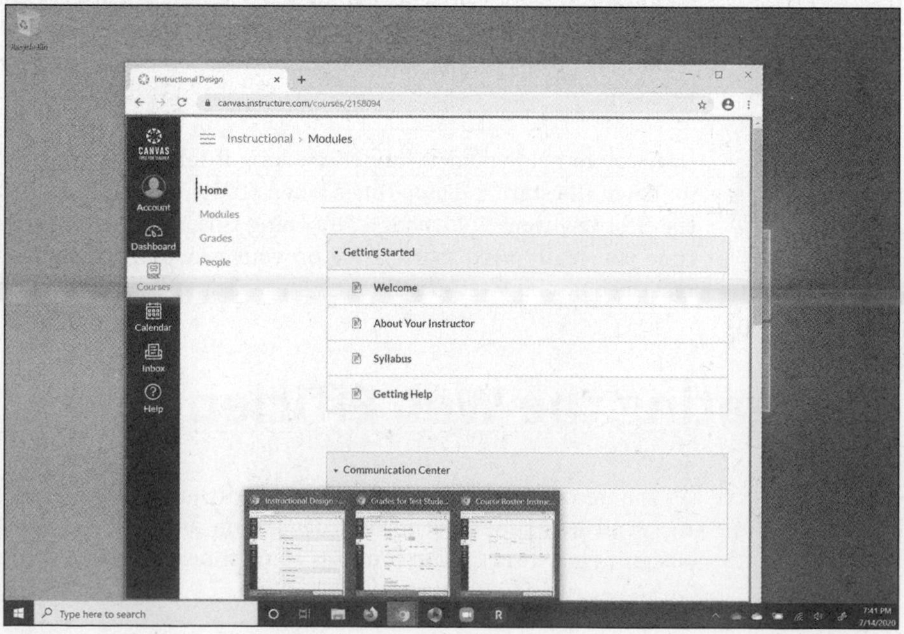

FIGURE 12-1: A full taskbar, showing multiple floating windows.

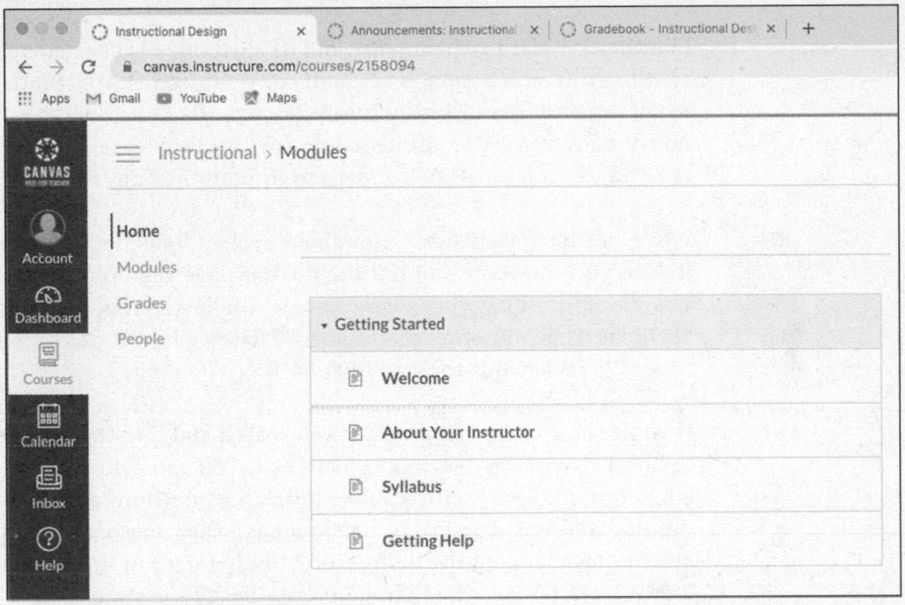

FIGURE 12-2:
A single window, with multiple tabs.

Permission for the use of this screenshot granted by the Board of Regents of the University of Wisconsin System on behalf of University of Wisconsin-Stout

How would you actually go about using separate browser windows to your advantage? Imagine reading a discussion post by one of your peers discussing a topic you recently researched for another assignment. You decide that you want to share with this peer a white paper you found during your previous research. While on the course page, you would open a new browser window (either a floating window or a new tab in the existing window), locate the resource on the web, copy the URL (web address), return to the window with your course information, and paste the URL in your reply. This saves you from getting lost in cyberspace by having to hit the Back button endlessly to find your course site.

TIP

When viewing course information, you may come across links to external resources. When you click on these links, they may open in the same window, overwriting your course information. You can force the link to open in a new window by right-clicking (Command+click for Mac users) and choosing either the Open in New Window or Open in New Tab option.

Avoiding time wasted by chasing links

Occasionally, when navigating within your virtual classroom, you click on a link and it sends you to a page with an error on it. This happens no matter how hard your instructor tries to share up-to-date information or how often they test those links before sharing them with you. It's just one of the challenges of utilizing web resources. It's easy enough to conduct a quick web search on the title of the article to see whether the URL may have changed. If a quick search doesn't yield results, notify your instructor immediately (privately, please, to spare embarrassment; see Chapter 11 for methods of private communication) and move on to other tasks.

TIP

When notifying your instructor about broken links, be sure to paste a copy of the link in your message and tell them what page the link was on inside the course. The more information you can provide, the faster your instructor can address the problem. This is another place where knowing how to take a screen shot can save time! We review this topic in Chapter 8.

If you're able to conduct a quick web search and find the working address, be sure to share it with the instructor via email. You can also share it with your peers if your course is set up with a public forum for questions and answers. When posting the updated link, be sure to use language that doesn't make the instructor look bad or place fault on the instructor. Simply mention that the link on a given page didn't work for you and that an alternative address was found.

Using social bookmarking tools

How many times have you come across the perfect resource on the web and then forgotten where you found it? This can be frustrating, not to mention time-consuming when searching for it again. We have an easy fix for you: Social book-marking tools are web-based tools that allow you to bookmark important web addresses and store them in cyberspace, not on your computer. (See Figure 12-3.) Yes, this means another login and password, but it's well worth the effort. Trust us!

Here are a few major benefits of social bookmarking tools:

>> **You can categorize your bookmarks using common search phrases, called *tags*.** Each bookmarked URL can have multiple tags assigned to it, making it easier to find in the future.

>> **You can choose to make each bookmarked address public or private.** If it's public, other Internet users can see your bookmarked addresses; some may find you because they use the same keywords you used to tag your resources. If it's marked as private, only you can see that bookmark associated with your account.

>> **You can get to your bookmarks from anywhere with an Internet connection.** So, if you want to get some homework done while on your lunch break at work, you don't have to worry that your bookmarks are on your home computer. A quick navigation to your social bookmarking tool brings all tagged bookmarks to your fingertips.

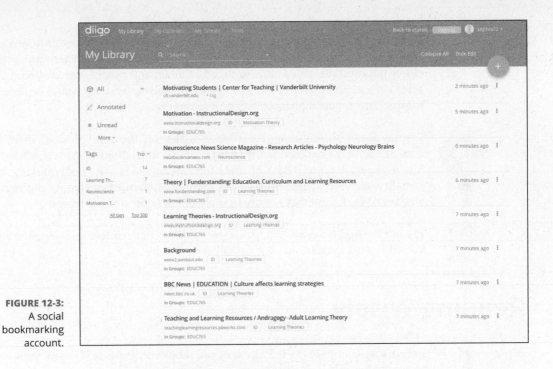

FIGURE 12-3:
A social
bookmarking
account.

Depending on your tech savviness, you can either have your social bookmarking website open in a separate tab or window and copy bookmarks to that site as you find them or see whether a browser plugin is available for your browser. A browser *plugin* allows you to add a toolbar to your browser whereby you can click a single button on any web page to add that page's address to your account.

Here's an example of a practical use for social bookmarking tools. Imagine researching the topic of conducting business in a foreign country. As you can imagine, tons of resources are available on the web about this topic. Some are good and others aren't so good. As you browse the web and find resources you want to read in more detail later, you can bookmark them and tag them with key-words (tags) such as Business, ForeignAffairs, or BUS120 if the assignment is for your Business 120 course. Later, when you're ready to review the resources in more detail, they're all in one place. The application is also set up in a manner that stores who else has saved the same URL. This allows you to link to that person's saved list, which gives you access to additional resources for your own research. You may find new material for your paper or project!

Newer versions of social bookmarking applications allow you to upload images, PDF files, and other documents to store and tag. This helps you keep all your resources in one place when conducting research.

By the way, you may have noticed that the ForeignAffairs tag doesn't have a space between the words. It's because tags often don't allow spaces. Therefore, you can either put multiple-word phrases together or separate them with a special character such as an underscore. If you choose the latter, your tag would be Foreign_Affairs. This tends to be more pleasing to the eye.

Several social bookmarking tools are available on the web. Most of them have similar features. Two commonly used tools include Diigo (www.diigo.com) and Mix (http://mix.com). Both of these tools provide adequate bookmarking functionality. However, Diigo offers a few additional features, including highlighting web text. We discuss this feature in more detail later in this chapter.

If you're using Microsoft 365, you have a built-in tool, called OneNote, that allows you to store, organize, and tag resources.

Reading Wisely

Because a majority of the information you receive online is text based, your ability to read efficiently is of the utmost importance. We're not just talking about reading comprehension here. We're also talking about your overall ability to navigate to and read important documents and posts quickly, as well as your ability to retain what you've read with note-taking and keep track of everything you've read so that you don't waste precious time rereading.

Finding the stuff you need to read

You can save time by knowing what information is in an online course and where to find it. The following sections introduce you to the type of information you find online and gives ideas for managing that information more efficiently.

News and announcements

Every instructor-led course has some kind of news-and-announcements section. This is often a one-way communication from the instructor to the learners, and it's required reading — no exceptions. Instructors use this feature to welcome learners to the course, remind them of deadlines, share additional resources, and assure students of the instructor's presence. (See Chapter 11 for more information about this method of communication.)

As instructors, this is one of our most utilized features within the virtual classroom. Our learners should expect to read a new post at least once every 48 hours — more during the first week or two of class. However, other instructors prefer other methods of communication, like email or posts within discussion forums. No matter what method your instructor uses, it's important that you read their posts and respond if necessary. You may be thinking that this might be a lot to manage, but usually these types of communication don't require a response and are for your benefit. Checking in with your class daily, as we suggest earlier in this chapter, and developing good tracking techniques can really help. Tracking techniques include filing messages in folders in your email and marking discussion posts as read (a feature found in most learning management systems).

Discussion postings

The heart of any online course is its content discussions. For example, one activity we use to engage students is to assign each student a discussion question pertaining to the current module's content. Students are required to respond to their assigned question, read other students' posts, and respond to at least two different student posts. Students are encouraged to read all posts, but respond only to those that interest them.

Using this example, simple math tells you that if you're in a class of 20 students, there should be a minimum of 60 posts at the end of this activity. Our experience says that you'll see closer to 200 posts. This is a good thing, assuming the posts are evenly distributed and don't come from four or five boisterous students. It means that students are engaged and dialoguing about the topic. However, it can be quite overwhelming if not managed correctly. Here are a few tips to consider when participating in such an activity (see Chapter 11 for additional information on discussions):

>> **Focus on your assigned question as soon as possible:** As soon as you know your assigned question, begin reading, researching, and formulating your response. The sooner you do this, the more time you have to focus on reading and responding to your peers (and the more time your peers have to respond to you).

>> **Set aside time to check in and read new posts:** When possible, take 15 minutes every day to check in and read new posts, as we suggest earlier in this chapter.

>> **Respond to posts:** If it's easier for you, based on your time schedule, respond to two students in one sitting.

>> **Check responses:** Take time to check and see whether anyone has responded to your initial post and whether a reply is needed. Also check the threads you responded to and determine whether further discussion is appropriate.

Most discussions occur while you're working on other course assignments in the background. Be sure to schedule enough time to manage both.

At times, you and/or your peers will want to discuss topics that don't relate to the course content. Most courses have a social forum for this purpose. This keeps off-topic discussion from interrupting the flow of content discussions. This can be a useful resource, but don't feel bad if you're too busy to read any new posts in this forum. Feel free to ignore them. You can always go back and read them later, when you have more time.

Assigned readings

Just like in the face-to-face environment, each online course uses a variety of course materials to support the curriculum. You may be asked to purchase one or more textbooks, download Internet-based resources, or link to "lectures" written by the instructor. It's not uncommon to be asked to read 60 to 100 pages per week. We estimate that our learners need to dedicate approximately two to four hours to reading the assigned materials in an 8-week, 3-credit course. If you want to succeed in your course, don't skip these readings! Be sure to block off plenty of time in your study schedule for them, as we suggest earlier in this chapter.

Depending on the course structure, you may find course readings in the syllabus or course calendar or at the beginning of every module. For example, in Kevin's course, you would find the readings in two places: in the syllabus and in an introduction page at the beginning of every module. This allows his learners to read ahead if they want (they have access to all readings in the syllabus) without being able to post discussions early (content modules are opened one at a time as needed).

Deciding whether to print online reading material

Printing isn't a requirement when working online. If you feel comfortable downloading everything to your computer and reading it from there, go for it. Portability is probably more important. If you're one of those students who likes to read whenever you get a free minute, printing can help. Printed documents are easier to take on the bus, stash in your backpack or briefcase, and pull out during downtimes. Printed documents are also easier to highlight and jot notes on. A friend who is a mother of two on-the-go children reads between chauffeur duties and during athletic practices. (We have more to say about working offline later in this chapter.)

Feel green with guilt? For the more environmentally conscious, print on recycled paper and print on both sides. You can also print everything in draft form and save ink.

Or, another idea is to buy an inexpensive tablet that allows you to read digitally but be portable.

Increasing the font size in your browser to help you read more easily

In an effort to squeeze as much information on a page as possible, some web designers use smaller fonts. Internet browsers allow you to expand the text size so that it's more manageable to read. You may have to use the scroll bars more, but that's better than eyestrain. Figure 12-4 shows how to zoom your text inside a web browser. In most browsers, the zoom feature is on the View menu in the application's toolbar at the top of the screen.

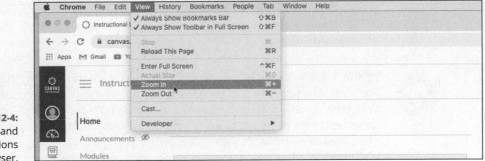

FIGURE 12-4:
The View and Zoom options inside a browser.

Taking notes on what you read

Taking notes while reading helps you organize your thoughts, recall information, and reduce the amount of rereading. Here are some guidelines for this task:

>> **Grasp the main ideas:** As you read, take note of the main ideas presented in the materials. Paraphrase this information in your own words and quote anything that you use directly from the materials.

>> **Test your knowledge:** While taking notes, ask yourself why you're reading this chapter and see whether your notes are able to provide you with a correct answer. Still not sure? Read the abstract or conclusion, which summarizes the material. Then go back and reread for more details.

TIP

>> **Note your opinions and experiences:** As you read, if you have an opinion about something or recall an experience that relates to the information, write it down.

>> **Decide whether to write in your book:** If you plan to resell your textbook, remember that highlights and handwritten notes in the margins decrease its resale value. Consider purchasing a notebook for each course for the purpose of taking notes while reading.

>> **Bookmark Internet resources:** As you search the web, bookmark articles you may want to reference again. Bookmark websites even if you decide to print the information. (See the next section.) Nothing is more frustrating than trying to find an article you remember reading last week.

>> **Save articles and citation information:** When conducting database searches within your virtual library, you can't bookmark results pages. Therefore, it's important to download the actual article, if possible, and/or document the citation information for future reference.

>> **Keep track of reference information:** Don't forget to write down the source information based on your instructor's preferred editorial style, such as APA or MLA. You'll need this information to give proper credit when referring to concepts and ideas gleaned from the source. We say more about citation tools in Chapter 15.

TIP

By this time, it should be no surprise that there's a digital answer to note-taking. For those who prefer to read everything online, you can use products that allow you to highlight and annotate documents, including PDF files and web pages. Some of these tools even allow you to make your notes public for others to read. Figure 12-5 illustrates an example of a web-based program, Diigo (www.diigo.com), that allows highlighting. Diigo has a browser plugin that adds a toolbar to the top of your browser. One of the tools is a highlighter tool that allows you to highlight text on the web page you're browsing.

Keeping track of everything you've already read

In the earlier section "Checking in every day for a short time," we discuss the need to establish a pattern of logging in. Well, this is where it pays off. To give you a little perspective, we want to share with you the number of discussion posts alone that make up our classes. After eight weeks of teaching, an average of 2,500 posts have been submitted by students and the instructor. This includes discussion posts, announcements made by the instructor, and social conversations held in the virtual student lounge. As you can imagine, it's important to know how to determine what's new and how to track what you've already read.

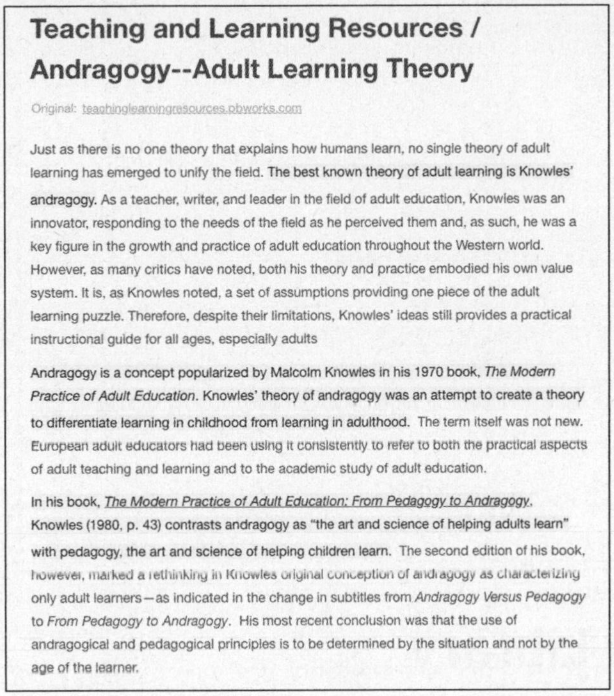

Teaching and Learning Resources /
Andragogy--Adult Learning Theory

Original: teachinglearningresources.pbworks.com

Just as there is no one theory that explains how humans learn, no single theory of adult learning has emerged to unify the field. The best known theory of adult learning is Knowles' andragogy. As a teacher, writer, and leader in the field of adult education, Knowles was an innovator, responding to the needs of the field as he perceived them and, as such, he was a key figure in the growth and practice of adult education throughout the Western world. However, as many critics have noted, both his theory and practice embodied his own value system. It is, as Knowles noted, a set of assumptions providing one piece of the adult learning puzzle. Therefore, despite their limitations, Knowles' ideas still provides a practical instructional guide for all ages, especially adults

Andragogy is a concept popularized by Malcolm Knowles in his 1970 book, *The Modern Practice of Adult Education*. Knowles' theory of andragogy was an attempt to create a theory to differentiate learning in childhood from learning in adulthood. The term itself was not new. European adult educators had been using it consistently to refer to both the practical aspects of adult teaching and learning and to the academic study of adult education.

In his book, *The Modern Practice of Adult Education: From Pedagogy to Andragogy*, Knowles (1980, p. 43) contrasts andragogy as "the art and science of helping adults learn" with pedagogy, the art and science of helping children learn. The second edition of his book, however, marked a rethinking in Knowles original conception of andragogy as characterizing only adult learners—as indicated in the change in subtitles from *Andragogy Versus Pedagogy* to *From Pedagogy to Andragogy*. His most recent conclusion was that the use of andragogical and pedagogical principles is to be determined by the situation and not by the age of the learner.

FIGURE 12-5: Highlighting a web page within a browser using a text highlighter tool.

Most learning management systems have an information section on the course's home page that alerts you to any new information posted since the last time you logged on. (See Figure 12-6 for an example.) This summary usually includes links directly to that information. When you click on the link, it takes you directly to the unread information. The system automatically tracks where you have clicked and updates the new information summary accordingly.

Other learning management systems provide you with more control by requiring you to manually mark information as read or unread. Either way, find out how your institution's system identifies newly posted information and take advantage of this feature. To find out whether your system has this feature, review the support materials often found by clicking on a Help button on the screen, contact technical support, or ask your instructor. Because your instructor must be able to manage a lot of information within the system (student posts, assignment submissions, and so forth), they're probably fairly well versed in using the tool efficiently.

Another feature your system may have is the ability to have new information emailed to you. Depending on your personal preference, this can help you keep up with new information as it's posted, or it can be a distraction from your daily activities. To find out whether your system has this feature, again, review the support materials often found by clicking on a Help button on the screen, contact technical support, or ask your instructor.

FIGURE 12-6:
Your learning management system can alert you to new information.

Visiting the Library

During the course of your class, you're expected to complete assignments that require you to conduct research and summarize your findings. Trust us when we say that searching on Google is not enough. As a matter of fact, most graduate courses are now adding a "No Google" clause in their syllabuses to discourage students from citing sources that aren't reputable.

So, you have a choice: Jump in the car and drive to your local library, or sit comfortably in your PJs at your computer and log in to your institution's virtual library. Don't get us wrong: We love libraries and feel they're an asset to any community. However, as an online student, you may need access at times when your local library isn't open. Knowing where your local library is and its hours of operation is a great backup plan, though.

This section explains how to access your institution's online library, provides some basic pointers on using an online library for research, and clues you in on the value of library tutorials.

REMEMBER

You should access the library whenever you need external resources to support opinions or positions and/or to provide cited materials as required by the instructor. Your experience helps you apply theory to practical situations. However, you shouldn't rely on your experience alone. Instructors want you to reference course readings and external resources so that they know you understand the material.

Accessing the library

Each institution has a different way for you to access the library. Some have a link to the library on their home pages, and others have links to the library in every course. If you didn't learn how to access the library in any of your orientation materials and it's not obvious within a few minutes of looking around, ask your instructor. When you find the link, it most likely takes you to the library's own home page or portal. Depending on how the institution connects to the library, you may or may not be required to log in using a different username and password than the one you use to access your class. Figure 12-7 provides an example of an online library portal. Notice that it has sections with tutorials, databases, and information specific to distance education students.

FIGURE 12-7: An online library portal.

Permission for the use of this Screen Shot granted by the Board of Regents of the University of Wisconsin System on behalf of University of Wisconsin-Stout

The nice thing about libraries today is that most of them provide 24/7 access to their online databases and resources. Therefore, the times that you can access the library aren't controlled by strict hours of operation. However, if you think you may need help, knowing the availability of help staff is important. Libraries use a variety of telecommunication devices to provide support to students and faculty. For example, coauthor Kevin's favorite method of contacting help from his institution's library is via its text-based, instant chat messenger. If he has a question when browsing the library site, he simply clicks on the Chat with a Librarian button, which immediately connects him to a live person.

If your library has a Chat button, it's usually on the library's home page or a static section of the site that follows you from page to page, such as the header or sidebar navigation menu. Most live Chat buttons use text to tell you whether a librarian is available. For example, when available, the button may read something like Chat with a Librarian Now, but it may say something like Chat Is Unavailable when staff aren't logged in. Sometimes the button disappears completely when librarians are unavailable. Check your library's home page for hours of operation. You can usually find staffing hours there, including live chat hours.

Doing research online

As an online student, you need the library primarily to conduct research for papers and projects. You may be surprised by the similarities between a virtual library visit and a visit to a physical library. You determine the kinds of materials you need, you search for them via databases and the card catalog, and then you determine what's worth checking out to take home. These processes require decision-making and knowledge of what makes a source credible and useful.

Begin the research process as early as possible. Just because you have access to the institution's online database doesn't mean that everything you want will be available in a format you can download immediately. You may be required to have materials mailed to you, get them from other sources such as your local library, or find an alternative resource. This process can take time.

Figuring out the type of material you need

Before you begin to search for resources for a course or an assignment, consider the type of material best suited for your research. Scholarly literature is often the most appropriate for college level research, so you should be able to identify it.

Scholarly materials appear in journals. They're academic or scholarly in nature and may be available in print or online. Scholarly journals can be easily accessed via academic library databases and usually have at least some of the following features. They

>> Have long articles (five or more pages)

>> Are written by scholars or authorities in their fields (and aren't anonymous)

>> Have a bibliography, references, citations, or footnotes

>> Contain jargon (language that pertains to the field)

>> Often (but not always) contain graphs or charts

>> Report original, scholarly research

>> Are written to relay information to other scholars in the field

>> Are often peer-reviewed or -refereed, which means that the article must undergo a review process of scholars in that particular field to be accepted into the journal

Accessing online library databases

Databases are electronic collections of information. Periodical databases provide citations and full-text articles for journal, magazine, or newspaper articles. Online catalogs are also databases that allow you to search for materials in a library by author, title, subject heading, keyword, or call number.

When your instructor assigns you the task of finding a journal article in your discipline, look first in a database specific to that field. In most cases, your institution's library portal will have specific links to find different types of resources, such as books, articles, reserves, and/or media, directly on the home page. These links take you to a search form that often allows you to search by keywords and subject. You also have an advanced search option that allows you to search by other variables, such as author, journal title, or year.

Conducting searches by subject or keyword

When you search for materials on a specific topic, you most likely need to begin with a subject or keyword search.

>> **When you search by subject, you're searching for items that have been identified with a specific and standardized heading.** If a subject heading is available that is closely related to your topic, this often produces more useful and relevant results than a keyword search. Subject headings are usually generic field titles such as Business, Education, Engineering, Physical Science, or Social Sciences.

>> **Searching by keyword allows you to use a combination of keywords that may appear in any of the fields within a record.** The keywords you use might appear in the titles, authors, subject headings, publishers, or abstracts, so your results will usually be broader and may be unrelated to your topic.

Keyword searches are more flexible, though, and subject headings may not always exist for your topics.

TIP

When doing a keyword search, use only the most relevant keywords for your topic. Don't include words like *effect, cause, relationship, pros and cons,* or prepositions (like *of, at, to,* or *in*), because these ineffectively limit your search. For example, imagine that you need to research the current state and perceived effectiveness of accessibility efforts in education. It's best to focus on the two main ideas: accessibility and education. Leave out the extraneous details in your search. Figure 12-8 illustrates an example of a keyword database search on this topic.

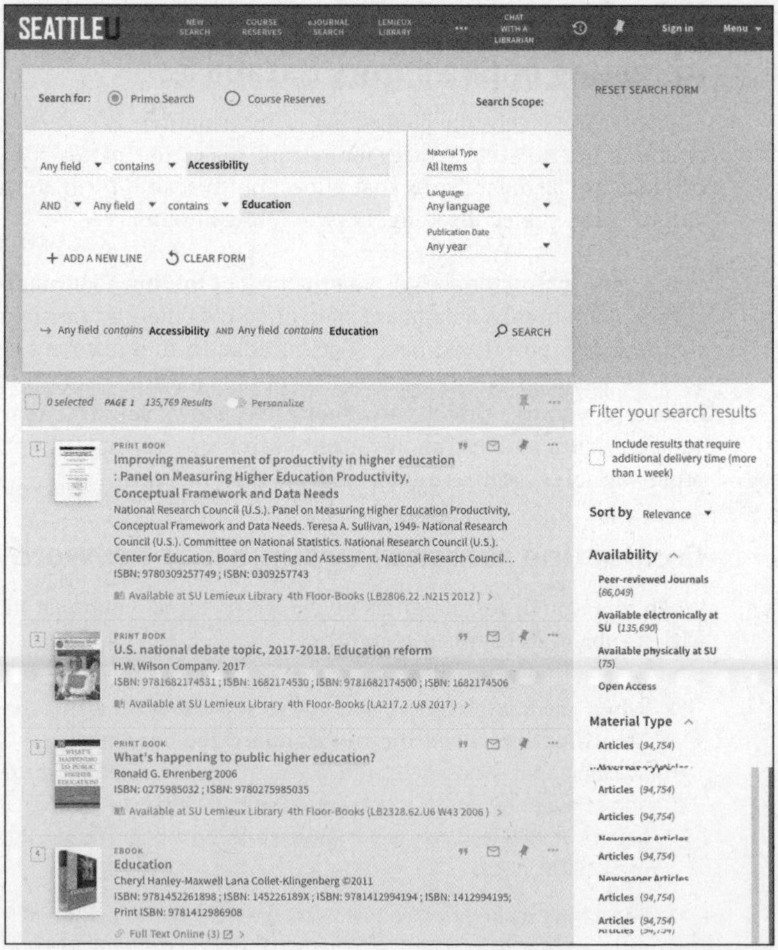

FIGURE 12-8:
An example of a keyword database search.

Determining the quality of your sources

When conducting research, you'll find several sources of information about your topic. However, don't just accept information at face value. As you search the web or library databases, critically evaluate each resource to ensure its quality. Here are a few questions you can ask yourself to help assess the quality of the resources you find:

>> **Accuracy:** Are there footnotes, citations, and/or a bibliography? Is the information free from error?

>> **Authority:** Is there an author? What are their credentials? Is the author well-known in their respective field?

>> **Objectivity:** Is there a minimum level of bias? Is the author trying to sway the reader's opinion? Why was the document created?

>> **Relevancy:** When was the document created? Is the information up-to-date for the subject?

>> **Coverage:** Is the information in-depth? Is the information valuable for your topic?

>> **Readership:** Who is the intended audience? Is the material appropriate for college-level research?

Watching tutorials on the library site

TIP

Most libraries have links to tutorials that provide additional tips on how to conduct database searches and check for quality. Take time to review these tutorials. The time it takes to review the search tips alone is returned twofold in the time they save you when conducting research. Pay attention to tips and tricks on searching using Boolean commands and truncation methods of searching. These help make searching more efficient and help you get the information you want by reducing the number of unnecessary search results.

Working Offline

The fact that you're taking a course online doesn't mean that you're learning only when you're logged in to your class. As a matter of fact, you may find that you spend more time thinking about your class and working on assignments offline than online. Working offline has a lot of advantages:

TIP

>> **Reading offline:** Printing documents or reading texts away from the computer allows you to take documents with you when you're on the go. It also saves on eyestrain from reading your computer screen. You can also take notes more easily on printed materials.

>> **Writing offline:** Some learning management systems time-out and cause you to lose your connection if you sit on the same screen too long. This means that you may lose all your hard work if you take too long to write a discussion post before posting it. Therefore, we recommend that you first type all your assignments, including discussion posts, in a word processor of your choice. By doing this, you can save as you go and then paste the final product into the learning management system when you're finished. This process automatically creates a backup copy of all your work. If for any reason the system fails to accept your post, you can quickly repost by opening your document and copying-and-pasting the information again.

Chapter 13

Getting a Handle on Group Dynamics

D o you smile or cringe when you hear the words *group project?* We find that learners have extreme views: Either they truly appreciate group projects or they really detest them. Those who appreciate working in a group have had positive experiences and see the value multiple people can bring to a project. Others have had a bad experience working with peers who have done nothing, leaving them to pick up the slack.

One of the most frequent questions we get from learners and other instructors we train is "Why group work?" Besides the typical "Because we said so" or the over-used cliché "Two heads are better than one," educational research supports the use of groups as a means of helping students amass and retain knowledge. Not to mention the opportunity it gives them to learn and practice marketable skills.

This book serves as a testament to the power of distant collaboration. Not only do we, your humble authors, live in different states, but so do the editors and other technical staff who put this book together. Some of us have no idea what the other contributors look like. Most communication occurs via email. So, when we ask our learners to complete online group projects, we truly are helping them learn marketable skills that easily transfer to the workplace.

Online collaboration takes time, communication, organization, and dedication on the part of all group members. This chapter provides you with strategies for successfully participating in online groups and communicating effectively with peers, including in times of conflict.

Making Your Online Group Successful

So how do online groups work? Just like in the face-to-face classroom, an instructor may ask learners to create a common document or product as a team. Learners may be able to pick their group members, or groups may be assigned by the instructor. (In most cases, the instructor assigns groups to save time.) Learners contribute to the final product by sharing research, writing, and editing responsibilities. The difference for online students is that they must be organized enough to do this from a distance. The following sections talk about how to make the overall collaboration process successful.

REMEMBER

It seems like the world changed in a matter of weeks, thanks to COVID-19, but many of us were already doing group projects online — as part of our work responsibilities. The world of work, especially in large corporations with multiple locations, requires workers to collaborate on projects across locations. What you're about to read pertains to online learning as well as online working!

TIP

Keep in mind that you'll do some of the following steps at the same sitting. For example, you may make your introduction and initial posts about establishing roles one right after the other — before others even have time to reply. Otherwise, the time it takes to wait for replies in the asynchronous environment can delay your progress to the point of no return. Take initiative, and don't be afraid to be the first to post your thoughts regarding next steps and the process for taking those steps. In most cases, others go along with ideas presented first as a way of moving forward with the project. Be sure to post in a manner that is respectful and doesn't seem pushy. Otherwise, your plan may backfire.

Introducing yourself in a group forum

After your group has been given its assignment, it's time to introduce yourself to your fellow group members so that you can begin organizing the project. Most likely your instructor will provide you with a private discussion forum to communicate with one another. From the students' perspective, these forums look and function like any other discussion forums. (See Chapter 11 for an introduction to discussions.) The only difference is that only you, your fellow group members, and your instructor can access it.

TIP

You can organize this forum by creating new discussion threads specific to conversation topics. For example, your first thread might be titled Group Introductions. Figure 13-1 illustrates an online discussion forum that's organized in this manner.

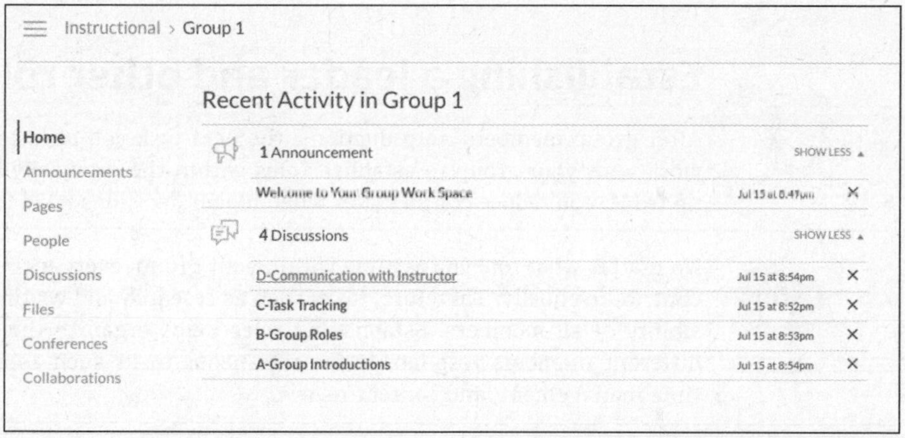

FIGURE 13-1:
An example of a discussion forum for a group.

> Instructional › Group 1
>
> ### Recent Activity in Group 1
>
> **Home**
> Announcements
> Pages
> People
> Discussions
> Files
> Conferences
> Collaborations
>
> 📣 **1 Announcement**   SHOW LESS ▲
> Welcome to Your Group Work Space   Jul 15 at 8.47pm   ✕
>
> 💬 **4 Discussions**   SHOW LESS ▲
> D-Communication with Instructor   Jul 15 at 8:54pm   ✕
> C-Task Tracking   Jul 15 at 8:52pm   ✕
> B-Group Roles   Jul 15 at 8:53pm   ✕
> A-Group Introductions   Jul 15 at 8:54pm   ✕

Before you jump too deep into the content of your assignment, it's important to set a collaborative tone among your teammates. We recommend introducing yourself as soon as possible. Your introduction should be brief and provide essential contact information. Provide the following information in your introduction:

REMEMBER

>> **Name and brief introduction:** Include a brief background of any experience you may have in the subject matter, your professional goals, and any skills that may help complete the assignment.

>> **Contact information:** Include as many methods for contacting you as possible, including your school email address and mobile phone number for texting. Feel free to include any parameters and conditions around this information as well, such as no texting after 9 P.M. your local time. Be sure to include your time zone so that your peers can respect any time restrictions you may ask of them.

>> For security purposes, we recommend not providing home addresses. If by any chance your group is able to meet face-to-face, choose a public location, such as a library or a coffee shop.

>> **Available times to meet synchronously:** Provide your peers with the days and times you're able to meet synchronously. (We discuss having real-time meetings in more detail later in this chapter.)

>> **Your desired role:** If you have a preferred role you want to take, this is the time to share it. Whether you want to be the group leader or the editor or take on another role, let the group know. The sooner you do this, the more likely you are to get what you want. (See the next section for more about the roles of group members.)

Establishing a leader and other roles

After group members' introductions, the next task you need to accomplish is to work with your group to establish roles within the group. By establishing roles up front, you reduce conflict later when bigger decisions need to be made.

REMEMBER

No matter what role you assume within your group, every member is expected to contribute equally. Therefore, tasks such as research and writing are the responsibility of all members. Establishing roles helps organize the group by making different members responsible for extraneous tasks such as content structure, time management, and content review.

Here are a few roles to consider when establishing your group:

>> **Leader:** The group's leader is responsible for the overall management of the project. The leader's job is to facilitate the processes for setting deadlines, delegating tasks, and staying on track.

>> **Editor:** The editor's job is to critically review each group member's contribution and comment on grammar, spelling, content quality, consistency in language usage, and so on.

>> **Submitter:** The submitter's role is to format and submit the final draft of the project to the instructor on behalf of the group.

If your group is communicating via the discussion forums, one member needs to initiate some kind of voting process for deciding on roles. We recommend that you take the initiative and post your preferred role as soon as possible in the appropriate discussion topic. For example, if you have leadership skills and want to volunteer for this role, simply write something like this: "Hey, everyone! I'm really looking forward to working with each of you on this project. I'd be happy to take on the leader role if no one is opposed to it. I recommend that we post our preferred roles and vote on them by Wednesday so that we can move forward with the project. Let me know what you think." If the group has more workers than roles to fill, that's okay. What's most important is that each person's complete workload is equal to the other members of the group. So the editor may do less research and actual writing as a way of leveling the playing field.

Setting up a group schedule

Whether your group plans to meet in real time (see the next section) or communicate solely in an asynchronous fashion (via email and your private discussion forum), creating a group schedule is important. Your schedule should include task benchmarks, deadlines, and formal progress check-ins. Be sure to document the schedule and post progress information in a location where your instructor can see it (such as inside a topic titled Group Progress). One way of making sure everyone understands the schedule and their responsibilities is to post the schedule within a discussion topic and ask all members to reply to the post with a simple statement such as, "I have read and agree to meet the deadlines provided within the posted schedule." This makes everyone accountable for completing their part. Table 13-1 is an example of what a group project schedule might look like:

TABLE 13-1   Example of a Group Project Schedule

Day	Task
Monday, January 25	Everyone conducts initial research on topic.
Wednesday, January 27	Everyone submits three ideas to include in the project in a private discussion forum.
Thursday, January 28 Synchronous session scheduled for 8:00 to 9:00 P.M. (Central time)	Leader compiles submissions to a single document and distributes the document via email to all members before the synchronous session. Everyone votes on the top five items to include in project in Collaborate (synchronous session).
Friday, January 29	Leader delegates research topics to group members in private discussion forum.
Saturday, January 30	Everyone conducts research.
Friday, February 5	Everyone posts draft of research in Google Docs.
Sunday, February 7	Editor edits draft and submits for group comment in Google Docs.
Wednesday, February 10	Everyone posts comments on draft in Google Docs.
Friday, February 12	Editor makes final edits in Google Docs.
Sunday, February 14	Submitter posts final project to public forum.

TIP

Not sure what Google Docs is all about? Don't worry: We talk more about it later in this chapter.

Meeting in real time

Completing tasks in an asynchronous environment can take a while, as you wait for peers to reply to posts, answer emails, and so on. Therefore, we recommend that you find a way to meet synchronously, or in real time, especially during the initial organizing stage. And, if you and your group have the ability to meet synchronously multiple times throughout the project, take advantage of it. (See the later section "Web conferencing" for details on methods you can use to meet synchronously.)

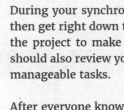

By scheduling definite start and stop times for your meeting and then sticking to the schedule, you force yourselves to stay on task.

During your synchronous meetings, you should briefly introduce yourselves and then get right down to business. Your first meeting should include an overview of the project to make sure all members of the group are on the same page. You should also review your established roles and begin to break down the project into manageable tasks.

After everyone knows what the project tasks are, the leader can delegate them to the group and set deadlines for each. Future meetings can be used to check in on each other's progress and discuss any problems or issues you may be having. These meetings are usually very short and are meant to keep everyone on track.

Want to impress the group and make your meeting run even more smoothly? Create an agenda ahead of time that provides your interpretation of the project and your recommended tasks and deadlines. The more you bring to the table, the faster you can complete the meeting and focus on completing the project. Consider doing this even if roles have not been determined yet and no one has been elected as the group's leader. A quick message to the group via email or discussion forum post to let them know you're planning to do this will help communicate your dedication to the project's success and reduce the chances of someone else duplicating work.

If your web conferencing tool has a Record option, be sure to record your meeting so that your group and your instructor can review it later, if needed. If recording isn't an option, a group member should be assigned the role of secretary, and that person should post a brief overview of each meeting, outlining tasks and deadlines, in your group's private discussion forum. This strategy helps your group and your instructor stay up-to-date on your group's progress.

Speaking of your instructor, feel free to invite them to your group's synchronous meetings. They may not be able to attend, but at least you're keeping them in the loop. If they do attend, conduct your meeting as usual and allow them to lurk in the background. However, don't be afraid to take advantage of their presence by asking questions, if needed.

Using collaborative tools

As you find out in the following sections, you can use quite a few web-based tools to collaborate and communicate with your group. These tools are often external to your learning management system. Many of these tools are free for public use.

REMEMBER

The key is to either use tools that are simple to learn or use only tools that every member of the group is already familiar with. Trying to learn a new tool in the middle of a group project can be frustrating and can distract you from completing the project on time.

Document collaboration

Suppose you and your fellow group members are asked to produce a written document such as an essay. In the "old" days, one person would write something and forward the document to all other group members. Then everyone would provide feedback and send back their comments individually. The originator would have to open several documents and do the best job possible of combining the input of the others.

No longer is this necessary, thanks to collaborative tools such as Google Docs and Microsoft 365. These web-based tools allow multiple people to contribute to the same document. In a group project situation, this means that you can collaborate on the same document at the same time as your fellow group members. The file is created by one of the group members who shares a link to the other group members with permission to edit the document. As a group member, you click on the link and are taken directly to the document, where you can start editing.

REMEMBER

Depending on the privacy setting determined by the original document creator, you may be required to log in with your account or create a new account with that service in order to access the document.

Technology has come a long way where applications on the web look almost exactly the same as they do when installed directly on your computer. Therefore, when you get to the shared document via your web browser, it looks and feels just like a common word processing, spreadsheet, or presentation program. It doesn't matter what software you have on your individual machines, because everything is handled online! Each of you can edit and download a copy. Eventually, one of you can save a final copy and turn it in for your assignment or link your instructor and class to the page. Online document sharing can be used for group projects, company policy documents, and much more.

TIP

In some corporate setups, you may have access to a product from Microsoft called SharePoint. If you have access and are working on an online learning course in your company's learning management system, SharePoint may be the best choice for you because you're probably already using it for work.

One of the more common online document sharing applications on the web right now is Google Docs (http://docs.google.com). With Google Docs, you can collaboratively create a word processing document, spreadsheet, presentation, or web form. This free service gives a document originator the ability to invite others to edit the document. Figure 13-2 shows a document created using Google Docs.

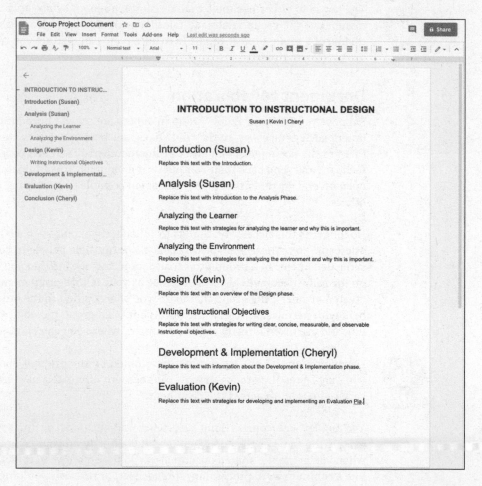

FIGURE 13-2: An example of a group project document using Google Docs.

For your essay assignment, one group member or the instructor would start the document. Then that person would invite the other group members to view the document as collaborators in order to provide them the permission needed to edit the document. Based on your group's organizational meeting, the editor might add headings to the document as a way of visually dividing it into pieces. Group members would then go in and begin filling in the blanks as they completed their research.

Web conferencing

REMEMBER

If your group decides to meet synchronously, a few tools are available to help facilitate the process. Consider the following variables when choosing a synchronous tool:

» **Availability:** Don't spend extra time looking for tools if your course provides them for you. For example, one institution Kevin teaches for provides each class with a virtual office space via Microsoft Teams. Students can access this space 24x7 from directly inside their virtual course.

» **Functionality:** Some tools are limited as to which features they offer. For example, the telephone provides voice communication, but you can't share documents via the phone. FaceTime allows iPhone users to call, talk, and share videos with each other. However, this is limited to iPhone users only. If you have an iPhone, you cannot FaceTime with someone who has an Android phone. Plus, it may not be the best tool for sharing screens and collaborating. Other, more multimodal tools, such as Zoom, provide interactive features that allow users to share voice, text, presentations, whiteboards, each other's computer screens, and more. Choose your tools according to what you need, or learn to work around your chosen tool's limits.

» **Cost:** These tools can be quite expensive for large-scale use. Luckily these days, many tools have free versions that may have some limitations compared to their paid versions that you can use and will work just fine for short, small-group meetings. For example, Zoom offers a free version of its Meeting tool that allows you to access almost all of its collaboration features. The limitations of this tool are that meetings are limited to 40 minutes and meetings cannot be recorded to the Zoom server in the cloud. You must record locally and find alternative ways to share those video recordings with others for playback.

Three available synchronous communication tools are Zoom, Microsoft Teams, and Google Meet:

```
https://zoom.us
```

» **Zoom** is what we call a *multimodal* web conferencing tool. *Multimodal* refers to the user's ability to interact using a variety of methods. For example, Zoom allows users to interact using voice, chat, video, whiteboard, application sharing, and more. The free version of Zoom allows you to meet with up to 100 participants for 40 minutes. The free version also allows you to record to your local computer so that you can later share the archive with members who may have missed the meeting or need a recap.

To efficiently use this tool, one group member needs to have a Zoom account. The individual with the account schedules a meeting and invites the group members via email. Group members receive a participant link in their email that they click on to join the meeting. Figure 13-3 illustrates a conference call using Zoom.

FIGURE 13-3:
A group call using Zoom.

Once connected, the group can use the voice and video features to see and hear each other. One member of the group can also share their screen so that the group can work collaboratively to create a document or presentation or another type of project. If you're not in the creation stage yet, it's also a good idea to share the agenda with everyone and have someone take notes during the meeting and then make the notes available in a place where everyone can access them.

```
www.microsoft.com/en-us/microsoft-365/microsoft-teams/free
```

» **Microsoft Teams** is a tool, similar to Zoom, that provides unlimited chat, video calling, file sharing, and 10 gigabytes of storage to share and collaborate on documents. Participants use the same process for accessing meetings as they do with Zoom. At least one member of the group must have a Microsoft 365 account. That person schedules the meeting and sends out the invitation to their peers.

Teams is fully integrated into Microsoft 365, and participants can seamlessly share Word, PowerPoint, and Excel files with participants. This can be helpful if your group is needing to collectively contribute to an essay or develop a slideshow in order to give a group presentation. Figure 13-4 illustrates a Teams meeting with group members collaborating to build a PowerPoint file.

>> **Google Meet** is the synchronous conferencing tool built into Google Suite. Like the others, one person must have a Google account and invite the others. If your school already uses Google Suite for email and document storage, you may as well use Meet. Imagine having a meeting with your voice, but co-editing a document! Figure 13-5 shows a meeting in Meet.

TIP

For conferencing tools such as Zoom, users need a microphone and speakers. We recommend a combination headset with microphone. A camera is optional, but it can give a more personal touch to the distant meeting experience.

If you have ever attended an online meeting, you know that the discussion can get out of hand quickly. People may unintentionally talk over each other, or there may be so many chats that you can't keep up with them. To help reduce this chaos, web conferencing tools assign different roles and permissions to different people. For the most part, there are three different roles: the meeting host, cohosts, and participants or attendees.

FIGURE 13-5:
A group call using
Google Meet.

- The *host* is the person who schedules the meeting and sends out the invitation link. Often, this is the chairperson of a committee or the group leader. This person has more permissions during the meeting to help control the chaos. They also have the ability to turn features on and off as needed. For example, the host can determine the people that attendees can chat with: everyone, only the host, or no one. This allows them to present information without interruption and then turn on the chat feature when there's a natural pause in the presentation. They can also turn on and off the ability for participants to turn on video, talk, share screens, write on the screen, and more.

- *Cohosts* are participants that the host assigns to help during the session. Cohosts can perform most of the same tasks as the host. A host might assign participants to cohost when hosting large meetings in order to ensure a more seamless experience for the attendees. In peer group situations, a host might assign all team members the cohost role to provide an equitable experience.

- *Participants and attendees* join a meeting with limited responsibilities and are able to participate based on the permissions sent by the host. For most smaller group meetings, features are not restricted.

REMEMBER

Tools like Zoom, Teams and Meet can take a little time to learn how to use, especially as the meeting host. The good news is that most product vendors provide tutorial videos and documents on how to use the tool as both a host and a participant. So keep this in mind when choosing a tool, and look for support options before making a final decision.

Being patient

Okay, time for a reality check. Even if you do everything we tell you to do in the preceding sections, not everybody in your group will be able to dedicate the same amount of time to your project. Inevitably, life happens: Kids get sick, work is busy, and other life events distract your group members from participating at the most desirable level. Therefore, patience is a must! Even the most dedicated group members may have a different work schedule or live in a different time zone. Therefore, communication may be delayed. At the beginning of the COVID-19 crisis, learners (and workers) were challenged by trying to study and participate in live sessions with kids sitting on their laps or playing in the background. So, a little grace and understanding may also be needed when working in groups.

REMEMBER

The sooner you can organize your group, the sooner you will feel more relaxed. After you're organized, you can work independently on your own time schedule — just as long as you meet established deadlines. (See the example of a group schedule in Table 13-1.) As you work alone, you need to trust that your fellow group members are doing the same. That's why having periodic check-ins is important. You definitely don't want to find out the day the project is due that a group member has done nothing.

Resolving Conflicts

Whenever people are asked to collaborate, the potential for conflict exists. The ability to be patient and strategically resolve conflict is an important skill when participating in an online course. The lack of participation of a group member or the misinterpretation of written text can lead to frustration and resentment — distracting you from the objectives of the course. As you read this section, don't just think about how to resolve conflict — consider how to prevent it as well.

Understanding the conflicts you may encounter (and handling them)

In our experience, conflict occurs between students in the online environment for three reasons: They disagree on the subject matter; a student says something that others find offensive; or resentment sets in when one or more students are perceived as not pulling their weight.

Disagreeing on the subject matter

Sometimes students disagree on the subject matter. In a classroom, you would think this would be the most prevalent source of conflict. However, this type of conflict rarely occurs online, and when it does (typically in a discussion forum), the instructor should step in to help facilitate a resolution.

If the conflict is initiated via text, contact your instructor and provide them with the specific forum where they can find the post. If the conflict occurred during a synchronous session, contact your instructor and provide them with as much detail as possible, even if you're merely a witness to the conflict. Use your instructor's phone number for issues that need to be resolved immediately. If you have to leave a message, follow up with an email as well. Some instructors, like us, read their email on their cellphones and receive information faster that way than from voice mails on their office phones. Information should be presented in a factual and professional manner.

Finding a submission offensive

One student may write something that other students consider offensive. Rarely are these incidences intentional. Students sometimes write before thinking about how others might interpret their written words.

If you encounter a post that you feel is offensive, don't assume that it was an intentional attack. Politely respond by asking for clarification, and explain why clarification may be needed — without pointing fingers. For example, "Jane, thanks for your response. I'd like to ask for clarification about your point on . . . the way I read it made me think you were saying. . .."

REMEMBER

If a post is blatantly offensive, don't fuel the fire by responding further. Contact your instructor immediately and allow them to facilitate the resolution process. (See the next section for tips on how to communicate effectively with your instructor in this situation.) The instructor will most likely delete the post and deal with the situation behind the scenes.

TIP

An ounce of prevention here is worth a pound of cure. To avoid offending others, think before you write and reread your posts before submitting them. A simple slip of the comma can completely change the meaning of a sentence.

Simmering over slackers

Resentment tends to build when one or more students don't pull their weight. This often occurs when organization or communication within a group is lacking. Even the most understandable situations can lead to conflict if not communicated correctly. For example, we have both witnessed a student who has had a family emergency to attend to, requiring the student to step away from class momentarily. However, because the student did not communicate this situation to the group, the other group members started resenting her, which began to destroy the entire group dynamics. Had the student explained the situation to the group before removing herself, most likely the other students would have supported her lack of participation. Not only would they have provided emotional support — they also would have gladly picked up her share of the work.

REMEMBER

To avoid this situation, be sure to communicate with your group on a consistent basis, even if it's just to say hello. Your virtual presence reassures your group that you're on task and on time. On the other hand, if you find that a group member isn't participating, try contacting that person semiprivately. We recommend that you include your instructor on all communication, especially when you're dealing with lack-of-participation issues — hence the phrase *semiprivately*. If your instructor wants to be less involved in the day-to-day communication, they'll let you know. Write an email to the group member who isn't participating and copy your instructor. Do not blind-copy (BCC) the instructor because you want the instructor's involvement to be known by your fellow group member.

If, after two attempts, you don't receive a response from your peer, let your instructor take it from there. Start making backup plans for completing that person's share of the project and then move forward. Don't let one person's lack of participation hold you up from completing the project and having a positive group experience. However, continue to keep the nonparticipating member in the communication loop as a way of documenting that person's lack of participation.

TIP

One activity the group's secretary (or another designated group member) should consider when first delegating tasks is to create a spreadsheet that lists what is to be done, who is to do it, and when it's due. Then as tasks are completed, the secretary can document who actually completed the task and when. This encourages all group members to be responsible for completing their part of the project and provides the instructor with a clear picture of each member's level of participation.

Bringing problems to your instructor's attention

A good instructor will most likely know when a problem is brewing, from having observed goings-on in the background, especially if you include your instructor in your group communications, as we suggest in the preceding section. However, a good instructor will also provide the group with some time to resolve conflicts on their own without stepping in at the first signs of a problem.

Whenever you need to contact the instructor about a group member not living up to expectations, you may feel like a tattletale, but it's okay. The classroom is a good training ground for people to learn responsibility and the social repercussions of not living up to that responsibility. A good instructor will handle the situation professionally in a manner that doesn't reflect poorly on you or other group members. Instead, the instructor will focus on the unwanted behavior and coach the student on how to improve that behavior.

REMEMBER

The way you approach your instructor when you're dealing with a group conflict is important. Follow these guidelines when communicating to your instructor:

>> **Communicate privately.** When you reach the point where you feel that communicating directly with your peer isn't working, communicate the situation privately to your instructor so that you can focus more on you and the next steps you should take to move forward.

>> **Be direct and use facts.** Politely explain the situation, and share with the instructor any communication you have had with the group member. The more information you can provide the instructor, the better. Hopefully, the instructor already has some idea about what's going on, though it never hurts to be thorough. Share the link to your group's tasks spreadsheet to demonstrate who is doing what, or who should be doing what.

>> **Don't complain.** Your instructor understands the repercussions of someone not participating in a group project. Complaining about the situation only distracts you from moving forward and makes you look needy to your instructor.

>> **Have a backup plan.** Assure your instructor that you're ready to move forward with a backup plan, and ask whether this plan should include the group member who is failing to participate.

>> **Ask for direction.** End your communication by thanking your instructor and confirming that it's okay to move forward with your backup plan.

You may be asking yourself who should ultimately be responsible for reporting conflict to the instructor. Generally, the leader should be the person who contacts the instructor about problems within the group. However, sometimes, other group members have problems with the leader. In this situation, if the other members of the group are communicating with one another, it's best if only one person is chosen to contact the instructor. Otherwise, if you feel there is a problem that no one is addressing, you have a choice: Either report the situation to the instructor privately or politely initiate the group's decision on who should contact the instructor, by posting something like this: "Hi, all. It seems that we may be at an impasse, which is blocking our ability to complete our tasks effectively. I'd like to propose asking our instructor for guidance. I'd be more than happy to contact them on our behalf, unless someone else would rather do it. I'm confident that, with the proper guidance, we can work this out and create an amazing project to turn in."

Chapter **14**

Recognizing We Are Global

I f COVID-19 has taught us anything, it's how much more the world is interconnected. This chapter deals with learners who live in other countries and study online. Some of these learners are US citizens who live abroad, for either work or travel purposes, and take online classes. Other learners are international students who seek the advantages an online education will give them. You can find many opportunities to learn online, and not all of them are within the United States.

Setting the Stage for Global Learning

This news might surprise you, but the US accounts for only 5% of the world's population. At the same time, it ranks at the top for having companies in the Global 500 in 2018 and 2019, according to *Fortune* magazine. The *Global 500* represents companies from around the world that produce the highest revenues. Most of these companies have offices throughout the world. For example, US-based Walmart has a technology lab in Bangalore, India, and the Japanese company Hitachi has offices in Tarrytown, New York. Companies that are global require employees who are educated beyond book smarts. They need employees who understand how to function with many different cultures.

Perhaps this awareness is what drove enrollments in study-abroad programs to increase. As companies ask for more culturally competent employees, US schools respond with opportunities across the globe. Students enrolled in these programs study while living in foreign countries. This sets the stage for some exciting learning. However, whether you live in Portugal temporarily or Buffalo permanently, everyone has something to learn about global competence.

REMEMBER

Cultural competence can set you apart from the rest of your peers. To be culturally competent means that you respect cultural differences and are able to build understanding with a diverse workgroup. The same definition applies to being a culturally competent online learner.

When it comes to developing cultural competence, online learners have more options than ever:

>> **Complete an internship abroad.** You might look for an in-person internship abroad, but in the post-COVID-19 world, you may be eligible for a remote internship.

>> **Teach English as a second language (ESL).** Teaching ESL has always been an exciting way to see the world and learn a new culture. This option, too, is available online for the right candidate.

Where would you learn about these opportunities? Start with a site like Diversity Abroad (www.diversityabroad.com) or Go Abroad (www.goabroad.com). These sites have up-to-date information on global opportunities, both in person and online. You can find information on paid and unpaid experiences around the world.

Meeting People around the World

Your online classroom may be filled with students who come from other countries. People choose online courses for many reasons, including convenience. How much more convenient is it to learn a skill without having to leave home? Imagine *not* having to secure a student visa, *not* having to find housing, or *not* having to make arrangements to move thousands of miles away from friends and family.

Colleges and universities in the US have policies and procedures specific to international students. These policies and procedures are federally mandated. However, the requirements for learners who travel to the US to study are notably different than for those who may want to take a course that is offered online from the same institution. If you find yourself as a global learner who is interested in one course from a particular institution, reach out to the office on campus that works with international students. They'll know how to advise you.

That said, you may be a global learner who enrolls in free or low-cost courses, known as MOOCs, to enhance business skills or learn for personal enjoyment. Massive online open courses (or *MOOCs*) are available by way of well-known companies such as Coursera (`www.coursera.org`), Udemy (`www.udemy.com`), and EdX (`www.edx.org`). Several of these companies join with established universities in the development of these classes, and not all these universities are US based. At a few of these companies, you can earn academic credit, and even degrees. Look carefully at each provider to see what may be available.

Recognizing the value of cultural difference

Now that we are coming to appreciate the interconnectedness of the planet, we can see that the inclusion of different cultures enriches online learning. Sharing your virtual learning space with people from other cultures means that you can ask questions and learn from them. When we're approached with a spirit of genuine interest (and not judgment), our human differences become fascinating. We are all better for that.

Cultural differences play out in some interesting ways in online learning. For example, without stereotyping, consider how the following different types of cultures make unique contributions to the learning environment:

>> A culture where collaborative learning is a primary method of learning contributes to group projects and discussions.

>> A culture where students routinely question authority may encourage students to ask the Why behind current political policies or historical decisions.

>> A culture that enjoys hearty personal relationships helps the class get to know one another.

>> A culture that is sometimes reserved and introspective may contribute a depth of analysis via discussions that would not have been expressed otherwise.

The online environment allows learners that represent these individual cultural characteristics to share their perspectives and learn alongside others with different perspectives. When put together, these differences lead to a richer space in which learners can explore ideas. If there is any disadvantage, it's that, online, you can't share the wonderful food from those different cultures!

REMEMBER

People and learning communities flourish when the instructor and learners approach cultural differences with a spirit of genuine interest and respect. Be careful not to stereotype or judge.

CULTURAL DISCOMFORT

Though we're convinced that learning about different cultures can be a fascinating experience, be prepared to deal with some awkward situations. Here are some questions to consider and ideas to help you over the hump:

- What if you find yourself in a study group where one individual appears intolerant of others based on cultural or language differences? Can you be the bridge, by pointing out what the others have in common? Can you offer another interpretation?

- What if you're asked a question that seems too personal? This answer is easy; You don't have to answer! It would be polite, however, to say, "That's a little too personal" so that the asker understands our culture a little better. Every culture has different boundaries.

- What if you're challenged about US policy or government? This is an opportunity to educate an international audience and tell them that most Americans are moderate and well-intentioned and don't want to come off as bullies.

- Most of all, remember that the best response is always to ask more questions and listen! That is how you learn about the world.

Accessing experts from anywhere

Not every online learning experience is US based, and not all experts are in one place, either. One of the powerful developments in online learning is the ability for experts from around the world to collaborate and present new information.

In Chapter 10 we discuss various guests in the classroom. Your instructor may invite a guest lecturer from another country, which is an opportunity to see how the material you're learning applies globally.

Accessing the Internet around the World

Any online learner needs a reliable Internet connection to succeed in online education. Where and how you find this type of connection may present challenges, and we discuss these in the following sections.

Considering residential expenses

How much does Internet service cost where you live? In the US, a basic residential, high-speed connection (cable or DSL) can range from $50 to $75 per month. Compared to Americans' incomes and other expenses, this is relatively little money.

However, depending on where you live, Internet service may be more or less expensive than in the US. In western Africa, for instance, the same service costs well over US$400 per month, whereas in Russia it's as little as US$10 per month. In India, the costs are comparable to US prices if you live in a metropolitan area. Online students must determine the relative cost of a reliable residential, high-speed Internet connection in figuring the overall cost of an online education.

TIP

If residential, high-speed connection costs are pricey in your corner of the world, investigate the following home alternatives before registering for an online course or program. The best person to ask these questions of is the course instructor, but a recruiter may be able to give you answers, too:

>> **Consider whether you can use a mobile phone connection.** Assuming that you have an unlimited data plan, see whether you can use your mobile device as a hot spot. Coverage and speed largely depend on where you live, of course.

>> **If the course requires high speed because of video or audio, ask whether alternatives are available, such as transcripts you can read.**

>> **Estimate how much work can be done offline and how much synchronous time you should expect.** Can you download assignments, work on them offline, and then connect for less time to upload? Will you be required to be online at specific times?

Getting connected outside your home

If you can't afford residential Internet service, what are your options in terms of connecting? If you're a student living abroad, you may find that you can connect where you work or in more public areas such as coffee shops, libraries, or community centers. The next few sections look at some of the advantages and disadvantages of these locations.

Connecting at work

If you work in a business that has a high-speed connection, ask your employer whether they can allow you to complete your coursework using company computers after working hours. This is a common solution for US online students whose future degrees directly relate to their professional lives. Here are some advantages to connecting via your workplace:

>> **You are focused on the coursework and are not distracted by family or friends.** Not that you want to rush, but you aren't as likely to multitask, because you want to finish your schoolwork and go home.

>> **Applying what you're learning to your professional situation is easier when you're sitting at work.** Not only is your mind on business, but if you need to reference a policy or procedure, you also have the resources at your fingertips.

WARNING

Of course, connecting at work has a couple disadvantages, too.

>> **You may be expected to repay your company's generosity via continued employment.** In other words, don't start looking for another job right away!

>> **You open yourself to privacy concerns and criticism.** Whatever you do on the company's computers is traceable. In theory, your boss can read what you write. As long as you're happy with your employer and honest in your communication, this shouldn't be a problem.

Connecting at coffee shops, libraries, and community centers

In developed countries, people who lack residential service at home often connect via free services. Okay, maybe they aren't free if you're required to purchase a drink, but coffee shops exist pretty much worldwide. Libraries and community centers often offer free Wi-Fi connections, too.

WARNING

Any free service comes with security risks. Unfortunately, hackers are everywhere. When using public Internet services, it's best not to shop online or log in to your online bank account where sensitive financial information (credit cards or bank account numbers) can be easily monitored and stolen. Invest in security software such as Bitdefender (www.bitdefender.com) or AVG (www.avg.com) that can alert you to risks.

In developing countries, you may find a community center sponsored by a nonprofit organization where Internet skills are taught primarily to children. Although their services may target younger students, these organizations may allow you to access the Internet by way of their satellite connections if they understand that education is the purpose. Again, you need to consider whether you have your own equipment or can use theirs, and to what extent you can work offline to save connection time.

Finally, don't forget public libraries. Most public libraries around the world offer free Internet connections. If you cannot afford residential service, the library might be a helpful option.

Being aware of restrictions

Because of political and sociocultural differences, some web-based resources may be restricted by your government. For example, coauthor Susan once shared with her graduate students in an education course a link to a video posted on YouTube. The student in an Arab country could not see the video because their Internet service provider had restricted access.

REMEMBER

You must understand any restrictions before starting an online course so that you can tell the instructor if you can't access certain course materials; they can then provide alternative information. You'll know you're blocked when you can't access the site or program and you receive an error message. If you want a thorough explanation of why you're restricted, ask your Internet service provider, who can then interpret your government's policies.

Making the Most of Your Class Time

After you decide on a program and find the Internet access you need, you still have a few details to work out. The next few sections introduce you to a little information about what to look for in a class that may be global, tips for navigating time differences, and pointers for joining study groups.

Recognizing what's different about online classes around the world

REMEMBER

Here are some considerations for you as you think about taking a course from anywhere around the world:

>> **There may be different expectations about how you should address your professor.** Americans tend to be a little more casual about relationships in higher education, and your instructor may ask you to call her by her first name (Susan) rather than her title (Dr. Manning). When your classes begin, ask your instructors how they prefer to be addressed. If you're taking a class in another country, you'll want to know your professor's expectations!

>> **Given the nature of online education, your instructor may not be highly active in-class discussions.** They may opt to say less and ask the students to think for themselves. The teacher isn't lazy — this is a deliberate educational strategy.

>> **Students are expected to speak up and to ask questions.** If you don't understand something, the instructor expects you to ask. Saying that instructions are confusing isn't considered impolite. We recommend asking privately (see Chapter 11 for information on private communication methods), but be sure to follow through until you understand.

>> **Some instructors expect students to critically example the ideas of experts.** In other words, finding fault with a theory or piece of work from another scholar, from your professor, or from a famous author is not only permissible, it's also how we believe students develop critical thinking. As long as you provide your reasoning, most instructors appreciate dissent. (This is another cultural area you'll want to ask about!)

>> **The definition of plagiarism is extremely strict in the United States.** This concept is so important to the integrity of higher education that a portion of Chapter 15 is all about avoiding plagiarism. The US system of education insists that other authors and works that help form your ideas must be acknowledged and cited. If you're taking a class based in the US, make sure you understand how to do this!

>> **Americans are extraordinarily punctual.** If a virtual meeting is scheduled for 7:00, the teacher will start talking at 7:00, not 7:10 or 7:20. Be prepared, and log in early! If you're taking a class outside the US, ask for clarification when it comes to live meetings.

>> **When working in student groups, students may have a different timeline for establishing trust and credibility.** Because some educational systems are fairly competitive, global students may be less skillful at collaborating in small groups and find it difficult to trust other members. Again, this is a cultural consideration — and something to talk to your peers about.

>> **Not every student is comfortable with interpersonal conflict.** In fact, when working with study groups, you may find students who ignore conflict or don't handle it well. Don't take it personally.

Adjusting for differences in time zones

What time is it? What day is it? It all depends on where you are! Getting a handle on date and time is critical so that you're not late with meetings and assignments.

Handling synchronous class meetings

Instructors may call virtual class meetings using synchronous (real-time) communication or web conferencing tools. These meetings usually give students the opportunity to interact in text and voice.

To ensure that you make all meetings on time, you first need to determine what time it is where you are compared to your instructor's location. You might already know about the World Clock site at www.timeanddate.com/worldclock. From this site, you can access the meeting planner, where you state your country and city and the location of the instructor. For example, if you live in Vietnam and the instructor is in Chicago and they call a meeting for 7 P.M. on Wednesday, you need to be ready at 7 A.M. Thursday!

REMEMBER

Figure out if the predominant culture is punctual. Plan to log in five minutes before the scheduled time so that you're not late to synchronous meetings.

Of course, synchronous class meetings may not be convenient if you're called to a meeting in the middle of the night. Politely explain the time difference to the instructor or your fellow students. We're confident they will tell you to sleep through the meeting.

TIP

This tip is for people who don't speak English as their first language: If you're concerned that you'll be asked for perfect English, don't be! Americans are pretty forgiving when they hear accents and grammatical errors from speakers of other languages. (You should hear the mistakes we make!) If you're more comfortable talking via text, let the instructor know in advance and make provisions to type in chat.

Figuring out assignment due dates

Your assignment is due by midnight on Thursday. What does that mean if you live on the other side of the world? It probably means either the next day or a day ahead! Don't be caught on the wrong day. Use the same world clock tool we suggest in the previous section to synchronize due dates.

Joining study groups

One of the advantages of having a global economy is the richness of diversity, and the same can be said of study groups with students from around the world. Don't be shy! Online education thrives on dialogue, and your unique perspective enriches everyone. If you're presented with this opportunity, go for it!

Study groups may form for a specific task, as we discuss in Chapter 13. Or, they can be informal groups of students who agree to share notes and additional resources. In fact, the group may choose to maintain its own wiki or a separate group space on Facebook. This provides another avenue for discussing what's happening in the class without the instructor present.

If you're a global student, you'll find when you interact with your classmates that some seem more open than others. The others aren't necessarily snobby or deliberately racist; instead, they're probably intimidated by their own lack of knowledge about the world. The US is a geographically large, ethnically diverse country, but it still has many homogeneous communities where students grow up interacting only with people like themselves. Consequently, they're unsure whether asking about your country, culture, or habits is polite, and as a result, they appear aloof.

There's no magic potion to make others like you, regardless of where you come from. However, this list describes a few aspects of the American culture that you may find helpful:

>> **We're fairly informal about communication.** Of course, you need to follow the protocol of the academic class, but typically you can address your classmates by their first names.

>> **We're okay with some personal questions.** It's fine to ask questions like, "Are you married?" and "Do you have a family?" but it's not okay to express disagreement with someone if their lifestyle doesn't match your beliefs.

>> **We pepper our language with many idiomatic expressions.** If you don't know what something means, don't be afraid to ask! For instance, to say someone runs a tight ship may not make sense in an education course, until you understand that it means the principal is strict.

>> **We are, generally speaking, punctual.** If a meeting is set to begin at 8 A.M., we almost always start at 8 A.M.

>> **Get to know us and you'll be surprised at the diversity!** It really is hard to stereotype an American when you recognize our many ethnic and religious groups.

>> **We love jokes!** Good, clean puns always catch our fancy.

TIP

If you have the chance to work in groups and are asked to select members, think about the students who display a natural curiosity and interest in your country. That welcoming behavior can make group work downright pleasant as you exchange ideas. Have some fun together by sharing cultural information and being open with each other. Chapters 10 and 11 provide pointers on introducing yourself to your classmates and communicating clearly with them.

Chapter **15**

Understanding Netiquette and Ethical Behavior

Ever hear of the Robert Fulghum book *All I Really Need to Know I Learned in Kindergarten?* In it, he states some of the simple rules from childhood, including how you really need to play fair and not take things that aren't yours. In a nutshell, that's what this chapter is about! Online learning should be a place where students are fair to one another and honest in their interactions. We look at how this concept plays out digitally and what tools you can use to help you stay true to your word.

Defining and Using Netiquette

Netiquette is computerese for a set of rules or standards that people follow to keep the online environment pleasant and safe. The word combines *etiquette* with the Inter*net*, and, just like its parent definition of etiquette, netiquette is all about communicating respectfully and politely and avoiding stereotyping.

Most good instructors convey their interpretation of netiquette along with expectations for its use in the early days of the course. You may see a list of "do's and don'ts" or a policy statement, and this may be referenced in the syllabus (a document we describe in Chapter 9). Setting those ground rules early can prevent misunderstandings and hurt feelings later.

Communicating politely and respectfully

What makes discussion board postings, emails, and instant messages polite? A few standard conventions work on all communication fronts, no matter the audience (Chapters 11 and 16 feature additional guidelines for discussion posts):

>> **Always fill in the subject line for discussion postings and emails.** Mystery messages make people nervous. When discussion posts have no subject line, make the first line of your post the discussion and bold it.

>> **Address the reader by name, if possible.** Who doesn't love reading their name in print, and how else will others know you're talking to them?

>> **Sign your name at the end of your posting.** Own up to whatever you write.

>> **Follow basic writing conventions and don't mix popular text-message lingo with your academic work.** Not only is that form of communication full of jargon and inappropriate for scholarly work, but many in your class won't understand the code.

>> **Don't type in all caps!** It's the equivalent of shouting.

Okay, if you need to add emphasis, you can do it *this* way (by adding asterisks before and after the text you want to emphasize) or use all caps occasionally.

>> **Too much colored font or too many busy images can detract from your message.** Keep the look of your postings, emails, and messages simple and clean.

>> **It goes without saying that name-calling is out.** Diplomacy is in. If you disagree with something, say "I politely disagree and here is why. . . ."

>> **"Please," "thank you," and other courtesies work well online!**

>> **Those little emoticons like smiley faces and winks can be used judiciously in replies to one another.** However, be sure you're not punctuating every sentence with an emoticon — a little goes a long way. For that matter, avoid the overuse of !!! and ???, too.

>> **Be forgiving.** Anyone can make a mistake and accidentally shout with all caps or forget to say thank you. Rather than publicly humiliate your peers by pointing out a transgression, politely disregard the occasional offense. If it gets

to be a habit, you can raise the question with the offending student (privately and politely, of course!) and cc the instructor. Is it possible that your instructor will be the offender? Not likely, although they may forget to address you by name in an email, or a reply may seem uncharacteristically short. If that's the case, let it go. Pointing it out makes you look like a high-maintenance student.

>> **Proofread your work before hitting the Send or Submit button.** You'll save yourself embarrassment.

All the preceding guidelines go a long way toward showing respect for others, but we make a few additional notes concerning student-to-student communication and student-to-instructor communication in the following sections.

Showing respect for other students

In the academic world, discussion should involve critical thinking, which means ideas have to be taken apart and put back together again — hopefully, for the better. In short, not everyone will agree! How you communicate those disagreements speaks volumes about how much you respect the other party.

REMEMBER

Your tone shouldn't suggest shouting at or belittling the original author. You should simply offer another view and the reasoning behind it. To strengthen your point, it helps to support your opinions with course materials and additional research. We demonstrate with a few examples in the following list — it spells out polite ways to disagree in discussion forums and in email and instant messages:

>> I hear what you're saying, but I see it another way, and here's why. . . .

>> That's an interesting point you make about the causes. Have you also thought about <fill in the blank> because I think. . . .

>> Respectfully, I'd like to add a few thoughts that might reshape your thinking. Here are my ideas. . . .

>> I'm still thinking about what you said. One of the issues (or points) I struggle with is <fill in the blank> because. . . .

Next, we contrast the preceding tactful examples with some that might be misread. Any of the following examples can be written tongue-in-cheek and with a note of humor. However, they can also be terribly insulting. In fact, we encourage students and instructors to use humor sparingly.

WARNING

What you think is funny may be interpreted as offensive by others. We aren't telling you to leave your personality at the virtual classroom door — Chapter 11 explains how to put forward your online persona — it simply means to post carefully and respectfully.

REMEMBER

Online communication is void of nonverbal cues and can easily be misinterpreted.

The following are the types of comments that could easily be misread:

>> You're so wrong and don't even know it!

>> How can you miss the other side of the argument?

>> What are you — goofy?

TIP

If you do feel strongly about what someone wrote, don't reply immediately. Draft a response and sleep on it. The next day, reread what you wrote and see whether you need to tone it down or whether you still feel the message needs to be sent. Swift and emotional responses almost always backfire.

WARNING

One more note: Most of your communication will occur within a learning management system or at least within the parameters of class. Therefore, forwarding chain letter emails to your class is inappropriate. If you make friends with one or two students and want to share something like that, ask their permission first and use discretion.

Respecting your instructor

Of course, you know that your instructor is a real person and therefore subject to the same feelings as your classmates. While you're exercising diplomacy with your peers, extend the same courtesy to your instructor. Teaching is quite a public activity, and it's impossible to get everything "right" when dealing with technology. You may also want to approach your instructor when you disagree with a grade. Here are a few circumstances in which you may want to respectfully approach your instructor:

>> **When you see typos or broken links, email the instructor privately.**
Sometimes they have no control over these, and a link that works one day can be broken the next. Say something like, "I'm having trouble opening the link to X. It says 'page not available' and I can't tell if the whole site is down forever or if I'm just hitting it at a bad time. Do you know an alternative URL?" Or, "Dr. Manning, I noticed that you have the word *resource* twice on the first line of the second paragraph on the instructions page for the assignment this week. Just thought you'd want to know."

>> **If you disagree with a grade or a score, approach the instructor calmly and with respect.** After all, they have more content knowledge than you. Asking for clarification without going overboard emotionally yields far more positive results. In these cases, try something like, "Dr. Manning, I wondered if I can get a little more clarification on my grade on the last paper. I want to

make sure I can incorporate the feedback into the next round. Can you please tell me more about how I can improve in that area?"

Before you ask about a score, determine the overall relevance. Is it worth haggling over 1 out of 15 points? Even if you approach the instructor respectfully, be prepared to not get the answer you were hoping for in return.

» **If you need more specific feedback, ask for examples.** Say something like, "I'm trying to better understand how I can improve in the future. Could I please have an example of what you consider an excellent post/paper/project?" Likewise, if your instructor gives individual feedback, take the time to read it!

Avoiding stereotyping

Many people realize that stereotyping is harmful. It may be obvious that comments of this nature do not belong in online discussions. And yet, sometimes we inadvertently carry our stereotypes into the classroom. For example, if you assume that someone with the last name of Gonzales can interpret the cultural significance of homeopathic remedies in a community nursing course, you may be surprised to find out that that person married into the family and is a member of the dominant culture, not the minority. (Furthermore, Gonzales could be a surname from either a Latin American or Asian country.)

REMEMBER

You simply cannot stereotype. In an online course, it's important to get to know your fellow students as individuals. Take the time to read any icebreakers or biographies that are posted, and, rather than fall back on a stereotype, ask questions.

Recognizing the Importance of Online Ethics

In the early days of online education, the primary concern for many faculty, administrators, and students was that it was too easy to cheat with technology. They feared that the value of the degree would become meaningless because you could copy papers, make up resources, and persuade your cousin to do your work. Of course, the same might be said of face-to-face education, so a renewed awareness of the importance of ethics has evolved.

Ethical behavior should govern how (and what) people communicate with one another, what work people submit with their names attached, and the extent to which they are true to their word. We examine these themes in the next few sections.

Being honest in the written word

REMEMBER

Because written communication is the primary way ideas are exchanged in an online class, what you say and how you say it must belong to you. Here are a couple of examples in which honesty is absolutely important:

>> **Presenting ideas:** Your instructor may ask you to read the work of an author or a theorist and then give your ideas about the work. If you answer a discussion question or write a paper for this kind of assignment, you're expected to give credit to the original authors when you use their ideas. If you don't, you're not being honest about your work — you're plagiarizing. (Later in this chapter, we discuss plagiarism in much more depth.)

>> **Being yourself:** Occasionally, a student misrepresents their ability or life experience. For example, John might write that he is a certified public accountant. Later, the class learns that John barely finished his associate's degree and lied about his achievement. John's integrity is now shot because he wasn't honest. It's true that you can be anyone you want online, but if you're in an academic setting, we suggest that you become a serious scholar and not a dishonest participant.

Showing integrity by following through

You may be part of a study group in an online course, where others depend on you to do your share of the work. If you say you'll contribute, your group expects you to follow through, and rightly so. If you fail to do your part of the work and become a "social loafer," you will quickly lose trust and respect among your peers by your lack of integrity. Your grade will probably suffer as well, because most instructors give credit for group participation. (We give many more details about participating in an online study group in Chapter 13.)

At some point, you may need to step away from the computer and focus on personal issues. In this situation, you may "contract" with your instructor to extend deadlines or receive an "Incomplete" grade until you have caught up on work by a specific date and time. You may be surprised at how many students do this and then never finish the work. Don't make it your instructor's responsibility to manage your time. Follow through with integrity by completing the work by the determined deadline, and communicate with the instructor privately regarding your status.

Respecting privacy and confidentiality

REMEMBER

As we explain throughout this book, students develop personal relationships in online courses. They communicate outside the parameters of the course management system by way of private email and messages. You may receive confidential information about one of your peers, and it needs to stay between you and your friend. For example, if Jane writes about her ugly divorce, you have no right to bring it up in a discussion forum. Even if you're a law student and the topic is divorce, this is Jane's business, not yours.

The same is true for information you receive from your instructor. Your instructor handles your progress and grades as confidential matters. Please do not post this communication publicly or share it with your friends.

Asking before you repurpose prior work

If you're enrolled in a degree program, chances are good that assignments you complete in one course will flow nicely into another. For example, in an introductory course you may be asked to write a paper that requires research on a certain topic. That background research may be quite helpful in your second class as you extend the theme. Is it wrong to take your first paper and repurpose it for your second assignment?

The answer depends on your instructor. Though we would say that building on earlier work is efficient and shows impeccable organization, your instructor may not agree with us. Therefore, always ask before you rework an old assignment. Tell the instructor what part and how much of the old assignment you want to repurpose, and what new information you plan to add to complete the new assignment.

REMEMBER

If you don't ask before you repurpose prior work, you may find that your instructor won't accept the work. In some programs, instructors coordinate assignments and will know if you try to pass off an assignment from another course. You don't want a failing grade!

Avoiding Plagiarism

Is plagiarism more rampant today, and has technology made it easier to borrow another person's ideas? Faculty wrestle with these questions routinely because, unfortunately, plagiarism happens all too frequently. At some sites, students even share their assignments from classes they've taken. This is perfectly legitimate.

What's not okay is for someone else to download that work and turn it in under their own name.

The only way you can completely avoid plagiarism is to write every word without ever thinking about, borrowing from, or referencing another person's work. Examples of original work may be original poetry, a musical composition, or an essay about your summer vacation that only you could have experienced. However, this isn't the case in most academic courses in which you're asked to research the topic or back up your ideas, so we need to scratch away at the topic a little further. In the next few sections, we define plagiarism, take you through the process of writing without plagiarism, and provide tools and tips to guide you. We also explain what happens if you're caught plagiarizing.

Defining plagiarism and related concepts

Plagiarism is . . . well, without looking, coauthor Susan can tell you that plagiarism is stealing someone else's ideas and passing them off as if they were your own. Does she need to quote someone here? Is this common knowledge and therefore something that can't be attributed to a single source? A little investigating may be worthwhile.

If you research the definition of *plagiarism* and come to the website `https://plagiarism.org`, you find a similar definition at `https://plagiarism.org/article/what-is-plagiarism`: "In other words, plagiarism is an act of fraud. It involves both stealing someone else's work and lying about it afterward."

REMEMBER

If you want to quote a source, as we have here, you need to provide enough of a reference so that the reader can go back and check it. Even if you summarize or use this publication as evidence to support your own ideas, tell readers where you found the information. The act of providing that reference is called *citing* or *giving a citation.* This keeps academics honest. (Later in this chapter, we describe in more detail how to cite sources properly.)

TECHNICAL STUFF

These two important concepts work hand in hand with plagiarism:

>> **Copyright is the legal status that says someone else owns the work.** You see it in the front of books, at the bottom of websites, and on the back of CD cases. It denotes that the creator is legally protected from you or anyone else stealing their work or any portion of their work.

>> **Intellectual property is creative work.** When you write a paper for Introduction to Psychology, that paper is your intellectual property. And once the work is in a fixed state, including blogs and websites, it's automatically under copyright protection.

Getting the facts on plagiarism

Having a thorough understanding of plagiarism makes you less likely to make a mistake. The resources noted in the following sections are places to which you can turn to further educate yourself.

Using online tutorials

TIP

Teachers truly want students to succeed, and for this reason you may be surprised at the number of resources available online to help students understand and avoid plagiarism. Search for *plagiarism tutorial* at your preferred search engine and see what comes up. Here are a few of our favorites:

>> **How to Recognize Plagiarism:** Tutorials and Test (Indiana University School of Education at `https://plagiarism.iu.edu`): The page was written primarily for university students and advanced high school students. It provides a lot of information supplemented by videos and certification tests.

>> **The Duke University Plagiarism Tutorial** (`http://plagiarism.duke.edu`): Taking a straightforward approach, this tutorial clearly defines plagiarism and provides examples of both intentional and unintentional plagiarism. The site also provides procedures for citing sources, strategies for avoiding plagiarism, and additional resources for learning more.

>> **Purdue University's online writing lab (OWL):** The Purdue site dedicates a portion of its website to plagiarism. At `https://owl.purdue.edu/owl/research_and_citation/using_research/avoiding_plagiarism/index.html`, you can find links and activities to help you better understand how to avoid plagiarizing as you write your assignments.

>> **The Media Education Lab** (`http://mediaeducationlab.com/code-best-practices-fair-use-media-literacy-education`): This site can't be beat for background information on copyright and fair use. It provides information for teachers, but if you drill down to some of the fun videos and songs, you can find a lot that applies to student work.

Finding help from the school library

TIP

Get to know your school librarian, and when in doubt, ask this person to guide you toward understanding how to avoid plagiarism. Many school websites contain their own tutorials and resources. For example, the University of Washington maintains a page full of resources and links at `https://guides.lib.uw.edu/research/citations`.

Most libraries also have an Ask a Librarian chat feature. This feature allows you to chat with a librarian 24x7 online and ask questions such as where to find resources.

Citing sources properly

When you give credit to an original author within the body of your writing, you're citing their work. Proper citation demonstrates that you have a respect for the author's intellectual property and understand the standard conventions of citation. In this section, we describe the information that goes into a citation, explain when to use citations, note some popular citation formats, and list some tools to help with citations.

What goes into a citation

A citation typically includes the author's name, the date of the publication, and possibly the pages from which your reference came. Most often, this information is included within parentheses after the quote or concept from the original author, but it can be referenced in an endnote or a footnote as well. The citation tells the reader that you used a source to support your work and points the reader toward that source for follow-up.

You may be curious why we didn't say that the citation includes the title and publisher (and, possibly, volume, journal number, and other details). Those details are included on the Works Cited, References, or Bibliography page, which is the detailed listing of all citations mentioned in the document. That's where the reader turns for the details needed to find the original source.

TIP

Taking good notes results in better citations. As you prepare to write any assignment, take careful notes as you read each source. Copy quotes exactly and note page numbers. Summarize ideas separately. Be sure to document all bibliographic information you need according to the style you're told to use.

When to cite

The rules for citation are pretty easy. You need to cite work when you

>> **Quote the work:** A quote may be a one-liner or a lengthier portion, such as a paragraph. An example: According to Manning (2009), "Just because you embrace online education, doesn't mean you like gadgets."

>> **Summarize a portion of the work:** This means putting it in your own words, not just changing a phrase here or there. An example: Manning (2009) says it's possible to learn online successfully with relatively few technology gadgets.

> **Refer to the work:** You may have previously quoted or summarized the work, or this may be one work of many on the same issue. An example: One of the authors who argues against frivolous use of technology tools is Manning (2009).

REMEMBER

If the idea was not originally yours and is not a well-known fact (for example, that George Washington was the first president of the United States), you need to provide a citation and a reference.

Citation formats

The style you use to cite sources depends on your instructor and your academic discipline. Your instructor should tell you which style they prefer at the beginning of class or the start of an assignment. This information is often included on the syllabus, but you may also find it within a rubric. Some of the common styles for citing work include:

> **American Psychological Association (APA):** This format is common for the social sciences, education, psychology, and sometimes nursing. You can find out more about APA style at https://apastyle.apa.org.

> **Modern Language Association (MLA):** The humanities and arts are more likely to use MLA formatting. Check out https://style.mla.org.

> **American Medical Association (AMA):** Students in medicine, biological sciences, and other health related fields may use the AMA format. See www.amamanualofstyle.com for further information.

> **Chicago:** This is what the real world uses. When you read an article in a weekly newsmagazine, its references are in Chicago style. For more details, go to www.chicagomanualofstyle.org/home.html.

> **Turabian:** This generic style can be used by any of the disciplines. You can explore Turabian style at www.chicagomanualofstyle.org/turabian/citation-guide.html.

Tools for citing

You are so lucky: Internet tools can do the formatting for you when you need to write a citation! (We used to have to buy the manual and learn the system on our own.) After you know which format your instructor prefers, visit one of the many free, web-based services that formats your citation for you. At most of these sites, you select the style (APA or MLA, for instance) and then the type of media you need to cite. Is it a book, a periodical, or a website, and how many authors are listed? In addition, you fill in other information, like the date or page numbers, and eventually you click the Submit button. Voilà! The site tells you the appropriate formats for inclusion within the text and at the end of the document on a Works Cited or References page.

TIP

Here are a few of our favorite tools. You may also find that your school's library has a tool built into its web page. Whichever tool or method you use, double-check the results:

>> **zoterobib:** `https://zbib.org/`

This site automatically creates a citation for you based on an ISBN, a URL, or another media ID type. You can also manually add information about the website, book, or journal. Zotero also has a desktop version that tracks and stores your research and citations at `www.zotero.org`.

>> **North Carolina State University Libraries citation tool:** `www.lib.ncsu.edu/citationbuilder`

>> **Researchomatic:** `www.researchomatic.com/citation-generator`

Checking your own work

If the best defense is a good offense, then the best way to avoid plagiarism is to learn how to write correctly. However, even good writers question their own work. After you finish an assignment, take the extra time to verify your sources and citations. You can do this using online tools or by having a friend check your work.

Using online tools

TIP

You may have heard about Turnitin (`www.turnitin.com`), a web-based service that schools subscribe to so that faculty can check student work for possible plagiarism. Before your instructor sends your papers through the cycle, why not check your own work? Here are a couple of tools:

>> **At QueText** (`www.quetext.com`), you can sign up for a free account and run your papers through a database that checks against other web documents. It compares what you wrote to what it recognizes from its sources. The result is an authenticity report that states how much it believes your document is original work.

>> **Grammarly** (`www.grammarly.com/plagiarism-checker`), another free tool that is simple to use, not only helps check for plagiarism but also helps you develop better writing skills. This application offers both free and paid versions, depending on the level of checking you want.

Finding a classmate to help

TIP

If you prefer to rely on the human eye rather than on a digital check, you can ask a friend or classmate to help. In fact, you and a classmate might agree to read one another's papers and ask each other questions of verification. This practice not only provides a service but also helps you learn about plagiarism when you have to look for it in someone else's work. In the end, you come out a better writer for having done this.

Institutional support

TIP

Check with your institution if you're taking academic courses online. Many institutions offer tutoring and writing support even for students at a distance. You may be asked to either

>> Submit your work via email to receive feedback via comments directly in your document

>> Meet with a tutor using a synchronous tool where you share your work in real time

Looking at the penalties for plagiarism

Can you *accidentally* plagiarize? Is this possible? Quite a few schools say no, there are no accidents — just sloppy writers. After all, the cornerstone of academia is the idea that students create new understandings of their own, based on integrity and truth. If you plagiarize, your ideas aren't your own and there is no truthfulness.

REMEMBER

If you mistakenly fail to cite someone else's work and someone notices, you *may* be in serious trouble. Every institution has an academic integrity or academic honesty policy for students. You can find it in the student handbook and in the orientation materials. Your instructor may link you to the policy as part of the syllabus or resource materials in your course. Trust us: The policy exists, and by enrolling, you agree to abide by it!

Every institution also has a process for handling possible infractions. Though the details change from one institution to another, the basic procedures include the ones described in this list:

>> **Notification of the concern:** Your teacher may call you or email you to discuss the problem.

>> **Documentation of the problem:** The instructor takes screen shots of the material you may have posted and any communication surrounding the incident, along with the plagiarized source.

>> **A hearing:** You have the right to a judicial hearing, if you want one. It may involve a university judicial hearing officer and is most likely to be held via a telephone or web conference for an online student. You would need to compile and present a case for why the plagiarism occurred.

Sanctions for plagiarism range from failing an assignment to being expelled from school. The degree of plagiarism and whether it's your first offense often determine the outcome. In some cases, the instructor may keep the penalty at the class level, give you a failing grade for the assignment, and choose not to have it become a part of your permanent academic record. In other cases, the instructor has little say in the matter and must refer it to a different administrator.

Your attitude and how you deal with the instructor and the process can play a role in what happens. Consider the difference between apologizing and taking responsibility versus blaming the instructor or the software. Also, if you're invited to schedule a hearing and fail to respond, recognize that the judicial officer has to make a decision without your input.

Chapter **16**

Finishing and Submitting Your Assignments

From earlier chapters in this book, you know the drill: how to log in, who's in class, and how and why you should communicate clearly with everyone else. But how do you get a grade? You're not there just to have fun and converse with strangers, are you?

Instructors have several methods of determining how you're doing in class. They may assign papers or projects or ask you to take a quiz or test. Some determine how you're doing on a weekly basis by way of your participation in discussions. Hopefully, your class will utilize all these methods!

With technology, getting work to your instructor may require taking a couple of extra steps or following different procedures than the traditional classroom environment. This chapter walks you through the basics of getting your assignments turned in so that you can get the grade. After all, if you do the work, you deserve the score! We also review the use of grading criteria and how to write different types of assignments effectively to help ensure the best outcome.

Understanding the Ramifications of Rubrics

Instructors face a challenge in explaining to learners what they want. In online courses without live communication, it's difficult for learners to ask — and for the instructor to answer — the many little questions that come up during an assignment. For that reason, instructors have a clever way of telling you what they want: They use rubrics. *Rubrics* are scoring systems that instructors use to evaluate student work. The next few sections give you the lowdown on rubrics along with insights on how you can use them to your advantage.

Breaking down rubrics

Rubrics sometimes come in chart form, although they may be formatted as lists as well. A rubric makes giving the teacher what they want workable by categorizing for you the important parts of an assignment that the instructor will judge and making statements about what earns full points. You may find rubrics in a couple of locations:

>> **On the home page:** At the start of the course, rubrics are sometimes included in the syllabus or as a separate link to a document with multiple rubrics (for example, one for discussions and one for weekly papers).

>> **On the assignment page:** Sometimes instructors post a rubric within each individual assignment. This is a big hint that they want you to review your own work before submitting it!

For example, look at the rubric in Table 16-1, which describes how a paper in a course will be graded. This rubric presents three levels of quality: excellent, average, and needs improvement. Within each level are specific criteria for judging. You can see that the paper will be judged on the quality of your writing as well as on the overall structure and mechanics of the document — not to mention the fact that the assignment must be turned in on time!

Notice, for example, that if you want full credit, you need to properly cite sources in APA style. (See Chapter 15 for more about citations.) As for critical thinking, if you identify two problems and don't offer possible solutions, you don't get all the points. On the other hand, if you clearly show the connection between theory and practice and give at least one example, you're home free in critical thinking.

TABLE 16-1 **An Example of a Rubric for a Paper**

Criteria	Excellent	Average	Needs Improvement
Development of ideas and evidence of critical thinking	Essay is well developed, and presentation is logical based on a clear thesis statement with supporting materials, such as course readings, outside research, and interviews.	Essay is developed in a logical manner; however, thesis statement and/or supporting materials require more depth.	Essay lacks logic in presentation and/or lacks a clear thesis statement with supporting materials such as course readings, outside research, and interviews.
	Essay ideas/examples demonstrate the student's ability to analyze, apply, and synthesize content outside the classroom environment.	Essay ideas/examples do not directly relate to content or adequately demonstrate the student's ability to analyze, apply, and synthesize content outside the classroom environment.	Essay lacks ideas/examples that demonstrate the student's ability to analyze, apply, and synthesize content outside the classroom environment.
	(15–20 points)	(10–15 points)	(0–10 points)
Institution format and structure	Essay demonstrates proper use of institution format and structure by having a properly formatted title page, body, and reference page. Formatting includes proper use of spacing and page numbering.	Essay has a few errors specific to institution format and structure regarding a properly formatted title page, body, and reference page. Formatting includes proper use of spacing and page numbering.	Essay has multiple errors specific to institution format and structure regarding a properly formatted title page, body, and reference page. Formatting includes proper use of spacing and page numbering.
	(4–5 points)	(2–3 points)	(0–2 points)
Mechanics	Essay uses standard English mechanics and has few or no grammatical and/or spelling errors.	Essay uses standard English mechanics but has some grammatical and/or spelling errors.	Essay has multiple grammatical and/or spelling errors to the point that meaning is obscured.
	(4–5 points)	(2–3 points)	(0–2 points)
Timeliness	Essay is submitted via the assignment's digital dropbox on or before the scheduled deadline as stated in the course calendar.	Essay is submitted via the assignment's digital dropbox within 24 hours after the scheduled deadline as stated in the course calendar.	Essay submitted via the assignment's digital dropbox more than 24 hours after the scheduled deadline as stated in the course calendar.
	(4–5 points)	(1 point)	(0 points)

Using rubrics to your advantage

From your instructor's perspective, a rubric takes the guesswork out of grading. (Many instructors love to teach but hate to grade.) With the predetermined categories in a rubric, the instructor simply measures your work against the ideal as stated in the criteria.

REMEMBER

If the instructor can create a rubric to establish what they are looking for when grading, why can't you use that to your advantage when completing your assignment? Here are a couple of guidelines:

>> **Anytime you have an assignment, first read the rubric.** Determine the major criteria and compare these to what you find in the instructions. Make a list that includes both the criteria in the rubric and the criteria given in the instructions. Sometimes instructors forget to put simple instructions like page counts in the rubric, which is why we advise double-checking and making a combined list.

>> **After you write your assignment, judge it for yourself using the rubric.** Review each category and ask yourself for evidence. Pretend you're the instructor and be critical! By writing out the expectations in the rubric, your instructor has told you what they will measure and how. You can do the same.

Writing 101

The reality is that most online courses are 95 percent text and little audio. That means instructors and students "talk" with their fingers. Writing skills become the language! Online learners write papers, discussion posts, emails, reflections — the list seems endless. How well you write, according to the assignment and your instructor's expectations, determines your success. To earn the best grades, you must understand the style you need and the expectations of a specific assignment. In addition, you must show critical thinking by way of your writing. We work through what each of these means in the next few sections.

Examining different writing styles

Think about everything you wrote today. This list may include a text message to your significant other, your grocery list, an introductory statement to a post you shared on social media, some discussion posts for school, and countless documents for work. Did they all sound the same in terms of style and form? We hope not!

What you write for class depends on the assignment and the audience. This section considers different types of writing you can use in an online course.

Academic or scholarly writing

You use academic or scholarly writing in assignments such as short essays, long papers, and group projects. This kind of writing calls for a different *voice* — a more serious tone with proper grammar and reference citations. It stands apart from everyday writing in several ways:

>> **The organization is obvious.** Whether you're writing an essay or a dissertation, academic disciplines have clear expectations for organized writing. At the essay or paper level, this means related paragraphs that begin with topic sentences and are held together with a main thesis. On a larger scale, this means chapters held together with a primary thesis.

>> **The vocabulary changes.** When you write about your academic area of interest, you need to use the correct vocabulary for the context. This is not to say that you have to use multisyllabic words to impress the reader, but you do need to be precise and accurate in vocabulary use. For example, in nursing you might describe a patient as being in a supine position, whereas in other contexts you'd refer to the person as sitting.

>> **You use outside references to support your ideas.** In an academic paper, simply writing your opinion isn't enough. You need to back up your ideas with legitimate sources from other authors. Anytime you quote, summarize, or refer to someone else's work, you need to properly cite the source. The format for citations depends on your discipline and your instructor's preference. We write at length in Chapter 12 about finding resources and discuss in Chapter 15 the need for citations to avoid plagiarism.

TIP

Read the rubric for any assignment carefully, as we suggest earlier in this chapter. Chances are good that it will mention that you need to appropriately cite references as a condition of the assignment.

>> **The grammar follows standard conventions.** In academic writing, punctuation, spelling, and syntax all count. What is passable in spoken English isn't always acceptable in written form.

TIP

If good grammar and citing sources correctly is a weakness of yours, we highly recommend that you seek assistance, by way of either an online service available from your college or a website you find particularly helpful. For example, Purdue University's Online Writing Lab (OWL) is a wonderful web based resource at https://owl.purdue.edu.

WARNING

The following items shouldn't appear in academic writing:

>> **Colloquialisms and exclamations:** Ya know what I mean? Gee whiz, like, you just gotta learn to write or ur gonna flunk! This kind of casualness is unacceptable in an academic paper.

>> **Texting language:** A whole new language has been invented, thanks to mobile telephones and text. Abbreviations such as LOL and IDK have almost become mainstream. (If you're out of the loop, *LOL* is short for *l*aughing *o*ut *l*oud and IDK means *I d*on't *k*now.) Emojis are also commonplace in our everyday communication. Yet, as mainstream as you may think these abbreviations and symbols are, they don't fit in academic writing. Texting language and emojis are inappropriate in online education. Keep it on your phone. No smiley face needed.

Casual conversation

REMEMBER

An online course has appropriate places for casual conversation. For example, if your instructor sets up a discussion area called Student Lounge or Cafe, you can pretty much assume they don't expect scholarly writing in those forums. Also, some instructors allow for more casual learner-to-learner responses within discussion.

Suppose that coauthor Kevin has to answer a discussion question about an educational theorist. Following the guidelines and the rubric the instructor provided, Kevin writes three scholarly sounding paragraphs, including references to two outside sources. He follows APA style as requested by his instructor.

In response, coauthor Susan writes, "Wow! I just had an epiphany! You're so on target with your analysis of this theory. I was just telling my sister yesterday about how. . . ."

Susan's style and tone is a little too casual for academic or scholarly writing, but it's appropriate as a response to Kevin's post.

Knowing what's expected in your writing

Before you plunge into a writing assignment, take a look at what's expected. You can find this information within the instructions and the rubric. Three important aspects that influence how you write are the type of assignment, the length or word count, and any formatting requirements.

TIP

Remember how we advise you to make a list of criteria based on the rubric plus the instructions in the earlier section "Using rubrics to your advantage"? If you do this, you can't help but meet the expectations.

Recognizing the type of assignment

Read your assignment instructions carefully so that you know what's appropriate to include in your writing. Although all assignments require academic writing (which we describe earlier in this chapter), some of them allow more of your personality to shine through.

Think about the differences among a journal entry, a critique, and a literature review. Each of these calls for a slightly different type of writing:

>> A journal entry is personal and written in first person, meaning it's quite appropriate to use the word *I*.

>> A critique is less personal but involves judgment. It may also refer to other resources and texts, thereby requiring proper citation.

>> A literature review is a little more cut-and-dried with no judgment, just summary and reporting. It obviously requires references and citations.

TIP

Nothing is wrong with asking for an example. If you're confused from the beginning and can't get started with an assignment, ask your instructor whether they can share an example from the past.

Counting words to get the right length

How many words or pages you're allowed for a specific assignment tells you a lot about the writing. If your instructor asks you to answer a discussion question in 300 to 500 words, they're not looking for a full-blown paper on the topic! This also means that you need to write succinctly. Get to the point as quickly as possible, and then add a few examples. We recommend that you restate a portion of the question in your first sentence and skip lengthy introductions or storytelling.

On the other hand, if you're assigned a ten-page paper, the instructor expects you to fully develop each idea and back it up with outside resources. You can take a little more time and space to add details and illustrations of your main ideas.

TIP

Most word processing programs can help you determine your word count. If the count doesn't show in the bottom taskbar, look for a button or link labeled File Information or Properties and see whether the statistics are available there.

Formatting correctly

Check with your instructor about institutional formatting requirements. Do you need a title page? What margins are standard, and is there a preferred font? Should you number the pages? Some institutions have specific guidelines, and you want to know what they are before you start.

If your institution or instructor has formatting requirements, this information is usually found in the syllabus and again within the instructions for each assignment. If it's an institutional guideline, the institution may even provide you with a sample document that you overwrite so that you know your formatting is correct.

Demonstrating critical thinking

Coauthor Susan remembers asking a student a question once in a traditional face-to-face classroom and seeing the student visibly think through the response. He took the concept she was discussing, broke it into pieces, related it to something he had read, and then gave a well-reasoned, theoretically grounded response with his own insights. His eyes squinted, he rubbed his chin, and he spoke slowly with a few pauses. This was critical thinking in action in a face-to-face classroom. How does this work online?

Online, your instructor may not see your quizzical looks or chin-rubbing, but they can tell whether you thought critically about the question before you gave your response. They determine this through the quality of what you write. Your thoughts become transparent through your writing.

If you're not clear on the definition, *critical thinking* is the application of disciplined, thoughtful analysis to a problem. It combines what the experts say about the situation, what you know from life experience, and a dose of rational thought. You first break down the problem and then reassemble it with your own evaluation.

REMEMBER

There is no magical formula for giving an A+ answer in critical thinking, but here are some telltale signs that you're on the right track. Do the mental stretch and you'll be rewarded with better grades! Try to incorporate these indicators into your written work:

>> **Look at the question from multiple perspectives and explain this clearly.** Some people rush to judgment, but if you can show the "other side" of an argument or perspective, you're in a better position to demonstrate critical thinking.

>> **Actively ask questions.** People with strong critical thinking skills ask questions like, "What if . . ." or "How could the author have stated this differently?" Asking a lot of questions before you write may help you organize your thoughts, too!

>> **Find support via literature or research.** Critical thinking requires you to look beyond your own opinion and compare what you believe or know to others' ideas. In most academic writing, this is where we expect you to weave in references to other studies, books, or literature.

>> **Figure out how this relates to you and real life.** Anytime you can put something in to today's context, it demonstrates critical thinking. It shows you've thought about an idea and how it can be correctly applied to a different context.

TIP

Instructors know when students don't think before they type, so don't just sit down and start typing away at your assignment. Organize your thoughts by outlining the assignment first. In your outline, define the problem, summarize the literature, clarify your thoughts and opinions on the topic, and note examples of past experiences or possible future applications.

Completing Different Types of Assignments

Instructors measure student achievement in many different ways, all of which come in the form of assignments. You may be asked to write a paper, put together a project, participate in discussion, or take a quiz or test. In the next few sections, we look at each type of assignment and what it means to an online student.

Mastering papers and projects

For college-level online courses, papers and projects are the most common assignments. They keep students busy throughout a portion of the course and are a good vehicle for having learners comprehensively review major course concepts. If you're asked to submit a paper or project, consider the following ideas for success.

Papers

One of the most common assignments online students receive is "the paper." The following are examples of papers you may be asked to write:

>> Write a ten-page essay on your philosophy of integrating technology.

>> Write a five-page paper on your theories related to the causes of the Civil War.

>> Compare and contrast in a three-page paper the structures and functions of animal cells versus plant cells.

Your instructor looks for several markers of quality:

>> **Organized writing:** As we explain earlier in this chapter, scholarly writing requires organization. Whatever your topic, develop a clear thesis and present it from the beginning. Then write in a manner that supports the thesis.

>> **Points of view other than yours:** Instructors want to see that you've done the research and can summarize or quote from the experts. Citation is required!

>> **Original ideas:** Though your instructor expects you to research and provide sources for your background knowledge, they also expect you to develop some original ideas. Don't just repeat what the experts say — add your own insights based on past experiences and intellectual speculation.

Here are a few of the most common blunders we've observed:

TIP

>> **Not answering the question that was asked:** Nothing is more heart-wrenching than seeing a student submit a paper that has nothing to do with the question that was asked. As teachers, we assume that you put some work into this, and we hate to think that you wasted your time.

Save your teacher and yourself some heartache and make sure you understand the question being asked! In fact, sending a private email to double-check that you have it right before you start writing isn't a bad idea.

>> **Failure to cite any outside resources:** At the college level, inclusion of research and resources is a basic expectation.

>> **Confusing writing or writing that's full of nothing:** Sometimes we see writing that's poorly organized or grammatically askew, making it difficult to understand what the author wants to say. Or, the learner goes on needlessly with little substance. (We're being polite here!)

TIP

You can check for confusing reading in a couple of ways. The first is to ask someone who knows nothing about the subject to read your paper. Clueless people are quite helpful, sometimes. Absent the extra reader, eliminate all the extra phrases and make the sentences short. Get to the point. Then see what sentences you can combine to make the piece read a little more fluidly.

Projects

Rather than assign papers, your instructor may assign projects. Like papers, these generally call for a comprehensive understanding of the course content, but you complete them with a variety of tools. Consider these examples:

>> Develop a web page that shows an image, a banner, and a table.

>> Create a spreadsheet you could use as a general ledger for a small business.

>> Design a 10-minute presentation to sell your colleagues on the idea of social networking.

Projects allow you to show a great deal of creativity. Unless you're told which tool to use, you can explore different kinds of presentational tools. For example, you might build a narrated presentation using a web-based tool such as Visme (www.visme.co). Or, you could upload images and slides to a service such as SlideShare (www.slideshare.net).

REMEMBER

Most projects come with a rubric. Especially if the activity is complex, instructors provide guidelines and rubrics to help you determine whether you're meeting all the criteria. In the same way that you need to carefully read the rubric for any written work (as we explain earlier in this chapter), you should do the same for a project in order to complete it successfully.

Participating in discussions

The heart and soul of many online courses is the discussion area. This is where students answer key questions and respond to each other by replying to each other's messages and offering multiple perspectives. We have a few ideas about how to make your participation shine in terms of quality and quantity, even without seeing your instructor's rubric. (Flip to Chapter 11 for an introduction to discussions.)

Quality

Quality always trumps quantity! Take the time to answer your question succinctly yet thoroughly. Introduce some of the literature you've been reading in class, or refer to other sources you know of. Of course, add appropriate citations.

A good pattern to establish is this: Restate the question, present your initial view in a single sentence, point to some of the literature on the topic, and close with an interpretation of what this means in real life. If you can do that in a grammatically clean and clear fashion, you'll be submitting quality work.

REMEMBER

Before you hit the Post button or Submit button, proofread and double-check for accuracy!

With respect to your responses to other students, the instructor looks for quality writing here, too. You may want to say, "I agree!" but your instructor expects you to add why you agree, with some depth of thought. Follow up with an additional point from the literature or an example that exemplifies some data the original author proposed. Don't just post, "Me too!"

TIP

A good rule of thumb is to ask yourself whether the work you post has instructional value. Can people learn something from what you have written? If not, consider reworking the response.

Quantity

How often you post responses to other learners depends somewhat on the nature of the class, the instructor's expectations, and the learning community. Typically, the instructor notes the minimum number of posts they want to see. Be sure you know the expectations, which are typically described in a rubric handed out at the beginning of your course or within the instructions for the assignment.

Reading and following discussions can become overwhelming in an online course if learners post too frequently. Plus, the conversations can become long and drawn-out and break down to little more than trivial responses. And yet, your presence on the discussion board is one of the few ways the instructor knows whether you're engaged. By all means, meet the expectations, but then nudge yourself to go a little higher.

TIP

Look at your postings and see whether you're monopolizing the discussion board. If you're authoring more than 10 percent of the total posts, you're probably over-active. Pace yourself!

Taking quizzes and tests

One final method of measuring learner success is the traditional quiz or test. Whether you're asked multiple-choice questions or essay questions, quizzes and tests are relatively easy for instructors to administer and, in cases where the computer does the scoring, results are immediate.

When an instructor decides that a quiz or test is an appropriate measure of learner achievement, they make several decisions concerning the administration of the test. These clearly impact the learner! You may encounter these types of quizzes and tests:

>> **Tests with all kinds of questions:** Most testing software allows the instructor to choose from multiple-choice, true/false, short answer, and essay questions. This is nothing new to you as a learner. The only aspect that may be new is clicking in a box with a mouse instead of filling in a form with a pencil.

>> **Tests that have a time limit:** You may be limited in how long you have to complete the test. Instructors commonly leave a test "open" for only a few days and then set the software so that you must answer all the questions within so many minutes. This is to discourage you from looking at other sources (like your book) for answers. You have to know the material and answer quickly.

>> **Self-quizzes with no score:** Sometimes instructors build "self" quizzes to test your knowledge before taking a test for points. Practice makes perfect, so if you have the opportunity, test yourself!

>> **Open book/note exams:** To be truthful, we advise faculty to assume that students will use whatever resources they have available, including notes, books, and browsers. Your instructor may tell you that using your resources is permissible.

>> **Mail-in pencil exams:** Believe it or not, in some cases an online instructor may ask you to complete a paper/pencil exam and mail it in.

REMEMBER

If you have a documented disability, you may qualify for added support for test-taking like receiving extra time. Contact your Access Services Department and your instructor to make these arrangements. The sooner you do this, the better – before class begins is ideal.

When you have an independent third party monitor your exam, we say it's *proctored*. Proctors are like exam police making sure you are who you say you are and that you're not cheating. For high-stake exams, institutions insist on proctors. For example, if you're testing for a technical certification or a credential from a professional association, you will be proctored. The methods for proctoring vary and it's the decision of the institution (or association). You may be required to take a test

>> **At a center with a restricted IP range:** If you're taking a course from your local college, you may be required to come to campus and take the exam on their computers in their assessment center. This may not be the most convenient method, but it verifies identity and prevents you from using materials you may have saved on your computer. Additionally, if you're taking courses for

personal and professional development, you may be asked to go to a certified testing center. An example of this is a Pearson VUE Testing Center.

>> **With a professional "contractual" proctor:** Your school may allow you to find a proctor in your city and get that person authorized to monitor you. For example, coauthor Kevin proctors for a student he used to work with. When she has an exam, she takes it in front of him, he signs the exam to verify she was honest, and then he mails it to the school. If a school requires a proctor, they'll give you guidelines for types of people who are acceptable. Library staff are always favorite choices!

>> **By using a web-based service with enhanced technology:** Some companies proctor exams online with technology such as web cameras. For example, ProctorU at www.proctoru.com has test-takers log in, talk to a live proctor at the other end of the technology, turn on a webcam, scan the environment where they're taking the exam, and then take the exam. All of this is an attempt to make sure the person completing the exam is really you!

TIP

Don't cheat, don't cheat, don't cheat! Some of the newer proctoring software monitors your voice and the web pages you view, for example. If you're instructed to not look at outside resources, don't.

REMEMBER

How well you score on an exam depends on old-fashioned study skills. Chapter 12 guides you through strategies such as setting aside time every day to keep up with coursework, reading effectively, and taking notes. But perhaps the most valuable tip is staying engaged and active to increase your chances of success. The more you work with the ideas, by either reading discussions, taking self-tests, or practicing problem sets, the better your retention. If you're engaged and prepared, there's no need to panic at exam time!

Submitting Assignments

Think back to middle school (if it isn't too painful to remember those days!). Did you ever complete a homework assignment and forget to take it to school and turn it in? The same thing can happen online; you do the work and forget to submit it. In the next few sections, we review several methods for getting your homework to the instructor. These include uploads, email attachments, and Submit buttons. We also provide some pointers for turning in any kind of assignment.

Where did you store that file?

In Chapter 3 we review how to set a series of folders so that you stay organized. If you follow our advice, you won't need to think hard about where you stored the file. Nevertheless, sometimes files end up in random places. Before you log in to submit an assignment, make sure you know where it sits on your computer (or in what cloud). Did you put the final version in OneDrive? Is it a Google Docs document? Is it on your desktop? Figure that out first.

Attachments! Uploading papers and projects

Some learning management systems use a feature whereby students upload assignments. Different from email, this feature lets you put the document in only one place, and you don't need to know the instructor's address. The instructor retrieves your document, downloads it, and reads it. They may then comment on it and add a score to the grade book, all within the same tool.

If there's a secret to using this feature, it's knowing how to upload and hitting the Submit button until you receive confirmation. In most systems, you look for a button labeled Add a File or Upload. This prompts you to browse your computer to find the file. (See why knowing where you stored it is important?) Usually, you click Open after you identify the file you want and then click Submit. The next screen you see should be a confirmation that the file has been uploaded! Figure 16-1 shows what this looks like from the Student view in Canvas.

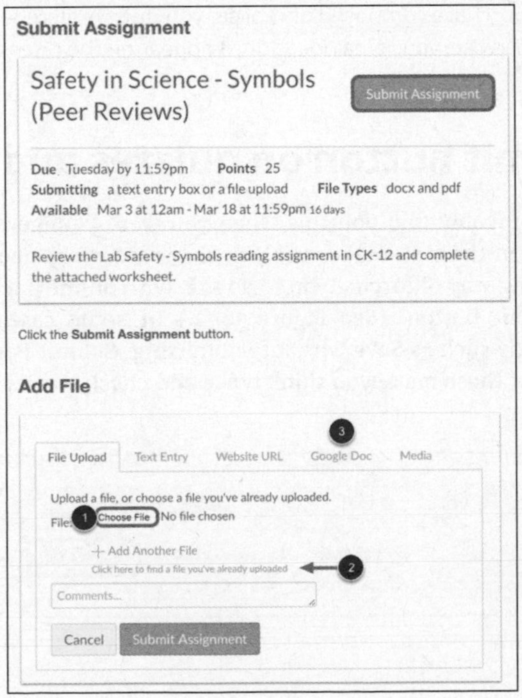

Submit Assignment

Safety in Science - Symbols (Peer Reviews)   Submit Assignment

Due Tuesday by 11:59pm   Points 25
Submitting a text entry box or a file upload   File Types docx and pdf
Available Mar 3 at 12am - Mar 18 at 11:59pm 16 days

Review the Lab Safety - Symbols reading assignment in CK-12 and complete the attached worksheet.

Click the **Submit Assignment** button.

Add File

File Upload   Text Entry   Website URL   Google Doc   Media

Upload a file, or choose a file you've already uploaded.
File   Choose File No file chosen
+ Add Another File
Click here to find a file you've already uploaded
Comments...

Cancel   Submit Assignment

FIGURE 16-1:
A dropbox
in Canvas.

If your instructor doesn't have this tool available, they may ask you to attach your work to an email. This process works the same as attaching photos to send to your dear cousin Ted. You find the Attachment icon (usually a paper clip), browse for the file, and upload. The uploading skill seems to be universal, whether you're attaching a document to an email or a discussion board posting. (Chapter 3 has the basics on fundamental email skills you should have before you enroll in an online course.)

REMEMBER

Some learning management systems connect to your Microsoft 365 or Google file structure, so you may be able to upload files from there.

Post, Emily! Submitting discussion posts

When you have a discussion question to post or respond to, the magic words change slightly:

>> **Compose:** Look for this button if you need to start a new discussion, one that isn't attached to anyone else's idea.

>> **Reply:** Use this button when you want to respond to something another person wrote. Here's a super tip: Copy-and-paste one or two lines from the original text (delete the rest) so that you can quote the first author and focus your comments.

>> **Post:** After you have composed or replied, you must remember to hit Post or Submit. Otherwise, your great ideas don't appear on the discussion board.

The Submit button on quizzes and tests

Your teachers probably told you this when you were younger: Check your work before you turn in the test. Make sure you answered every question. Technology has an interesting way of forcing you to do this with online quizzes and tests. It's called the Submit button. (See Figure 16-2.) In some cases, you'll be given additional options such as Save without Submitting, Submit Page, and Submit All and Finish. All of these make you think twice and check your work!

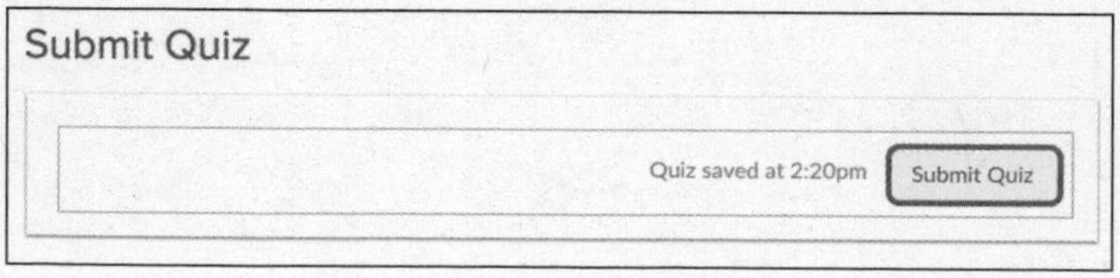

FIGURE 16-2:
A quiz page in Canvas shows different variations on the Submit button.

Submit Quiz
Quiz saved at 2:20pm   Submit Quiz

Tips for submitting any assignment

TIP

Whether you're working with papers, projects, discussion posts, quizzes, or tests, consider the following general pointers: Submit early, have a backup plan, and keep a copy. Here's why these are important:

>> **Submit early, when possible, in case of problems:** What if you plan to submit your assignment at 11:56 P.M. on the night it's due by midnight and the whole system crashes or your hard drive freezes? You don't have a lot of time to remedy that situation. A safer bet is to submit your work during normal working hours, well before you need to. That way, if you encounter a problem, you're more likely to contact a real-life tech support person who can assist you. (See Chapter 10 for more information on technical support.)

>> **Attach to email when technology fails:** Still on the 11:56 P.M. track? When all else fails, send the same assignment as an attachment to an email to your instructor. Include a polite note explaining that the system wasn't cooperating and that you wanted to be sure to get the assignment turned in, one way or another. This shows good problem-solving skills.

>> **Keep a copy:** Always, always keep copies of your work for the term of the course. You never know when you might need them. It's common for the system to freeze up when you're trying to submit a great discussion post (always when you've written something worthy of a Pulitzer), so if you first compose in a word processor and then copy-and-paste to the discussion area, you're safe in knowing that you have the original text. Should there be any question, you can find the file and resubmit it.

Understand How and When to Use Media

In addition to the written word, you may have the option of creating an assignment in the form of a video or an infographic. We refer to any assignment format that isn't exclusively written as *media*. Here are a couple of great examples:

>> **The assignment is to introduce yourself.** Rather than write the introduction, you record a quick video.

>> **The assignment is to explain the major principles of adult education.** Rather than write a discussion post, you create an attractive infographic.

>> **The assignment is to document the kinds of questions children ask at varying ages.** In addition to submitting a written lab report, you include audio clips of a dialogue with you and your child.

Using images

You know of a wonderful image that supports your assignment. For example, a map that shows migration patterns may be a nice addition to your paper about monarch butterflies. Why not add it to the submission?

First, a couple of warnings:

>> **Always provide the source!** Though you have a little more latitude in using a copyrighted image for the purpose of an academic assignment, you should not add an image that is copyrighted unless you're citing it as you would if you were quoting an author.

>> **Be certain your instructor is open to images.** That might sound silly, but you don't want them to think you're trying to get out of writing if you add the image. It can't hurt to ask.

TIP

If you're looking for an image that is available for use freely without concern for copyright, check out Creative Commons at `https://creativecommons`.

Images can be added to documents easily. Look for the Insert command on the top toolbar. Then choose Image or Picture from the submenu that appears and navigate to the one you want to include. After you have the image in the document, you can often drag and resize.

Using infographics

Infographics are a popular visual method to summarize information. Your instructor may give you the option to create one for a class assignment. You can use free tools such as Canva — available at `www.canva.com` — to create your own infographic.

If you choose to create an infographic for an academic assignment, be certain you still give credit and cite other works. For example, if you're referencing a study done by a professional human resources association, add a small citation or link to the article you're referencing. Above all, demonstrate your academic integrity.

TIP

It takes a true spirit of adventure to play with new tools. In Chapter 8, we talk a lot about the benefits of having a growth mindset. Here's an example where a growth mindset and spirit of curiosity can take you far using these tools. Just don't get so lost in the tool that you forget the point of the assignment.

Using audio

Including audio in an assignment might seem obvious for music studies. You can record yourself performing. However, you may want to consider audio for other reasons:

>> To document an interview so that the listener hears the tone and context

>> To demonstrate pronunciation or fluency in any language

You may be surprised that your computer has built-in tools for recording audio:

>> **On a Windows machine:** Choose Accessories ⇨ Sound Recorder.

>> **On a Mac:** Choose Applications ⇨ QuickTime Player.

>> **On a Chromebook:** You can add tools via Google Play.

>> **On your phone:** Even your phone can record audio, by using a voice recorder app, which can be easily found on Apple's App store or on Google Play.

In some instances, you can record audio directly in the learning management system. For example, in Canvas you can click a single button to record your voice inside the discussion forum. So, if your instructor is asking you to use vocabulary words in sentences, you don't have to write them. You can record your voice speaking those sentences so that tone and inflection can be heard and then submit the recording immediately afterward. Figure 16-3 shows you an audio submission inside Canvas.

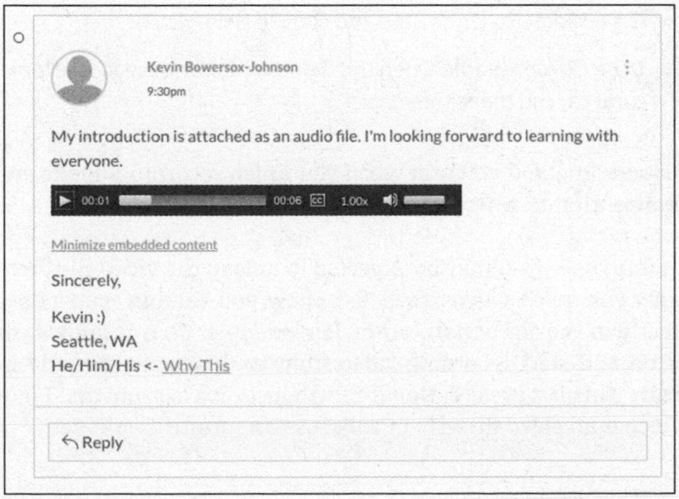

FIGURE 16-3: Audio submission inside a Canvas discussion forum.

WARNING

We aren't talking about audio editing in this section. That's another book! We are only referencing the ability to create a short audio file, unedited, so that you can upload it for an assignment.

In all cases, make sure your microphone is working and that you know what file format was used to capture the recording. After you finish the recording, pay attention to where you store the file. If you want to upload that file as part of an assignment submission, you need to know where it is!

Chances are good that an instructor who is asking for an audio file has provided you with tips to get started. Pay attention to those tips.

Using video

You may be given an option to record a video for a class assignment. You don't need to be a YouTube star to make that happen. Again, we are talking only about recording a 1- to 2-minute video, not editing it.

The easiest way to record video is to use a smartphone! Turn on the camera, steady your hand, and talk. Your phone is also a great option for going out in the field and conducting an interview to submit as a part of an assignment.

Of course, you can also use whatever built-in webcam feature you have if you're working on a laptop with one of the following operating systems:

>> **On a Windows machine:** Find the Camera tool, switch to Video, look into the camera, and record!

>> **On a Mac:** Use QuickTime and choose New Movie.

>> **On a Chromebook:** Open the Camera tool, choose Video, look into the camera, and make the magic!

Whatever method you use, when you finish recording, make sure you save it (and pay attention to where you're saving).

In some cases, you may be expected to upload the video file directly for an assignment. For quick videos that just show you talking, you may be able to record directly in the discussion forum. For example, Canvas allows you to press a single button and start recording video from your webcam directly into the discussion forum. This is a great option for introduction assignments. Figure 16-4 illustrates a video embedded directly in a discussion forum.

FIGURE 16-4:
A video,
embedded in a
discussion.

For projects that require a little more attention to detail and might be longer, a much, much easier way to deliver the video to your instructor is to put it on YouTube. Create an account, upload the file, and share the URL. We discuss audio and video options in Chapter 17.

REMEMBER

Not everyone accesses information in the same way. You may have peers in the class who are blind or deaf and are unable to see or hear your media submissions. So, it would be ideal if all images had clear, text-based descriptions, audio files had full transcripts, and video files were captioned. As instructors, we understand that not all students will know how to do this, so we ask that you provide a clear, text-based description or summary with media submissions.

Chapter **17**

Building a Portfolio of Work

n Chapter 5, we talk about finding a program and an institution that meet your needs. Why are you in school? The vision of your goal should be a constant driving force throughout your academic career. Keeping your main objective in mind helps motivate you to complete courses and stay on track.

If you plan to look for the perfect job after you finish your online education or you plan to put a newly earned credential to work, collecting a few artifacts throughout your journey can help you when it comes time to prepare for interviews. *Artifacts* serve as souvenirs of your trip. They should demonstrate your skills and abilities within the field. This chapter introduces some ideas on how to find and prepare for that dream interview through the creation of a body of work.

Developing a Body of Work to Take with You

A *portfolio* is a collection of artifacts that demonstrates a person's past work, either academic or professional. It showcases skills and abilities by providing sample work created in various work and school settings. Think of an artist and the kind of portfolio of their work you might expect to see. Now think of a web designer: The collection might be a website. Think of a writer: The collection might be essays and short stories.

If you store that work online, you have an ePortfolio. An *ePortfolio* accomplishes the same goal — to showcase your skills and abilities by way of artifacts — but rather than share a physical item with prospective employers, you simply provide them with the URL to a website where the same information is stored digitally, either for public viewing or by private invitation only. Figure 17-1 illustrates what a public ePortfolio may look like. The illustration displays a single project a student documented on his ePortfolio site. On this particular student's site, he allows visitors to interact with him by providing the ability to leave comments specific to the information being displayed.

FIGURE 17-1:
The public view of an ePortfolio.

In this section, we explain how you can use an ePortfolio to your advantage, and we describe its components. We also help you choose a method for building an ePortfolio, provide pointers for successful design, and tell you how to include items that aren't a part of your online coursework.

Understanding how to use an ePortfolio

REMEMBER

You can use an ePortfolio in two important ways:

>> **To satisfy educational requirements:** Many degree programs now require learners to build and maintain an ePortfolio throughout their academic career as a way of documenting growth and highlighting their academic accomplishments. In this situation, learners are often asked to also reflect on the experience of creating the artifacts added to the ePortfolio as a way of assessing the student's understanding of the project overall. (See the later section "Creating reflection statements" for more information.) As a degree program requirement, graduating is dependent on the completion of the ePortfolio. Some institutions even require a formal presentation to accompany the project.

>> **To land a job:** ePortfolios can also be used for promoting your knowledge, skills, and abilities to prospective employers. When applying for a new job or promotion, you can share your ePortfolio's website address (URL) with the hiring manager. The hiring manager can visit your site and gain a clear picture of your academic and work experiences to facilitate the hiring decision.

Checking out typical components of an ePortfolio

You can choose several items from your online coursework to add to your ePortfolio. Choose the pieces carefully and organize your site in a manner that's logical and easy to navigate. This section reviews different types of items and provides some examples of specific information to include.

Attaching artifacts such as papers and projects

Artifacts are objects created by you that can be added to your ePortfolio as attachments. When adding artifacts to your ePortfolio, ensure that your audience understands why you included them. Therefore, for each artifact, include a title and description and the context in which the artifact was created.

REMEMBER

Visitors may be downloading your work directly to their computer. Therefore, when adding artifacts to your site, consider whether you need to password-protect files before uploading and linking them to your ePortfolio. (We show you how in Chapter 3.) Then visitors can open and view your documents, but not edit them. Additionally, if you store your documents in a place like Google Drive, tweak the settings to View Only and not Edit.

Here are a few examples of the different types of artifacts you may want to consider adding to your ePortfolio:

>> **Document:** For example, an essay on the connection between Bloom's taxonomy and ePortfolios as it relates to education. Consider using text to briefly summarize the essay's contents with a link to click on if someone wants to download the document in its entirety.

>> **Image:** Perhaps a series of digital images that you shot and modified for an online photography course. Consider using text to describe the images and the purpose for taking them.

>> **Certification or alternative credential:** If you have a certification, add it to your portfolio. This is especially easy if your credential is represented in digital form such as a digital badge, where you can embed it in your ePortfolio. When a viewer clicks on it, they can verify that it was issued to you.

>> **Audio file:** For instance, an audio interview you conducted with a professional in your field. Consider adding a written transcript and general description of the assignment when attaching an audio file to your ePortfolio.

>> **PowerPoint presentation:** For example, a group presentation on the benefits and challenges of creating and maintaining a website for your web development course. Consider describing your contributions to the project and the tools you used to collaborate with your group in a reflection statement. (See the next section.)

>> **Video file:** For example, a video illustrating your ability to shoot, edit, and encode video for your Introduction to Video Editing course. Consider adding a written transcript and a general description of the assignment when attaching a video file to your ePortfolio.

WARNING

If your institution doesn't require you to use an ePortfolio system, acquire your instructors' permission before posting graded work with their comments on it. Instructors may ask you not to display their comments or grades publicly. The reason isn't that they treated you differently from other students — it's that it has the potential to stir up other classmates who may not have done as well as you.

Creating reflection statements

A *reflection statement* is used in the academic world as a way of helping the instructor assess your process as well as your final product. These statements can be quite helpful to both instructors and employers reviewing your ePortfolio for either academic or professional reasons. For example, by seeing your reflections on a project you completed in school, an employer can see how you organize and process information in order to obtain a goal.

The length of a reflection statement can range from one paragraph to multiple pages, depending on the context. A good rule of thumb is to briefly describe the project, the educational objectives it meets, how the project can be applied, and what you learned from completing the project. For example, the following is a reflection on an assignment requiring the creation of an ePortfolio website:

> *By requiring me to organize and document all my academic, professional, and volunteer experiences, I have been able to better understand where I have been, where I am currently, and where I am going. As a part of this project, I was required to learn about the resources and services available to create an online portfolio. The design process required me to develop a site that organizes my information into manageable chunks while maintaining an easy navigation structure for my visitors. This project also forced me to reflect on each assignment and how lessons learned can be applied in my life outside the classroom. As a living document, my ePortfolio will continue to be updated, and therefore require me to continuously reflect and grow with my field.*

TIP

As you write a reflection statement, try to weave in the same language you would expect a potential employer to use. That helps connect your work to their needs.

Providing informal transcripts of courses

Posting transcripts on your ePortfolio website lets your visitors see your level of dedication and provides a general sense of the quality of your work. You can let your visitors know the grade you earned for each course or your cumulative grade point average (GPA) for a program in a couple ways:

>> You can simply provide your cumulative GPA (for example, 4.8/5.0) on the program description page and the actual grade earned (A, B, and so on) next to the title of each course. In this case, the reader has to believe you.

>> You can scan your official transcript, adding it to your ePortfolio as an artifact and linking to it from your program's description page. Of course, scanning your transcript, even an official one, takes away its official status. Prospective employers may still require you to send them official transcripts directly from the institution in a sealed envelope.

WARNING

If for any reason you had a bad semester (and many people do), consider not adding this information to your ePortfolio. Most employers don't require this information, and if they do, you can supply them with official transcripts upon request. Being consistent in presentation and supplying this information for all courses and programs is better than posting it only for those courses you did well in.

Including recommendations from faculty

There are no better people to serve as your advocates than your instructors. They know the quality of work you produce and the level of dedication you put forth to complete your assignments. Therefore, be sure to build a professional relationship with them, and don't be afraid to ask them for letters of recommendation. Here are some guidelines to follow:

» **Be selective about which instructors you ask for a recommendation.** You don't need a recommendation from every instructor. One way to filter is to ask only those instructors who teach subjects that most resemble the type of work you're doing or hope to be doing in the future.

» **Ask in plenty of time.** Don't wait until you've completed your program to ask for a recommendation. Timing is everything. Think ahead and ask each instructor at the end of the course, when your participation and the quality of your work are fresh in the teacher's memory.

» **Provide instructors with an overview of your professional goals and a link to your ePortfolio.** Doing so helps them write a letter that matches your career goals. You can also send them your résumé if your ePortfolio is still in progress.

» **Provide instructors with two or three weeks to complete the letter.** Extending this courtesy gives them time to turn in grades and review your information more before writing.

» **Explain to your instructors exactly what you're looking for and specify that you want to publicly display the recommendation on your ePortfolio website.** Many institutions house instructor recommendations in the student's file, but these recommendations are anonymous to the student, making them unsuitable for your purpose.

Incorporating your résumé and work history

Have you ever wanted to add more details to your résumé so that prospective employers see what you really do on a daily basis? The nice thing about having an ePortfolio is that it gives you the ability to expand on information you can't fit on a two-page resume.

Though this feature is useful, don't forget to spread chunks of information across multiple pages so that everything isn't on the same page — you don't want to overwhelm the reader. Arrange chunks of information by dates of service and organization. Following is a list of components to add when including work history in your ePortfolio:

- **» Organization profile:** Provide the organization's name, geographic location, and mission.

- **» Position title:** Include the title of the position(s) you held within the organization and a brief description of the position's overall purpose.

- **» Dates of service:** Sequence your position titles within each organization by dates of services, in descending order. This strategy places your most recent experience at the top of the list.

- **» Accomplishments:** Provide a bulleted list of the accomplishments by stating the tasks you handled, the way you accomplished each task, and the result in quantifiable terms when possible. For example, you might say: "Created a database that analyzed recoverable charges to the organization, which led to the company's recovery of 1.5 million dollars."

- **» Project artifacts:** Provide artifacts for the accomplishments listed, when possible. For example, you might provide an empty copy of the database that was created to recover the $1.5 million noted in the preceding bullet.

REMEMBER

Always remove private information that might violate the law or have negative repercussions. For example, in the preceding database example, you'd want to share the database with either no data or fictitious data in it so that viewers can see what you developed without also seeing the private information used by the organization, such as names, addresses, and dollar amounts.

Sharing favorite resource links

Providing your visitors with a list of resources proves that you're aware of what's going on within your field. Plus, it provides you with a single location to return to when you need to find information yourself. Resources can include links to professional blogs, podcasts, journal articles, associations, conferences, citation style resources, career help, and other academic resources.

REMEMBER

Stick to professional links in your ePortfolio. This isn't the place to link to your favorite satire blog, cartoon site, or daily word puzzle.

Choosing a method for creating an ePortfolio

You can go about creating an ePortfolio in three different ways: Use institutional resources, subscribe to a service, or create your own from scratch.

Using institutional resources

Your institution may incorporate the use of an ePortfolio system in its program curriculum, which you're subsequently required to use. This system may be either built-in or external:

>> **Built-in:** Some institutions build ePortfolio programs into their learning management systems and tie them directly to each major assignment's rubric. The student can then upload the assignment and import the instructor's assessment with comments to the ePortfolio system.

>> **External:** Some institutions alternatively use an external service in a similar fashion, but it requires the student to log in to a separate website using a different username and password. The system may also have the capability to allow instructors to create rubrics to attach to artifacts. However, in this situation, the instructor is required to also log in to a separate system and copy-and-paste rubric elements and assessment comments to that system.

TIP

To find out whether your institution provides an ePortfolio system, first ask your academic advisor. If that person can't help, you can contact either your instructor or career services staff. Some institutions provide a career-oriented ePortfolio product, which is often available after graduation for a yearly or monthly fee.

Either way, this type of ePortfolio system allows the institution to dictate some of the artifacts to be added, along with their respective grades and instructor comments. Required artifacts might include course essays, final projects, or reflection assignments. By having all this information in one place, program faculty and deans can see each student's growth throughout the program as a way of assessing student performance and program effectiveness.

One benefit to using your institution's required ePortfolio system is that you're already paying for it by way of program fees. Therefore, you won't have an external cost to use it while you're a student. However, the possible downside is that you may be required to subscribe to that service after graduation in order to maintain your site and its contents. In some situations, you get to continue using the service for one year after graduation before having to decide whether to subscribe to that service or re-create your site by building it yourself or subscribing to a different service.

Subscribing to a service

TIP

You can subscribe to a service if your school has no required ePortfolio system or you prefer to exercise more control over its contents. Several subscription-based services offer web space for you to house and display your ePortfolio. These services offer templates for adding content and disk storage for uploading documents and other artifacts. Following are a few such services:

>> **PortfolioGen:** portfoliogen.com

>> **Behance:** behance.com

>> **Interfolio:** interfolio.com

One advantage to subscribing to a service is that it provides online templates for you to complete, requiring only web navigation skills and your portfolio content. Another advantage is the ability to lock down your site so that only invited guests can view it.

WARNING

Of course, these sites cost money, so prepare to pay for the convenience, and keep paying the bill. Imagine the embarrassment of sending a potential employer to your site and finding out that it's unavailable because you forgot to make a payment!

Creating your own ePortfolio from the ground up

Another method of building an ePortfolio is to create your own from scratch. The biggest advantage to creating your own ePortfolio is the ability to customize the design and navigation of the site to reflect your individuality. When you subscribe to a service, you're limited to the number of templates available from the service provider, which means your portfolio may physically look like those of other students who subscribe to the same service.

In the old days, if you wanted to create your own site, you'd need the following: a web hosting service, a registered domain name, and programming knowledge.

We are happy to report that there are now web building services that are easy to use. You can literally drag and drop in many cases to build your own ePortfolio site. Plus, many of them are free!

Designing a successful ePortfolio

TIP

Think about all your accomplishments as an employee, a volunteer, and/or a student. You probably have quite a list. The most helpful tip we can provide is to advise you to find a way to organize your information into chunks so that visitors can quickly access data without being overwhelmed. Here are a few more tips for designing a successful ePortfolio site:

>> **Create a top level navigation based on categories:** Organize information into logical sections and create a web menu and navigation system around that structure. For example, consider organizing your information using the following categories: Home, Overview, Education, Work Experience, and Community Involvement.

» **Create a sublevel navigation within your top level categories:** Arrange and sequence the information in each of the top level categories based on dates, organizations, job titles, and so on. For example, a visitor who clicks on Education should see a list of institutions you've attended, the dates you attended, a brief description of the program you were enrolled in, and links that give the option to see a list of specific courses, course syllabi, and course-specific projects. When a user clicks on Work Experience, a page should appear with a list of job titles, organizations, brief job descriptions, dates of employment, and links to specific job responsibilities and projects for each job. Figure 17-2 illustrates what sublevel navigation in an ePortfolio may look like. (Specifically, this figure shows sublevel navigation in an ePortfolio created with Weebly.)

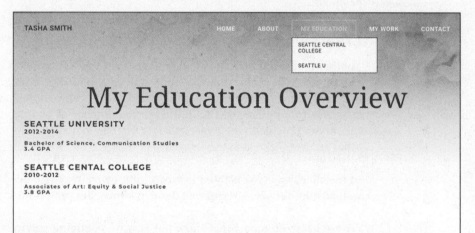

FIGURE 17-2: Sublevel navigation in an ePortfolio created with Weebly.

» **Create a welcome page:** The first thing a visitor to your ePortfolio site should see is a welcome screen with basic information such as your name, current position, contact information, and, possibly, a picture. Think of this page as a digital business card.

» **Create an overview page:** The overview page should include a brief overview of who you are academically/professionally, what you've learned from your school/work experience, and how your education has been applied in different situations. Think of this page as your digital cover letter, preparing visitors to view your digital résumé.

» **Know your audience:** Understanding why you're creating your ePortfolio can help you design for and write to your audience. For example, you may write differently for your instructors than you would for future employers. Because your ePortfolio may be shown to multiple audiences, be sure that the description of each component reflects the intended context. For example, when writing for instructors, provide an overview of each assignment along with what you learned specific to the objectives of the course. When writing for a more general audience, again provide an overview of each assignment, along with how you scored, what you learned from the project, and how the information you learned can be applied to other situations, such as a work environment.

>> **Be authentic and cite sources when necessary:** Displaying work that's authentic in nature and providing sources when you share non-original ideas is important. Remember that this site is a reflection of you, including your ethical standards.

>> **Keep your information up-to-date:** A portfolio is always a work in progress. However, unlike your physical portfolio, viewers may have access to your ePortfolio at any time. Therefore, it's important to keep your information current.

Transferring your existing portfolio to the web

You may have previous work, volunteer, or education experiences from an existing portfolio that you want to include in an ePortfolio. Great! The next step is to prepare that material for the web. Here's a list of the different artifact types and considerations to make when transferring them to the web:

>> **Word processing documents:** Consider converting short (one page or less) word processing documents to HTML so that visitors don't have to download them. Save longer documents as one of the more common file types so that visitors can view your work in multiple applications. Some of the more popular document types are .PDF, .RTF, and .DOC. Each of these formats can be opened with either a free document viewer or a basic word processing program that comes installed on most computers.

>> **Images/photographs:** Unless you're in the field of marketing or photography, consider reducing image size and resolution to a web-friendly configuration. Web files should be set at 72 dots per inch (dpi) and around 20 to 50 kilobytes. An excellent free program has been created for both Windows and Mac machines that can help you do this quickly: Gimp (gimp.org). Reducing image size and resolution allows for quick loading. Common image file types are .PNG, .GIF, and .JPG.

TIP

Avoid placing multiple images on one page. The fewer the photos, the faster the page loads for your visitors.

>> **Audio files:** Audio files are larger files and can take longer to download. Therefore, you should place them on a streaming site so that you can link to them or embed a player. Check out a free hosting site, such as Buzzsprout at www.buzzsprout.com/ or Simplecast at https://simplecast.com/.

TECHNICAL
STUFF

Streaming refers to how media such as audio and video files are delivered to a user over the Internet. Audio and video files are often quite large. If visitors are required to wait for the entire file to download to their computer before listening to or viewing the file, they may get bored and navigate to another site. Therefore, finding a free site to host your media is gold!

>> **Video files:** Video files are very large files that can take a long time for visitors to download. The most common place for hosting video is YouTube (www.youtube.com). However, you can also look at services such as Vimeo at https://vimeo.com/, where you may have a little more control over what displays after your video. After you upload your video, you can grab the embed code and put it in your ePortfolio.

TECHNICAL
STUFF

Embedding refers to taking a snippet of code generated by a streaming site and putting into a website. It sounds harder than it is. You can find videos on YouTube about how to do this.

TIP

If large video files are needed, consider providing visitors with a clip of the video online and then contact information to request a full-length video on CD or DVD via snail mail.

REMEMBER

No matter what type of artifact you choose to add to your ePortfolio, we recommend that each element have some introductory content that allows your visitors to quickly look at your work and choose which elements they want to explore in greater detail.

Getting Help with Finding a Job

Once your online coursework is done and your ePortfolio site is up-to-date, you may want to find a job that puts your newfound skills to use. Several resources are available to you online to help you in the job search process.

Benefiting from career services at your school

Most academic institutions have a career services department to help students who need career counseling, job searching skills, and other career resources. Most of these services are available online so that they're accessible by both campus-based and online students. If you're unsure whether your institution offers such services, contact your academic advisor. (We introduce the role of this important person in Chapter 5.)

Services provided by these career centers include the ones described in this list:

>> **Career counseling:** A career counselor may meet with you one-on-one or in a group setting over the phone to help provide direction in the areas of self-assessment, goal setting, and basic job searching.

>> **Job and internship listings:** Most career services departments have a private list where students can view jobs and internship possibilities posted by organizations. These listings are often organized by profession for easy searching.

>> **Career and internship fairs:** The fact that you may not live in your school's locality doesn't mean you can't attend a job fair. Online institutions are beginning to offer job fairs online. Organizations are asked to provide quick presentations via synchronous tools such as Zoom, and students are invited to join the session, ask questions, and submit résumés.

>> **Career resource webinars:** Career services staff may also offer webinars to provide tips, tricks, and other resources on topics such as searching for jobs, building a résumé, interviewing, and following up with prospective employers.

>> **On-campus recruiting:** Again, just because you're not local, don't assume that you can't work for the institution you're attending from a distance. Most likely, some of your instructors didn't live near the campus, right? Online institutions understand that work can be done even when co-workers aren't in the same physical location. So don't ignore those campus ads when browsing the career service's website. Your institution may provide both student jobs and full-time employment upon graduation.

Perusing general job search sites

Whether your institution provides career services or not, you can still do a lot of things outside of the institution to promote yourself. Specifically, several job sites post local, national, and international job opportunities. The advantages of these sites include the number of employers that utilize them and the ability they give you to filter searches by profession and location.

Job search sites usually offer these two types of services:

>> **Free services** provide you with general searching capabilities and give you access to several jobs available in your field.

>> **Paid services** usually include more customized features, such as the ability to create a profile that is placed in a database that's searched by employers.

Job search sites also offer free resources such as strategies for building your résumé, searching for jobs, and interviewing. Be sure to review each site's resources to gather a variety of ideas, and then customize those strategies to suit your personality and needs.

TIP

Here are a few job search databases to consider when conducting your employment search:

>> **LinkedIn:** linkedin.com/jobs

>> **CareerBuilder:** careerbuilder.com

>> **Indeed:** www.indeed.com

>> **Monster:** www.monster.com

>> **USA Jobs:** www.usajobs.gov

Establishing networks while studying online

TIP

As you attend your classes, be cognizant of all the networking possibilities you run into. These can lead to future project collaboration or jobs. Here are a few networking opportunities to keep an eye out for:

>> **Student introductions:** Pay close attention to the introduction of your peers. You'll probably find that they come from a variety of backgrounds and experiences. Befriend those who currently work in your field of interest and/or have a lot of experience.

>> **Partner and group work:** Much like the student introductions, you should also network with group-work partners. Take time to introduce yourself to your partner or group, and share your goals and your current situation. (Chapter 13 has the basics on working in groups online.)

>> **Volunteer and internship opportunities:** Look for opportunities to volunteer or intern within the field you're studying. By doing this, you connect with

professionals in the field, demonstrate the quality of your work, and gain experience to add to your résumé. Many students end up working for the organization where they either volunteered or interned. Don't assume that you have to be onsite to volunteer. You can find plenty of opportunities for online internships and volunteer experiences. Check out virtual internships at vitualinternships.com.

>> **Guest speakers:** If your online course has a guest speaker visit and interact with the class, document the guest's name and contact information. One way to get on that person's radar for future interactions is to send the guest a private thank-you letter with your contact information.

>> **Associations:** Professional fields are often defined by their associations. Though they cost to join, most associations have a student rate. Take advantage of it while you can, and join the professional organizations associated with your profession. Doing this provides you with access to professionals within the field, job bulletins, and conference discounts. Professional associations also offer online courses and certifications as well as opportunities to volunteer.

>> **Conferences:** Look for and attend conferences within your field. If none is offered locally, consider traveling and asking peers within your program to split travel costs such as gas and hotel. Attending conferences is a great way to hear presentations on trends and issues within your field. Conferences are also useful for networking with professionals and prospective employers.

>> **Networking websites:** Take advantage of professional networking sites. There's more than LinkedIn (although it's the most popular site). Look at other networking services such as Meetup at meetup.com or Opportunity at myopportunity.com. These sites provide networking opportunities on both social and professional levels. Curate a professional profile and share what you're looking for in terms of career enhancement. In fact, share your ePortfolio!

TIP

Creating a business card with your contact information and the web address of your ePortfolio on it is an excellent way to be prepared for those unexpected run-ins with prospective employers. For example, a friend of coauthor Kevin attended a conference in his field at the end of his studies and was provided several opportunities to network with professionals in the field. He was able to give prospective employers his business card, which directed them to his ePortfolio site. Within two weeks of the conference ending, Kevin's friend had two interviews, one of which landed him a job.

4

Special Considerations in Online Learning

IN THIS PART . . .

Access the online tools for academic success in the K-12 learning environment

See how online learning can smooth the path for differently abled students

Recognize the benefits of online learning for a diverse population

Chapter **18**

Educating Students from Kindergarten through High School

A s we are writing the revision of this book, many teachers and K–12 students are scrambling to teach and learn online as schools across the world close for the COVID-19 pandemic. Though this is a legitimate reason for online learning for K-12 students, many teachers and students weren't ready. Quality online learning takes time to develop, and it takes time for institutions to put the necessary support systems in place to ensure student success. Our hearts go out to all those having to react to such an event and who were not given the appropriate time to develop quality online solutions such as those we talk about in this chapter.

In Chapter 2 we briefly introduce the benefits of online learning for kids. This chapter examines why younger learners of all ages are taking courses online, and how this type of online education is different from that of their adult counterparts. We walk you through the various models of online learning for young students and discuss what you should know before signing up your child for an online course.

Understanding Why Kids Are Attending School Online

We could point you toward the Pew Research Center's Internet & American Life Project and their reports regarding Internet usage among kids ages 12 to 17, but you probably don't need research to know that kids are online. Granted, a lot of their time is spent checking social networking accounts and playing games, but a growing amount of time is spent learning. In the next few sections, we review some of the reasons that kids of all ages are attending online classes, either because they want to or because they need to.

Wanting to be online

The first category of kids who want to be online includes families who voluntarily move all or part of their children's instruction online. Notice that we introduce the idea of family decision-making; children rarely make this decision on their own. Nevertheless, here are a couple of popular reasons:

>> **Families are homeschooling.** Online education allows families who home-school to select curricula and programs that better meet their needs. Parents who aren't expert educators stand a better chance of introducing materials and methods that will truly help their children learn better because the online school provides a teacher who partners with the parent.

>> **Kids can learn at their own pace.** Because most online programs are set up to allow a child to complete the work independently, a fast learner can move at a fast pace. Gifted and talented children aren't held back by the pace of instruction. The same is true for children who need more time to master a subject. Because he's working independently, a child can take longer on a particular lesson, if he needs to.

Needing to be online

Sometimes the decision to move instruction online comes from an external force. Here are a few such circumstances:

>> **Health or family concerns interfere with traditional education.** Unfortunately, a child may have to deal with a significant health issue — for example, extreme epilepsy — that prevents them from attending a traditional school. Additionally, older children occasionally need to drop out of school to contribute to the family, by providing either childcare or medical care for

parents. Online education allows these kids to continue learning at home with a schedule that's more convenient. Online opportunities allow kids to make progress toward their educational goals despite such circumstances.

» **The course is only available online.** Advanced and specialized classes may not be available to kids who live in rural school districts or whose local public schools have limited resources. However, these students may find these types of classes online by way of virtual schools. Advanced placement (AP) courses are available via many online programs, for example.

» **The student has had disciplinary issues.** A child may have made some bad decisions that resulted in expulsion. When a child is expelled from school, families have few options other than homeschooling or extremely costly private schools. Online education may be a method whereby kids can continue learning.

» **The student has been bullied at school.** According to the Gay, Lesbian, Straight Education Network (GLSEN) 2017 Climate Survey, 59.5% of LGBTQ students report feeling unsafe at school because of their sexual orientation. Scenarios like these often lead to students searching for alternative learning spaces — including online programs.

» **The kid has a career.** Child athletes and actors lead unusual lives. We used to commonly read about child actors and their tutors, but today with online education, tutoring may be electronic. The same is true for athletes. A rising star in the ice skating world, for instance, may complete their education online while training for major competitions.

TECHNICAL
STUFF

» **The teacher sends the student online.** Traditional high schools may offer a portion of instruction online as a hybrid or web-enhanced course. The teacher may ask students to complete homework assignments or quizzes online so that class time can be used for other activities. Though this chapter doesn't go into details on this type of structure, we at least want to note that kids are partially online because their teachers have directed them there.

Seeing the Differences between K-12 and Adult Online Education

What makes online education unique for younger learners? After all, it can't be the same as online education for college students, can it? In the next few sections, we consider safety issues, extra parental involvement, synchronous meetings, and the need to work offline.

Safety concerns with children

REMEMBER

We won't kid you: Having children learn online is a reason for parents and guardians to be concerned about their safety. For starters, children tend to trust everyone and may not have the same sense of boundaries that adults do. Plus, creeps on the Internet prey on children. In the interest of avoiding hysteria, we want to frame some of these concerns with the positive solutions that online schools have put in place:

>> **Online education must be supervised by adults.** In the next section, we discuss enhanced parental involvement, and one of the primary reasons for this is to monitor what children do online, where they go, and with whom they communicate.

>> **Online programs must be password-protected with limited access.** Institutions establish protocols so that only the students and their adult supervisors can log in to the learning space. Coursework is conducted within that space so that a child has no need to interact with anyone else online. (Chapter 3 introduces the basics of password-protection.)

>> **Educators who work with children online must pass stringent background checks.** In the same way that teachers in brick-and-mortar schools must be blemish-free, online institutions ensure that their faculty are likewise squeaky clean.

Aside from addressing adults who prey on children, anyone with children online must also be aware of cyberbullying. *Cyberbullying* is the act of a child embarrassing, threatening, or harassing another child through online tools such as email, instant messaging, social networks, and public discussion forums. With adult learners, the same behavior is possible and disconcerting, but children need to be afforded special protection. (As soon as adults become involved, the language changes to *cyberstalking* or *cyberharassment*.) Schools help children understand what is acceptable communication with their classmates and encourage those who experience bullying to report it swiftly. Policies and procedures guide schools in addressing offenders and determining an appropriate punishment.

REMEMBER

If your child decides to study online, here are some pointers to keep in mind:

>> **Talk to your child about expectations.** If your child is going to learn or play online, you should talk as a family about rules for engaging online. For example, in Kevin's family, parents control their son's contacts list, and their son can engage only with people on that list. Parents also require login and passwords to all accounts, and no new accounts can be created without their permission.

>> **Beware of false identities.** One form of cyberbullying is tricking a person. A student may believe they are communicating with a friend when in fact it's a false identity. Help your child discern when and what to disclose online. Personal information should be off limits.

>> **Monitor social networking.** Classmates naturally form interpersonal relationships online. Your student may want to communicate with their classmates via email or social networking spaces such as Facebook. However, these activities should be monitored by an adult. In other words, if your kid has a Facebook account, make sure you can see what's going on.

>> **Report inappropriate activity.** If another child posts embarrassing or harassing statements or images, report this to the school officials immediately. It may be out of the range of their ability to discipline, but noting the behavior can have a significant impact on stopping it.

Then again, online schools know the types of behaviors that should be further reported to the police. For example, consider reporting to the police if personal information is involved in a threat against your child. You may hesitate, thinking that the incident is minor, but it's best to let the police sort it out. Don't immediately delete the offending messages. The authorities may need to see them.

Whatever you do, don't retaliate with the same kinds of threats or harmful messages. Getting involved in a verbal tit-for-tat will only result in your child being accused of being a cyberbully. Teach your child to walk away from the computer and cool down before reporting such an incident.

>> **Block bullies.** By all means, block communication with cyberbullies. Email programs and instant message software such as Yahoo! Messenger allow you to do this.

TIP

For more information about cyberbullying, consult one of these sites: Stomp Out Bullying at `https://stompoutbullying.org`, the National Crime Prevention Council's site on cyberbullying at `http://www.ncpc.org/resources/cyberbullying`, or the US government's `www.stopbullying.gov` site.

Enhanced parental involvement

In K-12 schools, parent–teacher communication is getting better, with electronic grade books and online learning portals that support the face-to-face classroom. However, direct communication between parent and teacher around specific areas a student needs to improve on can be difficult based on schedules, student-to-teacher ratios, and communication preferences.

Parental involvement is completely different with virtual schools. If you follow any of the virtual school links, you will quickly note that every institution requires greater parental involvement than traditional schools. Parents have access to everything: grades, feedback, and lessons. Adults who supervise at home are given various monikers by online schools — parent/guardian, home facilitator, and onsite instructional support, to name a few — but their roles are the same. The need for enhanced parental support stems from the age and abilities of the learner. Here are a few examples of the roles parents must play when their child attends school online:

>> Because most information is delivered by way of text online, the only way to survive in an online course is to read. That's impossible for the average 6-year-old! Adults serve as readers.

>> Few children are as self-motivated and disciplined as they need to be for online learning. Adults serve as watchdogs and taskmasters.

>> Because an online teacher may not see the whole family situation, routine communication becomes more important. Teachers schedule weekly or monthly communication with parents or supervisors, depending on the age of the learner and the structure of the school.

Pennsylvania Leadership Charter School has an interesting way of communicating parental expectations in its course catalog: It tells parents how much time and effort should go into their supporting role based on the grade level of the learner. For example, home facilitators with children in second grade are expected to assist the child 90 to 100 percent of the time that the child is working on material. In other words, if you have a second-grader, you'll probably need to teach the material and watch your child do assigned tasks. You can't expect a 7-year-old to read the computer screen and know what to do independently. As the child progresses academically, the amount of assistance decreases. By the time a student is in Grade 12 and takes more ownership of the learning process, the adult should be active no more than 1 to 10 percent of the time and not at all instructionally. Instead, the adult's role shifts toward holding the student accountable while continuing to provide motivation and support.

Any decent virtual school for kids requires parental involvement! Schools tell you this using some of the main links on their web pages — for example, a Parents tab or a link to parental involvement. It shouldn't be a secret. If it seems obscure, look at another school.

More real-time opportunities

The world of online education for children is more synchronous than their adult counterparts' experience (in other words, it takes place in real time more frequently). Students may be expected to participate in online meetings daily, weekly, or monthly. These synchronous meetings with instructors and other students reinforce the subject matter, build strong community bonds, and generally keep learners on task. Even schools that follow a self-paced model for curriculum usually back up their courses with regular synchronous meetings.

Synchronous meetings typically use web conferencing software (which we describe in Chapter 13) and call together multiple students in a class. These meetings can be a lot of fun! The teacher may present new information or reinforce what the students are studying. They can ask and answer questions about content or assignments. Perhaps the greatest value of the synchronous meetings is the feeling of interpersonal connection between the student and teacher, which is still vital in virtual education for children. Figure 18-1 shows what a synchronous interface may look like for an online K–12 course.

TIP

Don't forget that the telephone is a synchronous tool, too! Teachers often call students to monitor progress and talk about what's happening in class.

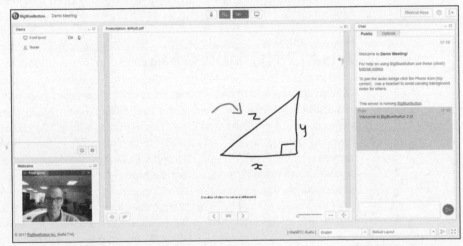

FIGURE 18-1:
A synchronous class interface.

PA Leadership Charter School

The need to work offline

Surprisingly, not all online education happens online. Although adults can work offline (as we explain in Chapter 12), such work is especially important for younger learners. Young learners need time away from the computer to accomplish academic tasks that involve the following:

REMEMBER

>> **Textbooks and workbooks:** Can you imagine learning to print numbers without having a pencil and paper in hand? Some early academic tasks have to be done away from the computer screen. Further, at the point when children learn to read for information (around fourth grade), they begin to access materials like books and periodicals offline.

Almost every virtual school uses textbooks. Flashy media may be available online to explain concepts, but online education for young learners also involves print materials.

>> **Old-fashioned, hands-on learning:** Curricula for young learners includes hands-on opportunities to experiment with concepts. For example, a child in an earth science class may be provided with rock samples to examine and evaluate. Or, the child may be asked to collect leaf samples for a botany unit. Exploring one's natural curiosity is part of learning, and good online curricula requires students to go out in the world and find these key relationships.

TIP

When you're researching online schools, ask how much learning occurs online versus offline. If a program seems especially off balance with no adequate explanation, consider looking at a different school. Kids need balance.

WHAT? NO DIPLOMA?

You may be surprised to learn that students who complete an academic program in a virtual high school may not earn a high school diploma, even though they take the same courses as their brick-and-mortar counterparts. Instead, they take the General Educational Development (GED) test to earn a diploma or certificate. Homeschooling families are familiar with this process and have a longstanding practice of documenting their children's academic progress annually by way of portfolios that provide examples of their work and show how their child is progressing. When it comes time to apply for colleges, a homeschooled or virtual schooled student takes the same entrance exams (ACT or SAT) as any other student and submits their portfolio along with a list of courses completed.

Note: There are a few colleges that offer a full high school diploma for credit without having to take the GED or have to carry the stigma associated with it. For example, Olympic College in Bremerton, Washington offers a High School+ program where they will evaluate a student's transcript and develop an education plan that leads to earning a diploma.

Checking Out Different Kinds of Virtual Schools for Kids and Teens

If online education interests you or your child, how do you go about finding a suitable program? The next few sections sort through the variety of programs available for families who want to learn online. A survey of existing programs reveals common structures, whether state funded or private.

State-funded schools

Many states have state-funded online schools. In the following sections, we explain the basics of how these schools work and describe a classic example of a state-funded school. We also touch on outsourced instruction and charter schools.

TIP

Looking for a virtual school in your state? We know of two methods: Use your favorite search engine and search for *virtual high schools in [your state]* or visit the K-12 corporate site at www.k12.com.

The basics of how state-funded schools work

Before we get too far into how the state-funded schools work, we need to clarify that there are two general types:

>> **Publicly funded and open to all residents:** This type of school may offer complete diplomas or only a few courses, and is generally accredited. These public schools are usually linked to a state's department of education, and therefore follow the state mandates on what to teach. However, this type of school may be outsourced and run by a major education provider, such as the previously mentioned k12.com.

>> **Charter:** This type of school is also paid for by the government, but is a little more experimental in nature. A charter school often targets a specific subject or group of students, such as technology, math, or performing arts. Many times, charter schools are also directly linked to a public school district, and enrollment may be available only to residents in that district.

Both types of state-funded schools must follow state standards. What a child learns in Grade 11 English, for example, should be fairly consistent whether they sit in West High or a virtual campus. It's the *how* that may vary when we consider online education.

Online instruction in a publicly funded school often blends videos, workbook, and reading time with viewing and discussion online. The student accesses lessons online, completes a good deal of work offline, and then logs back in to submit assignments. Older students are often required to discuss ideas with their peers via discussion boards. K–8 students are often required to meet consistently with their instructors to demonstrate skills, discuss assignments, and learn new concepts. They usually have opportunities for live or synchronous interaction with high school teachers, too. Parents monitor progress and communicate frequently with instructors.

So, what should parents ask if they're looking at this kind of schooling for their child?

>> If this is publicly funded, who is eligible?

>> How closely aligned to state standards is the curriculum? What courses are available?

>> What are the qualifications of teachers? Is the instruction provided by local teachers, or is it outsourced to a national company? The quality may be no different — you just may be curious about where the teacher is coming from.

>> What happens daily, weekly, or monthly? What kind of calendar would be followed? Can your child complete classes early or take more time if needed?

>> What are the minimum hardware and software requirements for participating in the program?

>> In what ways are parents involved? What expectations should they have about communicating with teachers?

TIP

Ask whether a computer and textbooks are part of the package with any state-funded school. In some states, students receive laptops or desktop computers along with textbooks and workbooks. Some even offer stipends to help pay for Internet service, if it's deemed necessary based on financial need and if the online program meets the student's academic goals.

You may wonder about the instructors for virtual schools. Virtual instructors for accredited schools must be certified teachers. They are real educators and have the same academic credentials as Mrs. Smith at the local public school. Some teachers may also be nationally board certified and, in quality programs, all will have received significant and ongoing instruction in how to teach online. Some schools also have robust professional development programs that focus on not only specific strategies for online teaching but also research-based teaching methods in general.

UNDERSTANDING CURRICULA AND STATE MANDATES

What children learn in school is often determined at the state level according to mandated standards. For example, if you live in Montana, the publication *Montana Content Standards for English Language Arts and Literacy* tells you that all students will be able to "Read closely to determine what the text says explicitly and to make logical inferences from it; cite specific textual evidence when writing or speaking to support conclusions drawn from the text." Each standard is broken down into a more meaningful explanation according to age level so that teachers understand what is expected by the end of fourth grade versus eighth grade, and so on. Teachers use this information to plan lessons and to select curricula that match the state standards. *Curricula* is a fancy term for what is taught, including the textbooks and instructional materials. For example, if you're the person in charge of getting kids to "reflect upon their literary experiences and purposefully select from a range of works," you select a textbook and materials that help you achieve that purpose.

The International Society for Technology in Education (ISTE) asks states to consider the role of technology in their state-mandated curricula. ISTE's National Educational Technology Standards (NETS) suggest that educators should get students to "critically curate a variety of resources using digital tools to construct knowledge, produce creative artifacts and make meaningful learning experiences for themselves and others," for example. Though the NETS technology standards aren't mandated, if you put them together with the state standards, you can see how online education may be a solution. Using the previous Montana example, an online educator could get students to reflect on their literary experiences and conclusions via online discussion boards.

In 2006, Michigan rattled the education chains by passing legislation requiring high school students to take at least one online learning course or participate in an online learning experience before graduation. Though not all states have followed with legislated mandates, the idea that schools should prepare students for a technologically rich future is gaining currency.

A classic example: The Florida Virtual School

Perhaps the best known and longest running (since 1997!) online school is the Florida Virtual School (FLVS) at www.flvs.net. Any child whose parents are residents of the state of Florida can take classes via FLVS for free — including home-schooled kids who are registered with their school district. As of 2020, FLVS offers more than 180 courses, and FLVS students have achieved 4.1 million semester completions.

Students at FLVS select courses from a standard curriculum that closely follows state standards. For example, the curriculum includes four levels of high school English along with two advanced placement English courses. Students earn the same half-credit per semester per course that students in traditional schools earn.

Students can attend full-time or take advantage of the FLVS Flex model, which allows them to take online courses on top of their face-to-face classes at their neighborhood school, charter school, or homeschool. Students can work at varying pace options, from accelerated (fast) to extended (slow). Even within a given pace option, students can speed up or slow down as needed, depending on how well they're grasping the material. Though pacing varies, students are by no means working on their own. Teachers are proactively involved in their day-to-day learning by way of assessment feedback, discussions, phone calls, email, chats, and more. Students may also communicate with one another and with teachers by way of discussion boards and synchronous meetings online. The blending of asynchronous and synchronous learning works effectively for most learners.

A typical online course at FLVS includes some sort of multimedia presentation, rich in visuals. The method of presentation engages young learners who bring sophisticated expectations to learning. (See Figure 18-2 for an example.) It has to look good, be relevant, and contain a fun factor. As the student works through a lesson, they communicate with the instructor or their fellow students either via discussion boards or synchronous meetings like webinars or chat sessions.

Outsourced instruction and charter schools

Other states have programs similar to FLVS's for their students, but they may outsource the instruction instead of having dedicated state schools. For example, Arizona provides free online opportunities for children registered with a school district. However, Arizona's courses are outsourced to the K-12 company (www.k12.com), a proprietary group that develops and sells curricula. Like FLVS's courses, K-12's courses are self-paced and include media. Here, the difference is simply in who develops the courses. The quality of instruction and expertise of their teachers are consistent.

In some states, charter schools deliver online courses to their students. A charter school is a publicly funded alternative to traditional school. Charter schools are often started by concerned parents or community groups and target a problem believed to be unaddressed by traditional means. In virtual terms, state charter schools are smaller online schools. For example, Wisconsin and Pennsylvania each operate several charter online schools. Each of these schools is open to any resident of that state, regardless of proximity to the home office.

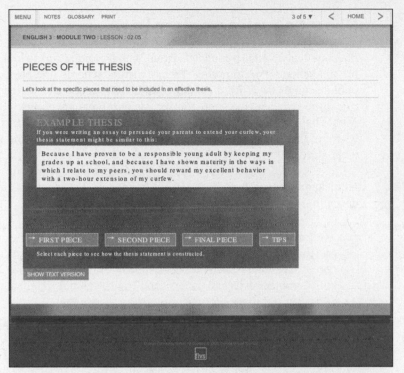

ENGLISH 3 : MODULE TWO : LESSON : 02.05

PIECES OF THE THESIS

Let's look at the specific pieces that need to be included in an effective thesis.

EXAMPLE THESIS

If you were writing an essay to persuade your parents to extend your curfew, your thesis statement might be similar to this:

Because I have proven to be a responsible young adult by keeping my grades up at school, and because I have shown maturity in the ways in which I relate to my peers, you should reward my excellent behavior with a two-hour extension of my curfew.

→ FIRST PIECE   → SECOND PIECE   → FINAL PIECE   → TIPS

Select each piece to see how the thesis statement is constructed.

SHOW TEXT VERSION

FIGURE 18-2:
A glimpse of what an online course for K-12 looks like.

Courtesy of Florida Virtual School

Because charter schools are smaller in scale, they may differ in curriculum. For example, in Wisconsin, more than one of the charter schools use K–12's curricula. In contrast to using proprietary curricula, Pennsylvania's Leadership Charter School (PALCS, www.palcs.org) uses curricula developed by individual teachers. Drawing from resources available in traditional print as well as from publishers of online media, instructors customize lessons according to grade and state standards. This results in a highly personalized method of instruction. Like the other programs, PALCS's program blends asynchronous and synchronous methods. The students receive a list of tasks to be completed by the end of the quarter and are also encouraged to meet routinely in synchronous sessions with the teacher.

REMEMBER

Some virtual schools are outsourced. The state subscribes to the services of a large provider. In many cases, this works to your advantage because you're tied to a vast network of resources and personnel. However, it's worth asking about so that you feel comfortable that your child's educational program matches your state's standards and expected curriculum.

Private online schools

If a state has no publicly funded virtual school or you want to look for alternatives, private schools are an option. Private virtual schools operate the same way the public schools do. With a combination of self-paced and instructor-led lessons, rich interactive media, and routine synchronous meetings, the public/private debate has little to do with qualitative difference in education and everything to do with funding bases! As long as you're willing to pay the tuition, it doesn't matter what state you live in.

REMEMBER

A quick online search yields many online schools, but what should you consider in decision-making? Following are some guidelines:

>> **Make sure the program is accredited.** This should be an obvious notation on the school's website. Two major accrediting agencies are the Commission on Colleges of the Southern Association of Colleges and Schools (SACS) and the Commission on International and Trans-Regional Accreditation (CITA). (See Chapter 5 for more information about accreditation.)

>> **Ask about the school's history and experience.** When it comes to online education and your child, you want to know that the designers and teachers have done this long enough to be confident that it works! The same questions we mention earlier about the quality of teachers, curriculum, and other aspects apply to these schools, too!

>> **Recognize that sometimes size is an advantage.** One of the powerhouses in private online high schools, for example, is Insight Schools at `https://wa.insightschools.net/`. Insight Schools is owned by the same parent company as University of Phoenix, the Apollo Group. As such, Insight can draw on the experience and resources of the behemoth university. Your child has access to research-based curriculum and best practices in instruction.

>> **Ask about the school's courseware.** Was it developed in-house? If so, is it aligned to state standards? How interactive is it? Ask to see a demo. You want to see a course that is highly visual, easy to navigate, filled with interaction, and full of options for students to "show what they know." Also find out how often the school's courseware is updated. Online courses should be updated regularly — that's part of the beauty of being online!

>> **Ask about teacher certification and training.** Choose a program that supports instruction by providing training specifically in online education.

>> **Find out what the face-to-face requirements are, and be sure you can meet them.** It's okay if there are no face-to-face requirements, but you should look for a program that strives to at least offer the opportunity for such communication.

>> **Inquire about the types of learning the school offers.** Look for a program that offers a healthy combination of synchronous and asynchronous learning opportunities. Too much synchronous time can be challenging for adults let alone young children who need breaks. In the same vein, it's hard to stay motivated if all work is expected to be completed asynchronously.

TIP

If you homeschool for religious reasons, you may prefer a curriculum that fits your beliefs. Online programs are available, such as that of The Morningstar Academy at www.themorningstaracademy.org. However, as you shop around for an online school, exercise the same caution we mention in the previous list regarding accreditation and experience.

TIP

If you homeschool your child and want online opportunities, there are several to choose from. For example, Khan Academy (www.khanacademy.org) offers a variety of courses in math, science and engineering, arts and humanities, and test prep. These courses are self-paced with no instructor. They are organized by age and often align to each age group's *common core standards* – the goals students should be able to meet at the end of each grade level. Many other educational sites are out there, too, that can support students as they learn how to type, read, write, spell, and speak another language. These programs usually require your student to create an account so that the progress can be tracked. When reviewing them, check to see whether they have a parent login that allows you to also be in control of your child's account and track their progress.

Going Through the K-12 Enrollment Process

If you decide that online education is right for your child, how do you sign up? The next few sections detail how you can find courses to meet your child's needs, confirm their credits, and confirm they transfer as you need them.

REMEMBER

Applying for an online K-12 school isn't much different from what we describe in Chapters 4, 5, and 6 for adults. You learn about the school and program online, ask for an application packet, and have the opportunity to talk with a real person about the school before committing to anything. The school typically wants records of prior work (similar to transcripts for adults). You also need to provide a birth certificate and maybe immunization records. (Yes, even for some online schools!) Some schools — for example, the Illinois Virtual School — require that you gain permission from your local school during the registration/application process before being approved to take online courses. In this same example, high school credit isn't granted by the virtual school but can be approved by the student's local high school.

REMEMBER

What's consistent between K-12 and adult schools is that you look at accredited programs and ask questions. If you're not finding the answers you need, move on!

Finding the right classes

How often have you heard of a student reaching the end of their senior year and being short one course for graduation? The solution is typically summer school, but if that student has access to online resources, an alternative may be to make up missing coursework through online education.

Or, how about a homeschooled student who really wants to take an elective in Chinese language, but whose parents can't find the right course material? Online education can fill this type of curriculum gap.

By searching what's available in your state or looking at proprietary curricula (as we suggest earlier in this chapter), you may be able to identify online programs that can help your student make up missing courses to get back on track or take courses that aren't otherwise available.

REMEMBER

Like colleges, virtual schools maintain course catalogs. These catalogs describe course offerings and the associated credit a student earns for completion. Schools make these freely available to interested consumers, but if you don't find a course catalog readily available online, call the contact number and request one.

Virtual schools are also available for children who need to complete *all* classes online. That's when you must examine the school's website to look for *full-curriculum* or *full-service* leading to a diploma. As you might expect, you should select an accredited school. Trust us: There are a lot of opportunities for earning a diploma online.

Confirming credits before taking classes

We mention credit several times in this chapter, and perhaps we should clarify what that means. American institutions "count" credit according to the Carnegie system, a well-established and accepted system for higher education and K-12. High school credit is counted in full or half units according to how long a student is in class — literally the time the student sits in their seat!

A full unit of credit is equivalent to 120 hours of contact time with an instructor, so in a traditional school where English class meets for 50 minutes five days a week, it takes roughly a year to earn a credit. (Schools factor in vacation days.) A semester-long course such as an elective in mythology may earn half a credit.

Obviously, this credit-counting method is antiquated for online education, but it's still the system in use. Virtual schools award the same credit as their brick-and-mortar counterparts by considering how long a student is engaged in learning activities (online or offline) and the amount of time the student is expected to be in communication with faculty or other students.

REMEMBER

Before registering for any online course, confirm how many credits that course will award upon completion. How many credits a course awards is listed in the curriculum. (For example, third-year English at the high school level earns one credit.) The school's admissions and registration personnel can verify this information, and it should be completely transparent to you as the consumer. Be sure that you're signing up for a course that counts toward your academic goal!

Understanding articulation agreements

An *articulation agreement* is a formal plan that details which courses will be accepted at which schools and under which circumstances. Suppose that your child is gifted and wants to take an advanced placement English course that earns dual credit for college and is unavailable at your local rural high school. You find that this exact course is available for free by way of a charter school elsewhere in your state. It would be easy to assume that your child could enroll in the charter school and have the credit count toward graduation at your local school. Don't make that assumption! Before you go any further, ask both schools about the articulation agreement so that you know the credit will count. The registrar at either school is the keeper of these documents.

REMEMBER

Checking articulation agreements is especially important for high school juniors and seniors who want to earn dual credit. You must verify not only that the brick-and-mortar high school will accept the online credit but also that the future college will honor the credit. We don't want to make it sound as if this is problematic, but the adage "Better safe than sorry" comes to mind.

CAN YOU GO TO HIGH SCHOOL AS AN ADULT?

If you didn't earn a high school diploma in a traditional fashion and now want to make up the difference, you can achieve this online. However, the virtual schools for traditional children that we discuss in this chapter, such as publicly funded charter schools, cannot accept you. Because they are state funded, provisions are written into their charters allowing students only up to a certain age to enroll. However, some online schools are available for adults to complete high school study. Mostly, you want to obtain the background knowledge necessary to take the General Educational Diploma (GED) test. Credit is not as important as passing the test.

Start by contacting your state board of education to see whether an online program is available for residents. If not, search for *online education for GED* in a search engine, and you'll find plenty of programs and services. Be sure to dig deep to find the kind of program that suits your needs.

Chapter **19**

Accessibility in Online Education

According to the American Association of Community Colleges, 20 percent of all students enrolled in community colleges in 2015–2016 reported having a disability. When it comes to accessibility for people with disabilities, we're being brutally honest in saying that the field of online education is still working on getting it right. Even the most committed institutions rely on individual instructors and outside vendors who aren't always familiar with the design and development strategies best suited for persons with disabilities. However, we can honestly say that this is a hot topic within the field and that more state and federal laws are forcing institutions to become more aware of the subject.

Does this mean you shouldn't attempt to take an online course if you have a disability? Absolutely not. The benefits of online education, as we explain in Chapter 2, definitely extend to people with disabilities. Federal laws prohibit any school that receives federal funding, whether private or public, from discriminating based on disability. These same institutions are also required to provide reasonable and appropriate accommodations to ensure equal access to all students. Plus, a lot of assistive technologies can help when needed.

TIP

We believe this topic is extremely important, and that's why we include this chapter. Here, we explain how to figure out the accessibility of courses you want to take and how to let your selected school know about your disability. We also describe assistive technology options to help you during class. However, a single chapter isn't enough to cover all that we have to say about this subject. Therefore, the following list describes a few additional resources that can help you better understand your rights and responsibilities in an academic setting:

>> **The Americans with Disabilities Act of 1990, as Amended (ADA):** The ADA prohibits discrimination on the basis of disability by public entities and has additional standards for public organizations. (We talk more about the ADA in the later sidebar "Defining 'disability' according to the Americans with Disabilities Act.")

```
www.ada.gov
```

>> **Section 504 of the Rehabilitation Act of 1973:** Section 504 prohibits discrimination on the basis of disability by schools receiving federal funds.

```
www2.ed.gov/about/offices/list/ocr/504faq.html
```

>> **Family Education Rights and Privacy Act (FERPA):** FERPA protects your privacy. This law allows information specific to your disability to be shared only with faculty and staff who are involved in the development and implementation of an accommodation plan.

```
www2.ed.gov/policy/gen/guid/fpco/ferpa/index.html
```

>> **The Individuals with Disabilities Education Act (IDEA):** The rules and regulations of IDEA require public schools to provide all eligible children with disabilities a free, appropriate education in the least restrictive environment. IDEA doesn't apply to postsecondary education.

```
https://sites.ed.gov/idea
```

Determining Whether the Courses You Want to Take Are Accessible

As promoters of self-advocacy, we provide you with a list of questions specific to accessibility and accommodations that you can ask the personnel at online schools you want to apply to. By asking the questions in the following sections up front, you can find out quickly how well-equipped an institution is to accommodate a variety of learners' needs. Unfortunately, what you find may not please you, but figuring it out before enrolling in courses can save you a lot of headaches.

TIP

Note that when you ask these questions, your academic advisor may not know the answer. Though we hope that the instructional design and technical staff are providing some level of information to those marketing the program and answering student questions, that may not be the case. Therefore, be patient if your advisor needs to find out the information and get back to you. On the other hand, if the advisor doesn't respond in a timely manner, you've received good information that will allow you to consider eliminating that school from your list of schools to which you may apply. (See Chapter 5 for additional questions to ask your advisor as you research online schools.) You might also want to see if the institution has a Disability Services Department website with a list of services and support offered to students. For example, the University of Illinois has a comprehensive website for its Division of Disability Resources & Educational Services (www.disability.illinois.edu).

Do the courses follow accessibility standards?

This question is of the tell-all variety. Institutions that are committed to making content accessible to all students are able to easily answer this question. The guidelines and standards for creating accessible websites and course content are so specific that any instructional designer responsible for developing content can provide you with specific examples of how the content meets those standards. It's easy for a school to claim accessibility. The level of detail it's able to give you in terms of the standards to which it adheres tells the true story.

Commonly used guidelines

Schools are required to follow federal guidelines when developing web content. A few organizations in particular are heading the pack when it comes to creating standards for web accessibility. This list describes those organizations:

>> **Section 508 Information Technology Accessibility Standards:** A federal law that mandates federally funded organizations to provide employees and members of the public with information that is comparable to the information provided to employees and members of the public without disabilities.

```
www.access-board.gov/guidelines-and-standards
```

>> **World Wide Web Consortium (W3C):** An international consortium where contributors work together in the development of standards and guidelines for the web. The organization has an initiative specific to developing web accessibility standards and guidelines.

```
www.w3.org/standards
```

>> **Web Content Accessibility Guidelines (WCAG):** Recommended guidelines for creating web content that is more accessible for persons with a wide range of disabilities, including blindness and low vision, deafness and hearing loss, learning disabilities, cognitive limitations, limited movement, speech disabilities, photosensitivity, and combinations of these conditions. These guidelines provide three levels of success criterion — known as *levels of conformance* — for each of their 13 guidelines. The three levels are A (lowest), AA, and AAA (highest). Each guideline provides strategies for how content designers can meet minimum standards (A) or the highest standards (AAA) for accessibility. In the state of Washington, an accessible technology policy was developed and approved in March 2016. The document is a statewide commitment for all Washington state community and technical colleges to comply with conformance level AA.

```
www.w3.org/TR/WCAG
```

TIP

The preceding standards are geared toward web-based content only. However, your online class may include links to external content such as word processing documents, PowerPoint presentations, and multimedia clips. Some states already have guidelines covering these types of content. For instance, all Illinois agencies and universities are required to implement the Illinois Information Technology Accessibility Act (IITAA) web accessibility standards in order to ensure that all web content, documents, videos, and other resources are accessible to persons with disabilities (`www.dhs.state.il.us/page.aspx?item=32765`). Ask at the institutions you're interested in whether all their content is created in an accessible manner, especially if you want to attend a school based in a state that has no guidelines similar to those in Illinois. For further information on the guidelines every state is required to follow, visit the ADA's Accessibility of State and Local Government Websites to People with Disabilities page at `www.ada.gov/websites2.htm`.

DEFINING "DISABILITY" ACCORDING TO THE AMERICANS WITH DISABILITIES ACT

The Americans with Disabilities Act (ADA) defines disability with respect to an individual as "a physical or mental impairment that substantially limits one or more of the major life activities of such individual." The act provides good examples of determining whether a person's inability to do something is due to a disability or other reasons. For example, a person's inability to participate in a program because of a lack of financial resources isn't considered a disability. However, a person who's unable to participate in a program because of a documented physical or mental condition such as dyslexia is considered by law a person with a disability. Find out more about the act at www.ada.gov.

Examples of accessibility

In this section, we give you a few examples of how institutions should be making content accessible to all students. These are the sorts of answers you should look for when you ask this question of academic advisors — see the later section "Using Assistive Technology Online" for more information about these options:

>> **Using heading styles inside documents:** *Heading styles* are text formats that tag important text. Headings are used to organize a website by importance. Each web page should have one Heading 1, which serves as the title of that page. Heading style 2 is used for topics within the page, and Heading style 3 is used for subtopic information. Heading styles help screen readers. (We cover screen readers in more detail later in this chapter; for now, just know that they are tools used by people who are blind or visually impaired.) With properly formatted headers and a screen reader, you can quickly navigate from topic to topic without having to read an entire page. This is extremely helpful, especially when you have your screen reader reread the same document multiple times. For example, someone who needs to check a course policy within the syllabus doesn't want to listen to the entire document via a screen reader — they want to scan for headings and subheadings to find the respective policy quickly. It's like an invisible table of contents.

>> **Providing transcripts for audio files:** Audio files bring a nice touch to a class and often reduce the psychological distance between the learners and the speaker. The files can be especially helpful to learners who learn better by listening. However, the files aren't helpful to students who are deaf or have hearing loss, so instructors should provide a transcript of every audio file used in class. Transcripts can also be helpful to students whose first language isn't English.

>> **Providing captions, auditory descriptions, and transcripts for videos:** Videos are another alternative way to deliver content to learners that stimulates visual learners. However, students who are blind or have vision loss and those who are deaf or have hearing loss don't benefit from these delivery methods. Captioning videos (displaying text on the screen as a subtitle in real time with the video) and providing an accessible transcript is a way to make the same content accessible to a lot more learners. Auditory descriptions are interspersed narrations of what's happening on the screen. This helps a person listening to the video to understand the context in which the dialogue is being used.

>> **Providing descriptions for content that relies on color to convey information:** Color is another great way to convey information. However, it won't help learners who are color-blind. For example, pie graphs that use color and a legend should also add titles within the graph itself so that it's clear what each section of the pie represents. Otherwise, each slice of the pie might look the

same to someone who can't see colors. Speaking of colors, web content should use tools such as the WebAim Contrast Color (`webaim.org/resources/contrastchecker`) to make sure your text color, text size, and background color choices have the best chance of being able to be read by individuals with visual disabilities.

TECHNICAL STUFF

You probably noticed as you were reading this list that accessible design benefits not only students with disabilities but also students with a variety of learning preferences, by providing multiple ways to access the same information. For example, someone who prefers to read information rather than hear it may choose to pay attention to a captioner during a live session rather than pay attention to the instructor's voice. Or, they may download a transcript of a video rather than watch the video. This is the goal of universal design.

Are the courses tested for accessibility?

Institutions that have a centralized process for course design usually have established standards for designing and testing new courses. In an ideal world, every institution would test each course before it goes live with a variety of learners. However, we don't live in an ideal world, and many institutions have no centralized process for testing. Courses are often developed by individual instructors with little to no understanding of accessible design. As accreditation becomes more prevalent specific to online courses (see Chapter 5 for more information), these types of courses are becoming less common.

Asking whether the institution's courses are tested for accessibility will help you understand the school's design and testing process. If your academic advisor doesn't know, ask them to help you contact someone who does. If course design isn't centralized, it's important that you work with your academic advisor to develop a schedule of all the courses you want to take. That schedule needs to be provided to someone who's responsible for coordinating your accommodations. That person should research your course list to determine what the challenges will be and what accommodations will be made to overcome those challenges. If you're unable to get this type of information from the institution, and staff haven't convinced you that accessibility is a high priority, consider looking at other institutions.

TIP

If you find that the courses you're enrolled in aren't as accessible as you thought they'd be, contact your instructor, academic advisor, and accommodation team leader as soon as possible. (See the later section "Understanding why and when you need to disclose" for more info about accommodation teams.) Provide a detailed description of the information that is inaccessible to you and explain why. In this situation, you may want to offer to help test changes to the content and/or course. Even though it isn't your responsibility to help the institution test the course, you'd be doing future learners a favor by helping the institution create more accessible content.

How will the school help me if I cannot access information in a course?

Depending on your specific needs, institutions can provide a variety of assistance types to accommodate your learning needs. Whatever strategy they come up with should be based on a comprehensive review of your disability, documentation, and discussions between you and your accommodation plan team. (See the later sections "Understanding why and when you need to disclose" and "Figuring out what information to disclose" for more information about this process.) During these sessions, you should share any experiences you've had and describe what has worked best for you and why.

REMEMBER

Here are a few examples of some accommodations that can be made for students taking online courses:

>> **Extended time on assignments and quizzes/tests:** For learners who need more time to access and absorb information due to their disability, institutions may arrange for assignment deadlines and testing times to be extended.

>> **Access to tutoring services:** Several institutions subscribe to online tutoring services that provide academic assistance in a variety of areas. Tutors can be accessed 24/7 via the Internet.

>> **Content in text form and large print if needed:** For content that isn't in text form or isn't scalable, printed and large-print documents can be mailed to learners needing these accommodations.

>> **Content in Braille:** For learners who are blind or have low vision, Braille versions of content can be printed and mailed when deemed necessary.

>> **Captioned or interpreted videos:** Some instructors may choose to use videos created by someone else that were not captioned. Colleges can work with third-party vendors and sign language interpreters to have the video either captioned or interpreted into ASL. Most schools determine this based on your preference as the learner. These two options are also available for synchronous sessions your instructor might choose to hold. It does take time to get these services arranged, so make these requests as early as possible if you know that they'll be needed.

>> **Early access to online courses and course materials:** Early access to the virtual classroom provides learners with access to course materials such as

the syllabus and calendar. By accessing this information early, learners can begin to organize and better determine what additional accommodations may be needed.

» **Oral examinations or assignments:** Institutions can request that instructors meet with learners via the phone or another audio device to conduct interviews as a way of completing assignments and exams orally. During these sessions, the instructor can ask the student to answer questions about the assignment to determine whether the student truly understands the material. Again, exam dates and assignment due dates can be altered on a case-by-case basis for students whose disabilities warrant that accommodation.

TIP

You can find third-party tools that can be integrated into learning management systems that help instructors and other content creators test the accessibility of their pages, images, and videos. For example, Seattle Central College, where Kevin works, uses Blackboard Ally, a program that not only points out trouble spots but also teaches content creators how to make the content more accessible. (You can check it out at `ally.ac`.) The tool also offers learners the ability to convert certain content for them on demand. For example, a student who prefers to hear content can have a Microsoft Word document converted to an audio file with just a few clicks.

Disclosing a Disability to Your Chosen Online School

In any academic setting, including an online course, learners want to feel independent and be known for their contributions to the class. Therefore, we understand the desire to avoid disclosing a disability to peers, instructors, or even the administrative staff. However, sometimes accommodations that are needed can be provided only if requested. This section provides some general information about disclosing a disability and devising a plan to create and implement appropriate and reasonable accommodations in a respectful and private manner.

REMEMBER

By the way, people with temporary impairments don't qualify for disability services under the law. For example, a student who breaks an arm and requires a cast over the hand they type and write with isn't considered to have a physical disability. In this situation, you should work with your instructor directly to see whether temporary accommodations can be made, such as oral exams or recorded presentations.

Understanding why and when you need to disclose

Simply put, institutions can't provide services if they don't know that the services are needed. Also, accommodations aren't retroactive. So, if you receive an assignment or course grade that reflects negatively on you because your accommodations weren't in place, the institution doesn't have to change that grade, even if you later document the presence of a disability. Therefore, disclosure is in your best interest if you need accommodations. For example, for the most part, a person who is deaf can easily participate in an online course without disclosing and without needing accommodations. But what happens when the instructor wants to use a synchronous (real-time) audio tool for meeting with students throughout the semester? Many synchronous technology tools have captioning capabilities; however, these tools don't automatically transcribe voice to text. They require a person with captioning skills to log in and type using a dictation device similar to the one you see in courtrooms. These people are often hired out-of-house and need time to gain access to your virtual course, test the technology, and meet with you to discuss logistics. (We describe captioning videos in more detail later in this chapter.)

When *do* you need to disclose your disability? Institutions should include a statement on either the application or acceptance letter that provides information on disclosing a disability and requesting accommodations. If you can't find the statement or it's unclear whom to contact, ask your academic advisor for direction. They can provide you with the proper forms and point you to the submission policy.

REMEMBER

If you know you'll need accommodations from the start, disclose as soon as appropriately possible. Institutions need time to confirm documentation and meet with experts who can review your specific situation and develop an accommodation plan to match. (See the next section.) This process can take a couple of weeks, depending on the staff and resources available. (For example, if you need a captioner for synchronous sessions, it may take two weeks to find a person available on the dates and times of your sessions.) If you wait until classes begin to request services, you risk not receiving the service in a timely manner and falling behind in your academic progress.

WARNING

If the question is a part of the application process, and you feel uncomfortable disclosing at that time, that's okay. Waiting until you're formally accepted is understandable. However, waiting can delay accommodations and possibly your start date.

In most cases, discussing your situation with your academic advisor first is perfectly acceptable. This person can help you complete the proper documentation or point you in the right direction regarding how to get additional help. And don't worry: Anyone you disclose to is obligated by law to share this information only with staff directly involved with creating and implementing the accommodations necessary for you to be successful. (See the later section "Keeping privacy in mind" for more about this topic.)

REMEMBER

Most institutions require you to request accommodations every term or at least once a year. This allows the accommodation team to reevaluate the accommodation plan and see whether anything needs to be modified.

Figuring out what information to disclose

REMEMBER

In most cases, when completing the disclosure information, you're asked to provide formal documentation regarding your disability. *Formal* means that the information is provided by a licensed professional who is familiar with you and your respective disability. Your academic institution will have specific requirements for documenting a disability (disclosed on the institution's website or outlined in a request-for-accommodations form provided by your academic advisor), but documentation may include the requirements described in this list:

>> **Diagnostic description of the disability:** This helps the academic staff understand your specific situation and provides them with the proper documentation to justify making the requested accommodations.

>> **History of diagnosis:** When you provide the history of your diagnosis, staff are better able to understand specific challenges you may face. For example, a person who recently lost their sight as an adult may need more assistance than a person who has been blind since birth.

>> **Academic history:** When you provide your academic history, staff are better able to understand specific academic challenges you may face. For example, a person with autism may be asked to show formal evaluation results in areas of reading and writing along with former accommodations provided and their effectiveness. What you provide is up to you, but the more information the school has, the better its staff can support your academic success.

>> **Functional implications of your diagnosed disability:** This extremely important information must be as detailed as possible. When staff know how your disability impacts your daily life, they can develop a more successful accommodation plan specific to your needs.

If you're blind or deaf, you may not have needed to provide this documentation in the past, due to the obvious nature of the impairment. However, online institutions aren't able to make such visual judgments and usually require all students requesting accommodations to submit formal documentation by a licensed clinician.

Keeping privacy in mind

REMEMBER

Specific to health issues and education, the Family Education Rights and Privacy Act (FERPA) protects your privacy. (See the reference to this resource in the introduction to this chapter.) Assuming that your institution adheres to FERPA requirements and properly trains faculty on how to implement an accommodation plan privately, your information will be only between you and the professionals charged with helping you succeed. As a matter of fact, your instructor should know only the accommodation plan to implement and few details about your medical record, unless you choose to share.

It may also help to know that your information isn't shared with other staff or students. Therefore, you may at times feel the need to disclose because the services you're receiving don't meet your needs. For example, your in-class resources may be accessible, but research materials found when conducting library research may not. Therefore, you may be required to ask a librarian for help in getting your necessary information in a more accessible format. This may require you to disclose your situation and provide staff with proper documentation.

On another note, at times you may choose to disclose to other students in your class — for example, if you're a person who is deaf and you've been assigned to work in a group. Your group members post that they would like to meet synchronously using the phone. You can consider a couple of options:

>> **Chat room:** Try to inconspicuously persuade your group to meet in a chat room.

>> **Disclosure:** Disclose to your peers that you're a person who is deaf and suggest using a telephone interpreting service.

WARNING

These requirements and accommodations assume that you're attending a public institution. You might find a different level of accommodations and support if you're attending a private school or taking professional development courses online from a private company. Always do your research and ask questions about support before signing on the dotted line.

WORKING IN A GROUP WITH SOMEONE WHO HAS A DISABILITY

If you're in a class where a person has disclosed publicly or privately to you that they have a disability, you can do a few things to help create a successful environment:

- **Maintain the person's privacy:** Whether your classmate discloses publicly or privately, that's their right. Maintaining your classmate's privacy is important. Don't share any information about the disability or medical history with anyone else — inside or outside of the virtual classroom.

- **Focus on the work at hand:** As curious as you may be, which is completely natural, keep focused on your coursework and refrain from asking personal questions about your classmate's disability.

- **Don't make assumptions about your group member's abilities:** Remember that the qualifications to participate in your program are the same for every student. You will only embarrass yourself if you make assumptions about your group member's abilities to complete the assigned work based on stereotypical conjecture. If the person isn't completing the work, address the issue privately and respectfully first with that person, and include the instructor when appropriate.

- **Be flexible and comply with special requests when possible:** If you're asked to communicate with your classmates using alternative methods, be flexible and positive about complying with this request. For example, if you've requested to meet synchronously as a group over the phone without knowing that a group member is a person who is deaf, be willing to conduct the meeting using text chat or an interpreting service. It may take a little longer, but it's the right thing to do.

When attending a synchronous session where an interpreter or captioner is present, follow these netiquette guidelines:

- Speak at a "normal" pace and articulate.

- Restate your name each time before speaking.

- If you reference something that was asked in the text messaging box, repeat the question and the name of the individual asking the question before answering.

- If applicable, when working in groups, use text-only chat upon request. (The captioner can't be everywhere!)

The decision is up to you. Some may interpret this as a teachable moment, whereas others may want to focus solely on the task at hand. Meeting with your accommodation team and discussing your preferences in these types of situations may help. If your instructor knows your preferences ahead of time, they can assign groups and dictate the technologies to be used without singling anyone out.

Using Assistive Technology Online

Assistive technology is the term used to describe tools that help people complete daily tasks. For example, the spell check on your word processing program is considered an assistive technology. It helps people write faster by automatically correcting most misspelled words and highlighting those it doesn't know. This helps speed up the writing and editing process.

People with disabilities can benefit from assistive technology when they take online courses. The following sections describe a few assistive technology tools that institutions should provide and/or design coursework for.

REMEMBER

Depending on the accommodations you need, your institution may be able to supply some or all of the assistive technology to you for free. This doesn't mean the institution will buy your computer for you, but other resources may be available for free or at a reduced cost, if needed. This is another reason it's important to communicate openly with the staff member in charge of your accommodations plan.

Reading web pages with screen readers

People who are blind or have other visual impairments often navigate the web via sound. An application that runs in the background, called a *screen reader,* reads the information on the web page using a digitized voice. Screen readers rely on good site organization and design to allow the visitor to quickly skim each site and navigate more efficiently. This technology is also helpful to students with dyslexia.

Think about how sighted people navigate a website. They go to the site, look to see what links are on the page, and quickly click on what interests them. The links they use may be the first item on the page or on a navigation bar on the left side of the screen. A screen reader goes to that same page and starts reading every word on the site, from top to bottom. If the site is designed appropriately, the user can ask the screen reader to announce all the navigation links and headings on the page. (For a discussion of how this works, see our comments on heading styles in the "Examples of accessibility" section, earlier in this chapter.) Good design allows the person to more efficiently browse the page and navigate to chosen links.

Screen readers are software applications that either come supplied with your computer or have to be purchased and installed separately. For example, Mac computers have a built-in screen reader called VoiceOver; you pay no additional charge for the application, and it works out of the box. Windows machines also have built-in accessibility tools, including a screen reader. However, the robustness of these tools is sometimes questioned, requiring users to purchase and download an external program. For example, Windows users can purchase and download a screen reader called Jaws for Windows from Freedom Scientific (www.freedomscientific.com/products/software/jaws). It's not cheap ($1,000), but if your accommodations require you to use a screen reader, you may be able to get a copy of the program from your institution at a discounted price or for free. Contact the person in charge of your accommodation plan for more information.

Transcribing and captioning audio and video files

A *transcript* is a text-based document that provides a word-by-word account of what was said in a separate audio or video file. Providing a transcript for audio and video files is one method for making content more accessible to students with a variety of learning styles and special needs.

Another option for video files is captioning, which provides synchronized text that matches the video in real time. This allows viewers to read what is happening while seeing an image that coincides with the text. This is helpful to students who are unable to hear the audio correctly or prefer to learn by reading versus listening. Figure 19-1 illustrates a video with closed captioning.

Courses that are designed with accessibility in mind caption videos and add transcript links directly within the course where everyone can easily access them. For example, you may click on a link that has a video pop-up on it. In an ideal situation, the video would be captioned, and a link to the video transcript would be directly under it. If this isn't the case, the institution may hire an internal or external resource to add captions to video or transcribe the audio on the spot. Once complete, the video is reposted and/or the transcript is provided by the instructor. Ask for captions or transcripts if you need them and do not see them.

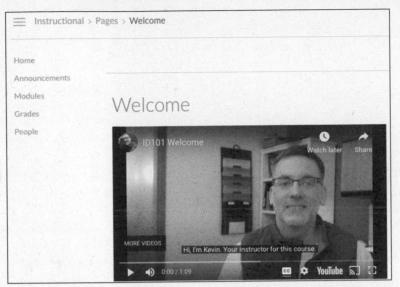

FIGURE 19-1:
An example of a captioned video.

Courtesy of University of Illinois Global Campus

Considering accommodation options for synchronous sessions

A person with a disability can attend a synchronous (real-time) session using any of the following assistive technology tools:

WARNING

>> **Closed captioning:** Programs that require synchronous sessions should provide either a captioner for those events or a live video of a sign language interpreter; these options benefit students with hearing impairments.

Videos occupy a lot of bandwidth and are often very small, making it difficult to see the interpreter's hand signs.

>> **Archive links and transcripts:** In case a student misses a synchronous session or needs to review the session to better understand a topic discussed during the session, each session should be recorded and an archive link provided to all students in the course. When necessary, a written transcript of the event should also be provided by the instructor.

>> **A telephone bridge:** A telephone bridge allows a person to connect to an Internet meeting by calling a phone number instead of logging on to a computer. For example, if you're blind or have other visual impairments, the screen display may not matter to you. A phone bridge allows you to call in and listen to everything that is going on without having to log in using the computer.

The Part of Tens

Chapter **20**

Ten Myths about Online Learning

espite the growing popularity of online courses, a number of myths related to online learning persist. People don't know what to make of studying and learning online. In this chapter, we bust ten of the most common myths about online education.

Online Learning Is Anytime/Anywhere

Asynchronous courses have no set meeting times, and you should be able to complete your assignments whenever it's convenient for you. In theory, as long as you have a decent Internet connection, you can access course materials and submit assignments at any time.

That said, learners sometimes fall into a trap with this statement because they fail to recognize that even an asynchronous course maintains a schedule. Your instructor expects you to turn in work by the stated deadlines. For example, you may be required to respond to a question on Wednesday and then read and respond to posts submitted by your peers by Sunday. Though you can decide what time of day to submit your posts, if you don't follow the class schedule, you'll probably find yourself losing ground in the grading scheme.

The other area in which this statement becomes problematic is the "anywhere" part. In theory, you should be able to travel and do your work as long as you have a decent Internet connection. However, our experience is that online education and vacations do not mix! If you must take a 2-week vacation in the midst of an 8-week course, consider rescheduling one or the other. Even if your hotel has free Internet, do you seriously want to stop playing on the beach to come inside and do homework? The reality is that you probably won't.

REMEMBER

Online courses come in two flavors: synchronous and asynchronous. In a *synchronous* (real-time) course, you meet at a prescribed time using web conferencing software. In an *asynchronous* course, you have no set time to meet, but you do have deadlines. You should know which of these two course types you're taking before you run into problems; see Chapters 2 and 4 for more about the distinction between synchronous and asynchronous classes.

Also, remember that a lot of workplace learning has shifted to an online format. Webinars abound! In some cases you can watch a recording after the fact, but find out first whether it's an option. If your company schedules the annual security compliance training at 10 A.M., plan to be there!

Only Kids Take Online Courses

Check the statistics for some of the larger online programs and you'll find that the average online learner is middle-aged. The convenience of studying while balancing work and family attracts slightly older students to online courses. Younger, traditional-age college students are also online, but they're more likely to be blending web-based and traditional courses at a land-based college (or they were forced online by the COVID-19 pandemic).

The notion that young kids know how to use computers to their advantage and slightly older students do not is an erroneous assumption. Don't overlook the computer skills of working professionals. Few of us complete the workday without email, shared projects, and collaboration. These are the same skills needed in online learning! Chapter 2 describes groups of all ages who can benefit from online courses.

An Online Course Is a Helpful Way to Learn How to Use Your Computer

This statement may be true if you're enrolled in a personal development course on using a computer. However, for the kinds of courses we discuss in this book, taking an online course to learn how to use your computer is a bad idea. People who do this spend so much time focusing on learning to use their computer that they waste money by not learning anything about the content area of the course. Why pay $300 for a geology course and not learn about rocks?

Additionally, the instructor may not have the time or patience to walk you through every little course related task. Even if you have 24/7 technical support, their job is to help you with software related to your course, not tell you how to use your computer.

REMEMBER

In fairness to the other students and your instructor, learn how to use your computer well before you enroll in an online course. Chapter 3 describes the technology and technological skills you need to succeed.

TIP

Contact your local two-year college or continuing education department to see what kinds of basic computer courses they offer. Chances are good that they have an introductory course that would be perfect for you!

You Must Be a Computer Geek to Take an Online Course

You do need to understand the basics of how your computer works as well as how to find files (see the preceding section), but you don't need to be a full-fledged geek to survive in an online course! Here's a short list of skills you should have before you enroll. You should be able to

>> Turn on your computer and start a web browser (the software that connects to the Internet)

>> Navigate the web, including opening links in new tabs or windows

>> Create a folder on your hard drive to store course-related information and know how to locate that information for later access

>> Open and answer email with and without attachments

>> Download and install applications and application plugins

>> Figure out some basic audio and camera settings if you're enrolled in a course that is synchronous and requires these tools

Flip to Chapter 3 for more details on basic skills you need for online courses.

Online Learning Is Easier than Face-to-Face Classes

Some people assume that online learning is easier than the traditional method, where you show up to a class with an instructor in front, but we don't know what *easier* means. To some people, it means less work, but guess what? In an accredited educational program, the amount of work expected of a student is the same whether the course is delivered in a traditional classroom or online.

Here's an example: If you attend a course offered once a week in a regular classroom, the instructor may lecture or guide activities for three hours and expect you to work on your own, completing readings or assignments for another six hours, resulting in a total of nine hours of active involvement in learning. The same course transferred online may deliver the lecture or activities by way of technology tools, but the assignments and the outcomes are the same. And, most importantly, you're expected to be engaged for approximately nine hours total.

Many online programs are accelerated, which has the potential of doubling your workload per course. For example, an on-campus course might take 16 weeks, whereas online, the same course covering the same amount of material may be only 8 to 12 weeks. We can't see how that's any easier. (Chapter 4 has more details on accelerated courses and programs.)

We will allow, however, that online learning can be much more convenient in that you can do the work when it suits your lifestyle and schedule — as long as you still meet required deadlines set forth by the instructor. (We explain this in the earlier section "Online Learning Is Anytime/Anywhere.")

Online Courses Are Lower in Quality than Face-to-Face Courses

In the early days of online education, some courses were little more than technology-enhanced correspondence courses with hardly any accountability for how well the students learned. We've come a long way since then, and today's online courses offer the same standards and outcomes as traditional courses. Research fails to reveal not only a statistically significant difference between online and traditional delivery methods but also that online courses are of lower quality. In fact, reputable institutions routinely review their courses using accepted standards of quality. Online programs are also beginning to participate in separate accreditation processes from agencies such as the United States Distance Learning Association.

That said, when COVID-19 began disrupting colleges, universities, and training providers around the world, some moved their programs online without having the time or luxury to redesign them and train faculty. Admittedly, the result wasn't good for the learner. Fairly quickly, quality standards were enacted and the situation is much improved.

REMEMBER

Look for an accredited program or institution. Chapter 5 reviews how to determine accreditation.

Online Learning Is Always Independent

Though you may do a considerable amount of work independently, such as reading or writing assignments, most online courses require students to interact with each other in a manner that's far from independent. This list describes two examples:

>> **In discussion forums, students read one another's submissions and comment on or reply to them.** This rich exchange of ideas extends everyone's understanding of the concepts. This manner of learning is hardly independent! In fact, it can't happen without participation from multiple voices, including the instructor's. (We cover discussions in Chapters 11 and 15.)

>> **Group projects are carried out online, too.** Often students collaborate with peers to create a final product. These situations may require even more time and commitment specific to communicating with others than traditional classroom projects. (Flip to Chapter 13 for more information on group work.)

REMEMBER

Taken directly from how people work in the 21st century (across distances and with others), teamwork rather than independence seems to rule in online courses.

Online Learning Is Less Personal than Traditional Learning

An amusing video on the Internet from the mid-2010s shows a professor refusing to accept a late exam from a student. The student asks, "Do you know who I am?" to which the professor replies that he doesn't. The student jams his paper into the middle of the stack of exams, smirks, and walks away. That's impersonal!

REMEMBER

You can't hide in an online course. Your instructor will get to know you and your ideas possibly better than they would have had you sat in a traditional classroom and said nothing. This is because the majority of online classes require participation — you can't log in and lurk and not do the work. In fact, if you try to approach your course that way, at the very least you can expect to have a few intimate conversations with your instructor!

There's another explanation why online education is not impersonal. Have you ever noticed that some people feel free to disclose information about themselves to strangers? Some instructors report similar occurrences with online students, indicating that learners are freer to share insights and personal details that support course concepts than they would if they had to face a classroom full of live people.

Plus, anyone who has lived, worked, or attended school during the COVID-19 pandemic has inevitably seen their co-workers' kids, teachers' spouses, inadvertent bathroom shots or similar. You can't say that's not personal!

You Need a Webcam for an Online Class

Determining whether to install a webcam for an online class kind of depends. On one hand, no one needs to see you sitting in your pajamas at the computer. Though webcams have real advantages for communication, they're rarely required in online courses. For starters, you only use a webcam if you have a synchronous component that accommodates video — for example, an office hour in a web conferencing tool. Even then, because webcams require greater bandwidth, instructors may ask you to turn them off. However, it doesn't hurt to go ahead and purchase a webcam for those occasional synchronous sessions.

In business settings, it's nice to have the option to turn on the camera. There's something reassuring about seeing the others in the room. Because laptops come supplied with this item as a standard feature, it's rarely an issue. Then again, in business webinars, because the focus is on whatever topic the speaker is covering, it may be less important for you to be on camera.

TIP

Most of the communication in an online course occurs on the discussion boards or via email. These aren't communication tools that require a real-time connection or video. If classmates are curious about what you look like, a photo works just as well. Chapter 11 introduces the basics of online communication methods.

Everyone Cheats Online

There is no evidence of greater cheating online than in a face-to-face classroom. Unfortunately, too much cheating takes place everywhere! However, smart online instructors now design their courses to minimize the possibility of cheating and use tools to help detect plagiarism. Cheating online simply doesn't pay, because the technology is on the instructor's side, as described in these examples:

» **Partial submissions:** Instructors ask for major projects to be submitted in pieces showing earlier drafts and revisions. Or they ask for projects that are based on personal or professional circumstances, knowing that no one else can possibly write about your life the way you can.

» **Software:** Some institutions use sophisticated software that checks written submissions for plagiarism.

» **One-on-one conversations:** Some instructors have these chats with learners where they ask questions to see whether students can properly articulate course materials.

REMEMBER

A working definition of *plagiarism* is presenting someone else's ideas as your own without giving proper citation. In Chapter 15, we give you lots of ideas for how to avoid plagiarism, along with excellent web links so that you can find out more about how to write correctly.

Chapter **21**

Ten Best Practices for Online Learners — Including Self-Care

I f you're reading this book and you made it this far, we assume that you want to succeed. We want you to succeed, too! In this chapter, we give you some practical advice on what we consider best practice when it comes to being an online learner. We throw in that self-care angle because you're making an investment in yourself, so show yourself some love!

Treat Learning Like It's a Job

Learning is work! There's no way around it. No matter how engaging a course may be or how interested you are in what you're learning, there's work involved.

Therefore, look at this as a for-hire situation. Set a schedule for yourself. Clock in and out at specific times, and decide whether this new job is ten hours a week or fewer. That also means you need to figure out a compensation package for yourself. What reward will motivate you to work? It might be as simple as a bubble bath.

TIP

For some learners, receiving a digital credential after a course is a bonus and quite rewarding. Especially for professional certifications, these gems can be career enhancing. We talk in Chapter 2 about alternative credentials and the benefits of having these in digital form.

While we're thinking about work, where is your office? It might be worth your while to invest in an ergonomic desk chair. Working from your sofa with your head bent down isn't sustainable!

REMEMBER

Asynchronous courses, especially those for academic credit, usually state how many hours per week you should expect to work. In Chapter 12 we explain this, but most 3-credit-hour courses would expect 9 hours of work per week. That includes reading plus working on assignments plus study plus posting.

It's Not a Sprint — It's a Marathon

As you approach each course you take, realize that it may be part of a bigger whole. Sure, there are fast training programs you may complete online, but for most true courses, you cannot log in and complete the program in one sitting.

Related to this is the idea that quality learning requires some time to let ideas percolate. Even if you could complete an entire course in a weekend, would the learning "stick"? Likely not. Enjoy the slow roll of learning something new, experimenting with new ideas, and seeing how it relates to the next chapter in your life. In fact, you may find that, as you have conversations with others (other people outside of class), it helps bring it all together.

Just in case you need a pacesetter, in Chapter 9 we explain how courses are sometimes organized by modules or smaller units, and the instructor reveals one module per week. The practice of releasing one bit of content at a time is a built-in pacer. For classes where the instructor reveals several modules at a time, you need to be your own pacer. The urge to get it done might be there, but, again, what will you have learned by focusing only on getting tasks done?

Manage Your Own Expectations

Coauthor Susan took up running years ago. She slowly progressed to being able to complete a 5K. (That's a little over three miles.) As she tells the story, it was one driveway at a time. She had no expectation to be able to run the entire distance at first, and she had no specific speed in mind. She managed her expectations.

This is not to say you shouldn't try to do your best, but when someone is new to a situation like learning online, everyone needs to manage expectations. Is it necessary to score 100 percent all the time? Is it possible that there could be feedback your instructor has to help you improve? Is it good enough that you did your best and tried?

We say yes. Give yourself a break and manage expectations. Otherwise, frustration can set in and you never make it to 5K.

REMEMBER

Pay attention to the syllabus and how you're graded. Look for opportunities to resubmit work if you're disappointed with your own performance, but please do *not* let yourself believe that you cannot succeed. We talk about the growth mindset in Chapter 8.

Your Calendar Is Your Best Friend

In Chapter 9 we talk about the calendar in a learning management system, and in Chapter 16 we reinforce deadlines. That said, both authors have seen wonderful students fail because they couldn't meet deadlines. Right from the beginning, find a way to follow a calendar and set deadlines.

Susan's calendar is on her phone, and it sends reminders for work projects. For example, at 8:50 A.M. every Monday, she receives an alert to check on a business project. She's never late — the time is blocked off on her calendar.

If you approach your learning like a job and schedule assignments on your calendar, you will never be late. The trick is to get everything organized in the beginning and then to respect what your calendar says.

TIP

Learn to coordinate with your personal calendar any calendar that might be inside the learning management system. You can find tips and tutorials to help with this.

Advocate for Yourself: Ask for Help

If this is your first experience with online learning, you may have a few questions. Of course, we're glad you invested in this book, but don't stop there! Ask questions. Ask for help. Here's a list:

>> If you have questions about how your specific course works, after you have read the syllabus and other course documents, ask your instructor.

>> If you have questions about the technology — specifically, the learning management system, look for tutorials on the school's website. If that doesn't give you what you need, search on YouTube!

>> If you're having trouble understanding an assignment, lean on your peers. Look for an area in the course where you can have learner-to-learner communication and see if others can help.

Be Present in Class (And Let Your Instructor Know)

We've seen a few inspirational posters that say, "Showing up is half the battle." When it comes to learning online, it's true! However, "being present" looks a little different online. It's often measured by how frequently you log in. Make certain you log in frequently (at least three times a week). That way, you'll see announcements and be more likely to keep on top of the work.

Alas, don't just show up. Leave some evidence that you've been in class. Comment on another student's post or submit an assignment. Your instructor will be paying attention to your level of engagement. Learning management system software gives instructors data such as how frequently students log in, how long they stay, and what pages they view. You can use this to your advantage.

TIP

Earlier in this chapter, we remind you about the calendar. Set yours to remind you to log in every two or three days.

Give Constructive Feedback

In the world of online learning, it's not uncommon to be asked to review the work of other students. You might be asked to comment on a discussion post or give feedback on a work project. You can develop a knack for giving feedback that's constructive. Here are some guidelines:

>> **Find something good:** Compare what you're reading to what was asked. Did the person follow the instructions, for example? Are they creative with their response? Start with something you like about their work.

- >> **Be honest and suggest:** To give constructive feedback means you're helping the author improve; you're helping them construct a better product. If you think the individual could go deeper in an area, or if you note a few issues with grammar, be honest but respectful. As a reviewer, it's not your role to fix the work, but feel free to make suggestions. For example, you might say, "I wonder if it would help the reader if you elaborate a little more about the difference between constructive feedback and praise?"

- >> **It's okay to disagree:** If you have a different viewpoint, as long as you present it with respect, share it! The world learns from diverse perspectives.

- >> **Close with goodness:** By *goodness,* we don't mean empty platitudes. It can be a comment as simple as "I enjoyed reading your paper/post. Thanks for giving me the opportunity to comment." Or, "I hope this helps you as you shape your work." Good manners go a long way!

TIP

The same method for providing feedback on student work applies to comments you might have for your instructor.

It's Okay to Take a Break

Up to this point, we have emphasized setting a schedule, using a calendar, and approaching learning like it's your job. We sound like taskmasters, but even workers get to go home! Sometimes the best response to stressful learning is to walk away. Take a break.

Take a break, whether it's a 5-minute stretch in the kitchen or 30 minutes playing *Fortnite.* Focusing elsewhere actually improves concentration later. Plus, ample brain research shows that you're probably still problem-solving and working it through, even when you're not sitting in front of the computer.

The idea of taking a break can also be applied to sitting out a term. If juggling work, home, and school is getting to be too much, maybe it's time to skip the next term or enroll in fewer hours. This is where a heartfelt conversation with your academic advisor can help.

TIP

Breaks come in varying sizes. For a 2-hour study session, 15 minutes makes sense, not 45 minutes.

Sleep Is Good for You

This is seriously Susan's favorite part of the book. Did you know that when you sleep, your body rids itself of waste build-up in your brain? It's amazing and true. That leaves your brain "rinsed out" for the next day and better able to handle new learning. (Apologies to brain scientists who have better explanations.)

Your brain is an amazing organ, and it needs sleep to thrive. As you approach your role as a learner, consider how you will preserve a regular schedule for sleep. For your health, please don't skimp. We know that kids can interrupt sleep as can irregular work schedules. However, if you can establish a sleep routine, you will find yourself performing better in all areas of your life.

TIP

Experts recommend a quiet, dark, cool room with minimal screen time before sleep. Of course, that doesn't sound like most households we know! A fan for white noise and foam earplugs are Susan's salvation.

Say Thank You

Not to sound like an awards show on TV, but there are a lot of people you may need to thank:

>> Your family, for freeing up your time and resources

>> Your instructor, for their patience

>> Your employer, for supporting your learning journey

>> Your peers, for their encouragement and camaraderie

We owe a lot to the many people who have worked with us through countless online courses. It's nice to be remembered, so, as you reach a point in your own online adventure, say thanks.

Index

D

kids
  appeal of online learning to, 320–321
  blocking bullies, 323
  candidates for online learning, 22
  with career, 321
  curricula, 329
  necessity of online learning for, 320–321
  private online schools, 332–333
  protecting from cyberbullying, 323
  real-time opportunities, 325
  researching virtual schools for, 80–81
  safety concerns with, 322–323
  special situations for, 22–23
  state-funded virtual schools, 327–330
  state mandates, 329
  virtual schools for, 327–333
kinesthetic learners, 43
know-it-all, 44
Kumon, 196

L

laptops, 51
late policy, 175–176
Latitudes & Attitudes magazine, 147
leadership qualities, showing off, 207–208
learner-to-instructor communication, 204
learner-to-learner communication, 201–202, 204–205
learning curve, 95
learning disabilities, 35
learning management systems (LMSs)
  accessing syllabus in, 87
  explained, 150–151
  flagging posts in, 219
  learning curve, 95
  messaging in, 202
  new information alerts, 232
  restrictions, 191
  saving documents, 155–157
  setting discussions in, 212
learning methods, 43–44
learning styles
  auditory, 42
  kinesthetic, 42–43
  preferences, 41
  tactile, 42–43
  visual, 42

letters of recommendation, 119
levels of conformance, 340
librarians, 190
libraries
  accessing, 233–234
  consulting about plagiarism, 273–274
  databases, 235
  determining quality of sources, 237
  doing research online, 234–237
  figuring out needed materials, 234–235
  Internet connections, 260–261
  overview, 232
  subject or keyword search, 235–236
  watching online tutorials, 237
LinkedIn, 110, 214, 314, 315
literature review, 285
Litmos, 150
live sessions, attending, 178–180
loafing, avoiding, 30
loans, 16, 125
local schools, 14
logging in
  to portal, 165–166
  setting aside time for, 218–219, 366
Lynda.com, 195

M

Mac users, 48, 52
  audio recording, 297
  opening multiple browser windows, 222
  right-clicking, 60
  taking screen shots, 153
mail-in pencil exams, 291
manners, online, 20–21. *See also* netiquette
massive open online courses (MOOCs), 73, 257
master's degree, 70
media
  audio, 297
  defined, 295
  examples of, 295
  images, 296
  infographics, 296
  video, 298–299
Media Education Lab, 273
Meetup, 315
memes, 207

T

About the Authors

Susan Manning is the Chief Success Strategist for Credly, a digital credentials company. On her way to that position, Susan was best known as an online professor, developing faculty and preparing them to teach online. She taught online courses in online learning, instructional design, technology tools, the synchronous classroom, and group work online for the University of Wisconsin-Stout and the Illinois Online Network at the University of Illinois. She also taught English as a Second Language at Waubonsee Community College.

Susan's online career began when she was asked to investigate the possibility of training literacy volunteers online. Knowing that she needed additional training and skills development herself, Susan became an online student and earned her certification as a Master Online Teacher from the University of Illinois. It is from that world that she recognized the value of alternative credentials, and these dovetail with her work at Credly. As a lifelong learner, Susan continually studies and earns new credentials that say more about her current skills and competencies than her patina'd degrees do. That said, she holds a doctorate in Adult Education from Ball State University, a master's in College Student Personnel from Bowling Green State University, and a bachelor's degree in Communications from Truman State University.

Kevin Johnson is the Director of Distance and eLearning at Seattle Central College. Kevin uses he/him pronouns and has more than 30 years' experience working in education and figuring out how to use technology to his advantage.

Kevin's interest in technology began when he was 14 and taught himself how to program, which led to being a computer programmer for the University of Illinois at 15. Anyone remember PLATO terminals? Since then, Kevin has developed curriculum and taught in academic and corporate environments. He has also held administrative positions overseeing eLearning, supervising instruction, and developing and supporting faculty.

Kevin met Susan after receiving his master's in Education working for the University of Illinois' Making the Virtual Course a Reality (MVCR) faculty development program. Together, they taught many classes individually and together, around online pedagogy, technology tools, web design, and synchronous communication. They did this all while working distant from one another, which is a testament to the power of distance education and work.

Dedication

We dedicate this book to our families and the communities who have supported us in our journeys. We didn't get this far without good foundational guidance from parents, followed by lessons learned through children, work, and personal buddies. You know who you are.

We'd also like to give a shout-out to those working in the distance and eLearning field. During the COVID-19 pandemic, our friends and colleagues came to the rescue by quickly training faculty, providing student support, and even helping staff learn how to work remotely. They worked tirelessly for months to help both their faculty and students be successful. They are more than deserving of our praise. THANK YOU!

Time and Space

An interesting thing happened on the way to this update: the COVID-19 pandemic. Now more than ever, people are working and learning online, and many of you need guidance. This edition addresses the changes as of this time and space. However, both authors are sensitive to how fast things change! We are also aware that some readers come to this online world without having had a choice. Neither of us has a crystal ball, but we predict learning and working remotely will become even more commonplace post-pandemic, so whether you read this in order to succeed in an academic course or to figure out how to keep up with workplace training, we're here for you.

Author's Acknowledgments

We didn't write this book alone! We first want to say thanks to the entire editorial staff at Wiley for making us sound so smart, especially Elizabeth Stilwell, Paul Levesque and Becky Whitney. We also had help, encouragement, and insights from the following people (listed alphabetically):

Christie Fierro, our technical reviewer, for her review of our work. Christie's experience in the field provided amazing insight that contributed to a better book.

Joan Vandervelde, Online Professional Development at University of Wisconsin-Stout, who works tirelessly to support students and faculty and graciously wrote the Foreword.

We also want to thank our respective work teams. Both of us are grateful for teams who support, critique, and cajole us into doing our best work.

Finally, we'd like to thank our families. Occasionally, we may have been a bit distracted or crabby, and you were always there for us.

Publisher's Acknowledgments

Acquisitions Editor: Elizabeth Stilwell

Senior Project Editor: Paul Levesque

Copy Editor: Becky Whitney

Technical Editor: Christie Fiero

Production Editor: Tamilmani Varadharaj

Cover Image: © damircudic/Getty Images

Leverage the power

Dummies is the global leader in the reference category and one of the most trusted and highly regarded brands in the world. No longer just focused on books, customers now have access to the dummies content they need in the format they want. Together we'll craft a solution that engages your customers, stands out from the competition, and helps you meet your goals.

Advertising & Sponsorships

Connect with an engaged audience on a powerful multimedia site, and position your message alongside expert how-to content. Dummies.com is a one-stop shop for free, online information and know-how curated by a team of experts.

- Targeted ads
- Video
- Email Marketing
- Microsites
- Sweepstakes sponsorship

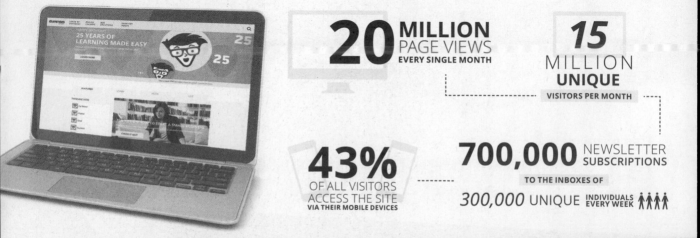

20 MILLION PAGE VIEWS EVERY SINGLE MONTH

15 MILLION UNIQUE VISITORS PER MONTH

43% OF ALL VISITORS ACCESS THE SITE VIA THEIR MOBILE DEVICES

700,000 NEWSLETTER SUBSCRIPTIONS TO THE INBOXES OF

300,000 UNIQUE INDIVIDUALS EVERY WEEK

# of dummies

Custom Publishing

Reach a global audience in any language by creating a solution that will differentiate you from competitors, amplify your message, and encourage customers to make a buying decision.

- Apps
- Books
- eBooks
- Video
- Audio
- Webinars

Brand Licensing & Content

Leverage the strength of the world's most popular reference brand to reach new audiences and channels of distribution.

For more information, visit dummies.com/biz

PERSONAL ENRICHMENT

Staying Sharp dummies
9781119187790
USA $26.00
CAN $31.99
UK £19.99

Facebook dummies
Carolyn Abram
9781119179030
USA $21.99
CAN $25.99
UK £16.99

Guitar dummies
Mark Phillips
Jon Chappell
9781119293354
USA $24.99
CAN $29.99
UK £17.99

Investing dummies
Eric Tyson, MBA
9781119293347
USA $22.99
CAN $27.99
UK £16.99

Beekeeping dummies
Howland Blackiston
9781119310068
USA $22.99
CAN $27.99
UK £16.99

Digital Photography dummies
Julie Adair King
9781119235606
USA $24.99
CAN $29.99
UK £17.99

Meditation dummies
Stephan Bodian
9781119251163
USA $24.99
CAN $29.99
UK £17.99

Pregnancy ALL-IN-ONE dummies
6 Books in one!
9781119235491
USA $26.99
CAN $31.99
UK £19.99

Samsung Galaxy S7 dummies
Bill Hughes
9781119279952
USA $24.99
CAN $29.99
UK £17.99

iPhone dummies
Edward C. Baig
Bob "Dr. Mac" LeVitus
9781119283133
USA $24.99
CAN $29.99
UK £17.99

Crocheting dummies
Karen Manthey
Susan Brittain
9781119287117
USA $24.99
CAN $29.99
UK £16.99

Nutrition dummies
Carol Ann Rinzler
9781119130246
USA $22.99
CAN $27.99
UK £16.99

PROFESSIONAL DEVELOPMENT

Windows 10 dummies
Andy Rathbone
9781119311041
USA $24.99
CAN $29.99
UK £17.99

AutoCAD dummies
Bill Fane
9781119255796
USA $39.99
CAN $47.99
UK £27.99

Excel 2016 dummies
Greg Harvey, PhD
9781119293439
USA $26.99
CAN $31.99
UK £19.99

QuickBooks 2017 dummies
Stephen L. Nelson, MBA, CPA, MS in Taxation
9781119281467
USA $26.99
CAN $31.99
UK £19.99

macOS Sierra dummies
Bob "Dr. Mac" LeVitus
9781119280651
USA $29.99
CAN $35.99
UK £21.99

LinkedIn dummies
Joel Elad, MBAs
9781119251132
USA $24.99
CAN $29.99
UK £17.99

Windows 10 ALL-IN-ONE dummies
10 Books in one!
Woody Leonhard
9781119310563
USA $34.00
CAN $41.99
UK £24.99

SharePoint 2016 dummies
Rosemarie Withee
Ken Withee
9781119181705
USA $29.99
CAN $35.99
UK £21.99

Fundamental Analysis dummies
Matt Krantz
9781119263593
USA $26.99
CAN $31.99
UK £19.99

Networking dummies
Doug Lowe
9781119257769
USA $29.99
CAN $35.99
UK £21.99

Office 2016 dummies
Wallace Wang
9781119293477
USA $26.99
CAN $31.99
UK £19.99

Office 365 dummies
Rosemarie Withee
Ken Withee
Jennifer Reed
9781119265313
USA $24.99
CAN $29.99
UK £17.99

Salesforce.com dummies
Liz Kao
Jon Paz
9781119239314
USA $29.99
CAN $35.99
UK £21.99

Coding dummies
Nikhil Abraham
9781119293323
USA $29.99
CAN $35.99
UK £21.99

dummies.com